A Conjugation of Art and Science

Iqbal Haider

February 22, 2014

Published By:

Josh Literary Society of Canada
1728 – 46 Street NW
Calgary, AB   Canada T3B 1B2
Website: WWW.joshsociety.com
Email: eternalquest2014@gmail.com

Printed By:

CreateSpace – A Division of Amazon

Suite B, 7290 Investment Drive

North Charleston, SC

USA 29418

To Order:

www.createspace.com

ISBN-13: 978-1492929376

Email: eternalquest2014@gmail.com

A welcome Surprise from Dr. Ammar Turabi

My Dear Iqbal Bhai,   January 19, 2014

I think it is great news itself that your book about renowned Josh Sahab will soon emerge on the horizon. Writing in English will be reaching out to a bigger audience globally.

poet is a maker of verses, a creator with words and an artist that uses words instead of paint. But Josh Malihabadi is not only a poet with a vision; rather he is a vision in totality. In fact, in reality he is a bigger "STATESMAN" with no comparison. Josh Sahab is a role model for today's political figures. He has much greater qualities than just painting with words. He cares for the poor, understands unity and teamwork, and is a voice of common people. Today's politicians call themselves the voice of the people. It hurts me to say this, but they are not. They couldn't care less about what happened to the people.

But who is a statesman? Is it the man that bows out silently into near oblivion after he has completed his term of life? Or is it the one who, after leaving apparent life continues to make his voice heard and live eternally?

Late Ajmal Khattak, a visionary legend and a dear friend of mine, once in our discussion said that the key difference between a politician's mind and of a statesman's is that "politician mind is often thought about getting re-elected, whereas a Statesman think about the welfare of the next generation." I remember, Ajmal Khattak had a great respect for Josh Sahab's vision of global unity. He admired Josh Sahab's educating importance of combined success, formalities of classes of people to be removed from different walks of life and poor to be more sovereign. Khattak sahab cherished the versatility in Josh and his powerful impression in life.

According to another living legend and my dearest Sahabzada Yaqub Khan, Josh Sahab's exposure and the wealth of knowledge acquired over the years made him able to look beyond the narrow limits of past lives into one life, one future and one world.

Henry Kissinger further strikes a distinction between the statesman and the ordinary leader. Of the latter, he notes that they only consume while statesmen create. He goes on to note that the statesman is not only satisfied with ameliorating the environment, but transforming it. For him, the statesman is both a visionary and an educator.

From his view, at least it is safe to say that it is still possible to have a Josh like statesmanship in public and private offices. Josh Sahab commands the respect and admiration of all across the political and intellectual divide. Josh is much more responsible and concerned with leaving logical legacies and creating deep impressions in the minds of those alive and those yet unborn.

I do not for once think that Josh is anything else but a statesman. And his vision, after his apparent death, has left an awesome impact, making him intellectually desirable and more acceptable. Sadly, the same cannot be said for today's selfish thinkers, policy makers and decision makers. Despite negatives versus Josh, his central role in our history, year after year has seen his charismatic image only bigger. His constant criticisms on close minds, his persistent claims and challenges in his explosive poetry has further promote his image as an individual who is capable of influencing people from diverse political and religious heritages towards a common missing heritage of mankind, the love & humanity. His contributions towards awakening, love and humanity are certainly something the Intelligentsia can't afford to do without. And he achieved all of this by his independent following of divine & divine people. And It is true as he is visibly passionate and inspired by Imam Hussain (a.s.), Prophet Mohammed's Grand Son and the Prophet's like minded Family.

The plight and well-being of the people also were a key concern of his. The impact he desires to make and the causes he intends to achieve will remain possible, if all of us reassert to get close to one another as the universal family, capable of engaging with others, irrespective of difference, ability to reach out even to bitter rivals and further heading towards oneness.

In the past couple of years, the tribute to praise the oneness of mankind, we the Allamah Rasheed Turabi Foundation incorporated 'Universal Family' in the memory of Josh and other master faculties to reach out to maximum frontiers with each other.

There is a lot to be proud about Josh when it comes to his poetry & ultimate words of wisdom. Our responsible members of universal family can and should strive to be the best statesmen that we all expect them to be for the health and future of this world. Today, we talk about splitting up nations, provinces, and separate states. Josh wanted unity and peace among all. Whether they are Hindus or Sikhs, Shia or Sunni, Christian, Muslim or Jewish, Josh would like everyone to live in harmony.

Josh Sahab always thought that we should work together. In his poetry and his life he expressed that more will be accomplished together not separate. The world should follow the footsteps that Josh has laid out for us. We should discuss and debate about Josh on every caring forum of the world including think tanks. As a President, Think Tank International, I would love to work with such people who desire to live with Enthusiasm and JOSH.

Josh has received many awards throughout his lifetime. In recognition of his great services to Urdu poetry and literature, in 2013, Josh has received Hilal-e-Imtiaz (the Crescent of Excellence), the highest prestigious civil award from the Government of Pakistan. I am grateful to you Iqbal bhai that you shared with relevant world of Josh, a little and humble role played by me.

Now I would like to request you to treat this as a letter only & not as an article, as I am only a student of Josh but he is my voice as well.

In conclusion, the late Shabbir Hasan Khan Josh Malihabadi is "the biggest statesman of the poetic world" and will always be present, without being late in life. God willing, he will be nurturing many generations hereafter.

With Regards

Dr. Ammar Turabi
Secretary General - Allamah Rasheed Turabi Foundation & Trust Int'l,
President - Think Tank International,
Managing Director - Universal Family

Table of Contents

Translations

Admirable Research

Inspiring Youngsters

Dedicated to:

The Man of the Century Nelson R. Mandela

1918 -2013

Gratitude and Acknowledgement

The words do not always succeed in transforming the heartfelt gratitude, but one must attempt. On behalf of Josh Literary Society of Canada I would like to thank all the individuals, Guests, Friends, Family Members, Organizations, Video and Audio Producers, participants, performers, Scholars, Volunteers and above all the Audience without whom this three day event would have not been possible. We are truly indebted to the University of Calgary for all their support, guidance and encouragement in organizing and holding this inimitable conference with their co-sponsorship.

The history will behold that it was Calgary, Canada where the first major convention was held with the objective of conjugating Art and Science while paying tribute to one the greatest Urdu poets, Josh.

Fortunately, this conference was attended by some eminent scientists and scholars who took time out of their very busy schedule. We do not have words to thank them for attending, welcoming and supporting us. I am sorry that a couple of papers could not be included because the presenters failed to provide us with a printed copy in spite of our reminders and wait.

Apart from the conference, the printing of this book also required a lot of help and support from some genuinely gifted people with extensive IT experience. Fortunately, we have an abundance of support there. I would like to thank them all for putting up with the peculiarity of the "Ebbs and Flows" that is more evident in uncharted waters. It wasn't easy to train a baby-boomer in familiarizing himself with the tricks of the trade of publishing. Very special thanks to my friend Tahir Jamal who created unique software for electronically challenged people.

Also, I must apologize for the insertion of some not-so-good Urdu Text, because working with the low print-quality of the dated and damaged source material was a daunting task. Honestly, it came to a point of going without the original Urdu version. But in the end we decided to sacrifice the optics for the essence. I sincerely apologize if it frustrates some of our readers.

I would also like to thank the principal of Math Corporation of Atlanta, USA who captured and painstakingly transformed the theme of this book into an art form. The conceptual title of this book would have never been possible without him. We must also thank the well known Artist, Zahid Ali Khan for the portrait of Josh and Bilal Khan Sahib for his devoted guidance and sincere contributions.

We also thank our youth volunteers for their help and creative contributions. A few of them could not finish what they started but a few others did, and it's all included in the book. We thank them all and hope to see a substantial increase in their contributions in future. The most notable, accomplished, and prominent amongst them is a young research scholar, Stephen Bauhart, from the University of British Columbia, who was so inspired by Josh's vision and poetry that he wrote a fairly long research paper for the book.

As I was getting ready to upload the book, was pleasantly surprised by an unexpected letter from a dear friend welcoming the news of the upcoming book. Since this letter contains some important names and references pertaining to our subject, it is included in the book as "A welcome Surprise". Since not only the book but even the Index was formatted so it is included in the initial pages.

In the end it's customary and necessary that all the volunteers, including myself, sincerely thank their families and spouses for the ongoing support and understanding.

Iqbal Haider

A conjugation of Art and science

Iqbal Haider

Founding President of Josh Literary Society of Canada

* A part of this article was delivered as welcoming speech at the conference

Honorable chief guest, Rose Goldstein, Vice President University of Calgary, Honorable Wayne Cao, the Deputy speaker of Alberta, his Excellency Andre Chabot, the Deputy Mayor of Calgary, distinguished scholars and scientists, and the overseas audience watching this program live on the Internet, ladies and gentleman; on behalf of Josh Literary Society of Canada and the citizens of Calgary, I welcome you all to this unique and august gathering.

We are certainly very fortunate to have so many great minds and prominent thinkers amongst us today. A more of a rarity is the fact that it is the very first time that these eminent and leading neurophysicist and nuclear scientists have been invited to speak on the subject of Fine Arts and Poetry. I guess this discourse can rightfully be called a conjugation of Art and Science.

We are all aware of the challenges that we face in this post 9-11 world, the fragmentation of society, the disintegration of ethical values, involution of moral fabric, ebbing of collective wisdom, a tidal wave of religiosity and the disillusionment of conscientious beings are definitely fostering a gravely paranoid mindset. No doubt the future looks bleak, but then again the humanity has survived worse. We have walked out of the quagmire of history, time and time again. So let's not despair, the question in front of us is "how to get out of this mess" and "how to sheath this double-edged sword of paranoia. I guess we have to work from within and instead of being overly concerned with the mitigating external forces we must focus on how to cultivate our inner self and work to strengthen the smallest unit within. We must cleanse ourselves, our families, our household and work outward from there.

We must believe, practice, and inspire others to accept that whatever is good for the betterment of masses is good enough for the Gods. We must not submit to the mindset of trying to appease some ecclesiastical being. We must see the good in other and then sincerely step forth with the goodness in ourselves. By doing so, if we not completely erase, we will definitely reduce this state of paranoia. We got to find the healing touch that will congeal us into a unifying force to counter the forced of division and fragmentation. We must turn to a Humanistic sage who can take us to the next level and beyond. We are gathered here today to remember and celebrate one of those sages, Josh. He was most definitely one of these more distinguished humanistic sages.

Thus the purpose of this seminar is to:

- Celebrate Josh and share his vision of Oneness of Mankind, with the Western audience and media. His relevance was never more so needed than now.

- Replenish and restore the true and natural characteristic of Urdu. We must revive the true Urdu Diaspora.
- To assemble a group of intellectually independent and fair minded secular scholars to provide an alternative thinking forum.

In fact, all the three above, are inter-connected like mind, body and soul.

Poetry is an ancient art that parallels the antiquity of Gods. There have been zillions of poets and there be many more. But it also a fact that we can name only a few in every era and fewer yet in every century that would stand out and become immortal. It seems what distinguishes a great poet from a good poet is the treatment of their craft and having an exclusive and intricate diction. But then again, what make a great poet immortal is that independent and indelible vision and the conviction of expression thereof.

Josh is revered and respected for what he represents what he stands for - the ever objective and undiluted rationality, and the deep-rooted, subtly crafted, multifaceted meaningful words to articulate and engage the sense data of human consciousness.

Evidently Josh's poetry would add unique dimensions to any literature, let alone Urdu. He had this very rare combination of a diversified and panoramic vision and profoundly intricate diction. An observation so keen and sharp that it will not spare a thing and a diction so potent and comprehensive that will become the most sensitive and aesthetic articulation of emotions, feelings and events alike.

He started as fiery revolutionary poet and remained revolutionary in the true sense of its meaning to the last day. He gave a fresh and most objective perspective to all the domains and topics that he touched, and he did not leave many untouched either.

He gave new meaning to life and new life to the meaning. He accorded a new level of consciousness to the art of aesthetics and poetry. He has the capacity of intellect to rationalize and analyze, and the integrity of character to fearlessly question and discard. And some of those questions were cutting too deep and too close to the core of the matter, hence he was punished. It is solemn, stirring, compelling and while given least credit, strangely life affirming.

 Josh may not be the slickest or most popular poet in recent times, and for obvious reasons, nonetheless definitely the most important and relevant one. Let's see how uniquely he urged his people to live rationally.

بوسیدہ روایات کی حُرمَت نَہ کرو

تَحقیق و تَجَسُّس کی اِہانَت نَہ کرو

دینِ آبا وبھی ، تُم کو لاحِق ہوجائے

ماں باپ سے ، اِتنی بھی مَحَبَّت نَہ کرو

Do not revere tattered traditions

Do not look down upon inquisitions

You even embrace their religion as such

Do not love your parents ever so much

It has always been common, but more so evident now than ever before, that the hardest poets and writers to remain popular amongst the masses are the Non-conformist ones. Well who wants to read about a voice of reason if it does not conform, nor share the same life experiences and do not have the same point of view.
Some more common characteristics of these seemingly unpopular intellect-surfers and wordsmiths are that they do not share the prevailing social values, do vocally and emphatically

question the majority belief system, are extremely blunt about their own beliefs or non-beliefs, have layered and multifaceted diction, live in very dogmatic society where generally people and specifically scholars are not very fond of reading from the source. Where critics rather listen to or read a couple of articles to form their opinion or write their own piece. Josh, fortunately or unfortunately, was victim of all of the above mentioned trends.

Hence there is a common public misconception about josh that he was somewhat of a temperamental reactionary rather than a deep rooted and well entrenched visionary. Whether widely praised or not he always commanded a grudging respect.

Thinkers and poets like Josh once they are introduced in an enlightened society they immediately flourish like a budding plant in a fertile soil.

Of course he did not fit into any established classification, may it be of a religion or an ideology. He was disliked by the clergy and ideologues both and more or less for the same reasons. His intellect refused to settle, he tirelessly kept moving ahead in search of the absolute truth. He was a constant reminder of life's dynamism.

Life being fluid in nature, detest stagnation, so should any true embodiment of it. And there is no better embodiment of life than the Real Art. Thinking is the essence of "Being".

The thinking must not stop, the intellect must not rest, the spirit must not acquiesce and the soul must not die, because we are not only part of our own consciousness but also part of a larger consciousness. One must continuously endeavour to establish that harmony with the cosmos and when you do, you really have attained

جب دشت میں، شب کی زلف ہوتی ہے دراز

کھلتا ہے سکوت، سنتا ہے گداز

اس وقت لرزتے ہوئے سناٹے میں

آتی ہے کہیں سے گھوڑے کی آواز

As the night opens its glossy locks
Suffocates serenity, Simmers pathos
Precisely then in throbbing silence
I hear the creaking of tł

میرے چاروں طرف سے ہے اک طرف خروش
اک قوس ہے پشت پر، لشکل آغوش
آخر یہ تعاقب میں ہیں نظر یں کس کی؟
یہ کون مجھے ڈھونڈر ہا ہے اے جوش؟

I am surrounded by a strange clamour
Behind my back is a bow-like bosom
Whose eyes are following me around?
Who is that looking for me O' Josh?

But he does not stop there, because deep down, he knows that
it is far too colossal a task to affirm, given the prevailing
limitations.

میں ،طرفہ کشاکش میں، گھراہوں معبود!
مکار حواس، اور وہ بھی محدود
بالفرض اگر کشف عطا بھی ہوجائے
پھر بھی نہ یقین آئے کہ تو ہے موجود

I am drowning in a rare perplexity O' God
Pretentious senses, restricted and imperfect
Suppose, all the veils are lifted off my sight
I still cannot firmly believe that you are

عیشیار ، اے آگہی کے طالب انسان
دریائے حواس ، مکر کا ہے طوفان
خلّاقیٔ وہم کے نہاں خانے کا
مالِ مسروقہ بیچتا ہے وجدان

Beware o' you, so fond of awareness
This stream of senses may be a flood of deceit
The stolen goods of superstitions' catacomb
Is all that offered by perspicacity

It seems plausible to think that our visionary-poet in his logical
thinking is as indifferent to saying no as he is to yes. But he is
not despondent

عجلَت نہ کر اے مسافرِ دشتِ شعور
نفیٔ و اثبات کا ابھی شہر ہے دور
ہاں ساتھ چلا چل کہ کہیں ٹھہرے گا
یہ قافلۂ علّت و معلول ضرور

Don't be so anxious O' trekker of reason
The Mecca of "Yes" and "No" is still far
Simply come along brother, because
Somewhere this caravan of Cause &Effect will stop

If anything he relies on deeply it is imbedded knowledge and
analytical Intellect that may provide answers and that is why
says:

جودت کا گہر، مہر مبیں سے بہتر
حکمت کی حلاوت، انگبیں سے بہتر
عالم کا دیا ہوا گمان بد بھی
جاہل کے عطا کردہ یقیں سے بہتر

The Pearl of Ingenuity is far better than Galaxy of stars
The suavity of Wisdom is better than the taste of honey
A doubt created by an erudite is better
Than the belief contrived by an unwise

His love for humanity, peace and fairness is insurmountable.
And his whole philosophy, that includes spirituality and gods,
is man-centric. Hence, Man he knows and the God he is
looking for.

To him every man who stood up for mankind, helped the cause
of humanity, boosted the collective wisdom or enhanced the
meaningful growth of societal progress and social
consciousness, regardless of whatever path he chose, was
venerable. To him, that is the genuine "spiritual soul" of
existence.

حبِ نوعِ بشر ہے، میرا ایمان
ہر چہرہ زشت و خوب، میرا قرآن
اللہ کو آغوش میں پا یا میں نے
جیسے ہی مری گود میں آیا یا الانسان

The unconditional Love of Mankind is my Faith
Distorted or charming every face is my holy scripture
I find God in my bosom
As soon as a person is comforted in my lap

But it is unfortunate that when he looks back to the history, he witnesses that most of the miseries, infighting, bloodshed, wars and other atrocities are waged against humanity in the name of religion and then he cries out in pain and declares with vengeance.

ایمان کو ، لَذَّات کی خواہش سے شَدید
ہر خیر ہے، اَسبابِ طَرَب کی تمہید
حُورانِ بہشت و دُخترانِ کُفّار
باقی نہ اگر رہیں تو غازی ، نہ شہید

The faith does have a penchant for indulgence
Every deed seems to be a prelude for Gratification
If not for the "Houries" of Paradise or the conquered Virgins
There may not be any Heroes or Martyrs at all

کم زور ہے، مستحقِّ دار و زنداں
شہ زور ہے، شایانِ سریر و ایواں
اِک کوچہ اُڑا لو، تو ذَلیل و سارق
کُل شہر چُرا لو، تو عزیز و خاقاں

Only the week deserves the wrath of law
The powerful is entitled to luxuries of life
Steal a backyard and you are condemned as thief
Steal the whole conurbation and be praised as Baron and king

Apart from acclamation of his creative brilliance, there is at least one more thing about Josh on which all his admirers and detractors e seem to agree alike, that he was an extraordinary man with an acutely peculiar Intellect. He was certainly one of the most difficult visionary-poets to objectively asses or to agree with. Let's face it there wasn't anything ordinary about the man.

A huge part of the problem might be that complex experiences are only simple if they are discussed or received with an open mind. And the open-mindedness is simply not one of our virtues.

We seldom entertain the idea of an open-ended pursuit. For example when we talk about the universe, spirituality or truth, it is always with a pre-conceived notion. At times it seems that we are so busy trying to prove our righteousness that we forget to explore.

An open-ended approach often leads to infinite spirituality as opposed to confined religiosity. It is simply a state of mind that we are talking about here, so we need not to worry about hurting someone's feeling.

Let us look at it in a slightly different way, if one simply set out to prove or disprove an idea that is easy, and can be achieved within a timeline and with a degree of certainty. But if someone is just overwhelmed by the vastness of "what is not known" to "what little is known" then he would never stop exploring. He travels far, real far.

Josh belongs to that same community; his logical hypothesis compelled him to ask that when the unknown is zillions of times bigger than the known, then why or how do we claim one thing or another?
The universe is constantly unravelling itself, so anything is possible why quarrel over it.

پُشتِ ایماں کا خم نکالا ہے کبھی؟
اقوال کو، افکار میں ڈھالا ہے کبھی؟
اقرار کے ساحل پر اکڑنے والو!
انکار کا قُلزُم بھی کھنگالا ہے کبھی؟

Ever tried straightening out the hump of faith?
Or tried transforming precepts to the vision?
O' you vain and haughty at the shore of assent!
Have you ever tried plunging in the Ocean of dissent?

کھولا ہے تو ہر ایک گرہ کو کھولو
منطق کی ترازو پہ ہر اک شے تولو
مانا کہ یہ عالم ہے کسی کی ایجاد
اور، علّتِ ایجاد ہے کیا؟ اب بولو

If you want to untangle then untangle all the knots
Let the notions be weighed in the balance of logic
Agreed, the cosmos is created by someone
And what's the reason behind it, do tell me

انسان، ازل سے ہے جہُول اور ظلُوم
لے دے کے ہے بس ایک شعُورِ مَوہُوم
طفلِ ناداں ہے، آ ئینے کے آگے
کس کا یہ عکس ہے، اُس سے کیا معلُوم

Since eternity the man is ignorant and unjust
After give and take there is this fancied wisdom
An innocent child is in front of the mirror
Whose reflection it is, how would he know?

افکار میں جب غوطہ لگایا میں نے

آفاق کو، پلکوں پہ جُھلایا میں نے

ادراک کی میزان میں تولا جس وقت

سائے میں بھی، وزن و حجم پایا میں نے

When I plunge deep in my thoughts

I feel the universe swinging by my eyelashes

When I weigh in the balance of Sagacity

I found weight and volume in the shadow even

T. S. Elliott once wrote that "Only those who risk going too far can possibly find out how far one can go". But I do not think Mr. Elliott even attempted to live this profound thought. And the people, who do, pay a huge price for doing so too.
It is people like Ghalib, Josh, Firaq, Iqbal, Rousseau, Voltaire, Blake, Shelley, Byron, Ismat, Rashid, Munto, Miraji, Jaun Aliya and myriad others like them who, of course at different levels and with varying impact, objectivity, sensibility, courage and range, were willing to pay the price to not only determine how far one can go but also to promote and augment the social conscience and collective sensibility.

We know that in creative Arts often the most important thing is the treatment of the subject and with layers, nuances and shades hidden behind the surface or the meaning behind the meaning. But then again there must be an eye so to see beyond the surface.

Anyhow, another very potent but once again somewhat controversial and misconstrued aspect of Josh's poetry is his treatment of the "First Person" with all its dimensions, variances and shades.

Depending on the complexity of thoughts and intellect behind it, First Person (singular and plural) narratives do involve convoluted multi level formation to create a stream of consciousness, and so did he. But alas, due to a certain animosity towards his religious or social beliefs or non-beliefs it was callously ignored.

A fabulous master of nuances he beautifully and frequently juggles and juxtaposes between the "universal self" and the "personal self" also including all that falls in between. There is no doubt like many other great minds and people he was a narcissist, and it's very hard not to, when one is who they are. It's only human and almost everyone, from an ordinary soul and up, looks at his virtues more than the follies.

I suppose being a narcissist, his subconscious mind must have thrived on the attention and the confusion created by these stream of consciousness. But isn't it the beauty of art, and I mean great art. Let us enjoy a few of his superb verses:

Hum aisey ahle nazar ko subut eHaq keliye
Agar Rasul na hutey tu subha kafi thih
(Not Translated)

هم ایسے اہلِ نظر کو ثبوتِ حق کیلئے
اگر رسولؐ نہ ہوتے تو صبح کافی تھی

مجھ کو، انعامِ حق پناہی دے گا
میری نیّت کو، تاج شاہی دے گا
میرے سینے میں، انبیا کا دل ہے
اللہ سے پوچھو، وہ گواہی دے گا

He will reward me for upholding the truth

My intentions will be crowned for Fairness

I have the heart of prophets in my chest

Ask the God he will witness

فردا کی زمین پر مکاں ہے میرا
امروز، اک عصرِ بے زباں ہے میرا
بویا ہی نہیں گیا ہے اب تک جو شجر
اُس کی چوٹی پر آشیاں ہے میرا

I live in the soil of future

Present is a mere mute phase of mine

The Tree that hasn't been planted yet

Atop its branch is abode of mine

اُف، میں یہ کہاں ہوں، بول اے شہپرِ تاک
ماہ و خورشید میں، نَہ اَرض و اَفلاک
کیسا ہے، لُجھی ہوئی دُھنک کا یہ دُھواں؟
کیسی ہے، جلے ہوئے ستاروں کی چِلک؟

Where am I O' you, O' lofty feather?

Where is the moon, the sun, the heavens?

What is this smoke of ashen Rainbow?

Why is this cinder of scorched Stars?

یہ اوج، یہ اجلال، یہ اعزاز، یہ جاہ
شانوں پہ مرے مہرِ نتیلی پہ ہے ماہ
"دیکھو، دَستک پہ دے رہا ہے جبریل"
"جبریل، نہیں، قبلۂ عالم ۔۔۔ اللہ"

All this zenith, this acme, this grandeur

Sun rest on my shoulder the moon on Palm

Look someone, knocking maybe Gabriel

Not the Gabriel, It's the almighty the God!

Now as we read these lines from Josh or another thought provoking masterpiece by some other poet we must realize that first and foremost they are poets. They say things differently because they are capable to see, feel, internalize and express them differently. At times it may have any or all of the following; tongue-in-the-cheek mischief, dare-devilish boldness, pinch-the-hypocritical-brain defiance -that's poetry that's life.

But what remains steady is an undercurrent which is constantly functioning to expand the intellectual boundaries and human discourse.

I only cited four examples but when we read them in connection with all of his other work and his overall thinking it's fairly easy to know where he is referring to "himself alone" and where he is not, and also when is talking about the future-man and the universe the way he expects and sees it unfolding. He has this unique way of looking at things and more unique way of articulating them.

No discussion on Josh is ever complete without talking about his revolutionary poetry. But I think I will just make a quick reference to his concept of revolution and progress itself.

In the real sense Revolution and progress both are perpetual and fluid. Because if the life is not static how can any of its cure be. Progress is nothing but moving ahead continuously, tirelessly and perennially.

The moment we stop we become regressive because life marches on.

Revolutions are waged in the minds, intellects and souls before being waged on the grounds, in the society and amongst the people.

Anything short of that is the same dogmatic entity, religion disguised and wrapped in an even smaller package of ideology.

Josh was first discarded by the religious zealots and then by his so called progressive and revolutionary disciples and Comrades. Because they thought they found progress based on Marxism in the same fashion that religionists think that they have attained without making a positive difference to everyday life.

In a way the Progressives did worse than them because if nothing else at least there is a promise of better life hereafter. The Progressives do not even have that because their philosophy is definitely for this world here.
It appears that this "New Testament" failed to help them once again without having gone through any metamorphosis to get rid of their dogmatic nature. So it became frozen in time quicker than the other ones.
The Brian trust of the commune in the subcontinent were so anxious to bow that they did not even bother to determine the huge difference between the two regions and their exploiting forces.

The result is that to this day there has not been any positive change let alone a revolution. In Europe the deity was not the massive exploiting force, in the East particularly in the subcontinent it was and still is.

To summarize this brief discussion, my question is who we see fighting selflessly the real oppressive force. Who went after the real exploiting forces, whose intellect relentlessly kept moving forward and who refused to submit to the subversive forces. And who was left alone and by whom.

کچھ وہم گداؤں کا ہے، کچھ شاہوں کا
کچھ وسوسہ محلوں کا ہے، کچھ راہوں کا
اس طنح شدہ شور کو تاریخ نہ کہہ
یہ تو فقط، اک نوڈہ ہے، افواہوں کا

Some horror of clergy, some terror of Rulers

Some dreads of mansions, some of passing day

Do not call this frightened collection history

It is nothing but a chronicle of rumors

جس وقت ..... بفیض مشق فکر جولاں
،انسان ..... آفاق کا بنے گا سلطاں
مجھ کو نہ ہلا..... تو ..... اے نگار کونین
بچ کر ..... مری اولاد سے ..... جائے گا کہاں

When with the help of sparkling wisdom

The man will become the universe sovereign

You, the darling of both worlds, if I don't see

How would you escape my Children's attention?

I would like to close my article by quoting one of my most favorite verses, an astonishingly unique quatrain of Josh. What a noble and original concept.

Judging from the chronology of printed material, it must have been written in the late fifties. The idea represented in this Rubai (Quatrain) was definitely alien to Urdu literature and possibly to any literature, at the time:

انسان کی توحید کا مشتاق ہوں میں

شمعِ حبِّ عمیم کا طاق ہوں میں

مشرق کا نہ پابند، نہ مغرب کا اسیر

انسان ہوں، باشندہ آفاق ہوں میں

I yearn for the dawn of the oneness of mankind

Like a niche on which the candle of humanity glows

Neither bound to the East nor tied to the West

Being a man, Citizen of the Universe I am

(All Translations by Iqbal Haider)

Rose Goldstein, Vice- President (Research)

Dr. Rose Goldstein joined the University of Calgary on July 1, 2007

Experienced clinician scientist to join senior leadership team

The University of Calgary today announced the appointment of a new vice-President, Research who will play a significant role in enhancing the university's national and international reputation as a research-intensive institution.

Dr. Rose Goldstein, a medical doctor who specialized in the area of rheumatology and who also has extensive leadership experience, will join the U of C as the Vice- President, Research, for a five year term beginning July 1, 2007.

Goldstein will fill the portfolio held by Dr. Dennis Salahub, whose five year term as Vice- President Research & international ends June 30. This senior position is a key to the ability of the U of C to continue its success as a Top 10 university recognized on the national and international scenes. Over the past several years, the U of C has significantly increased its research funding to 252.5 Million, which ranks seventh among the Top 10 in Canada.

The senior international portfolio at the U of C will become a new Vice- Provost position that will operate as part of the office of the Provost and Vice- president, Academic.

"Dr. Goldstein is a leader in her field" said of U of C President Dr. Harvey Weingarten. "But more importantly, she has an outstanding history of leadership and academic accomplishment that will benefit and further engage U of C students, faculty and staff, and the Calgary community."

Dr. Goldstein is currently a professor and vice- dean, Academic Affairs, in the University of Ottawa's Faculty of Medicine. In addition to her role as Vice- Dean at the University of Ottawa, Dr. Goldstein has shown considerable vision and is known for engaging and energizing those with who she works. Many of innovations and programs she has implemented have been emulated by other universities and organizations. In addition to her administrative appointment at University of Ottawa, Dr. Goldstein is also a practicing rheumatologist (a medical doctor who specializes in the treatment of join and connective tissue-related diseases such as rheumatoid arthritis, osteoarthritis, fibromyalgia and lupus). She obtained her BSc and MD degrees from McGill University and has done residency and fellowship training at the University of Toronto, University of Ottawa and the University of Texas at Houston.

As a clinician scientist, Dr. Goldstein has held a series of research grants and has served on editorial boards and scientific review panels in her area of research. She has also received grants to support her work in medical education, including exploration of gender and health topics in the training of medical student. Dr. Goldstein will maintain a limited clinical practice in rheumatology in the Faculty of Medicine/ Calgary Health Region in Calgary.

"The plans and aspirations of the University of Calgary appeal to me personally," Dr. Goldstein said. "This is a university that is full of innovative ideas and is moving very quickly. It's exciting to be a part of that vision and energy.

Inaugural Speech by Dr. Rose Goldstein

Vice President, University of Calgary

Ladies and Gentlemen, distinguished Guests, welcome to the University of Calgary.

We are honored to be hosting this two-day conference on esteemed Urdu Poet, Josh Mahhabadi. I also want to welcome in advance the several specials guests joining this two-day conference. Members of Legislative assembly, ministers, representatives from the Mayor's office and particularly Honorable Minister of Culture and Community Spirits, Lindsay Blackett, who will be joining the conference. We also have with us today, distinguished speakers who came from as far as India, Pakistan, the UK, and USA. So welcome all of you.

The first thing I want to do is to bring you greetings from the President and Vice Chancellor of the University of Calgary, Harvey Weingartner. Harvey wanted to open the conference himself actually, but unfortunately he had to be out of town today.

This conference celebrates and investigates the many contributions of Josh Mahhabadi. As you all know, he was a great poet, writer, philosopher, and scholar of the Indian sub continent.

Josh was born in 1898 in British India. A life of letters and teaching led to his receiving of the Padmabhoshan Award in 1954. This was the first year of the inaugural year that this civilian was awarded, so it was very distinguished. I understand that this award is similar to the Order of Canada and it recognizes the distinguished service to the Nation.

Concerned as he was with challenges facing the Urdu language and culture in Independent India, Josh migrated to Pakistan in 1956, where Urdu was an official language.

As you already heard, he wasn't received as warmly as he had perhaps hoped as his socialist views and his inclusive worldview ran odds with pervasive divisiveness and parochialism of the time.

He passed away in 1982, a celebrated, revered and, often times, controversial literary and academic figure.

Over the next two days, I understand you will have the opportunity to hear some of the most learned scholars who will highlight Josh's contributions toward human value, dignity, and respect for all living beings. His bold, open-minded, forward-looking philosophy has not only influenced the literary world, but also inspired fair-minded people to reject the cults of personality bias, racial & regional discrimination.

Josh's command of Urdu combined with truly masterful poetic sensibility means that his work is particularly difficult to translate. But translate it you must, because without that his word does not reach as many people as possible. So this is exactly the challenge that the members of this conference are proposing to explore. In this way, Josh's idea can be shared even further afield and have greater impact.

As I learn more about Josh, as I have over the last few days, I feel messages resonate with what we uphold here at the University of Calgary. We encourage and teach students to question the world around us. Our faculty members in meaningful scholarships and researches, that reach beyond our walls and doors, to improve our community in many ways. We value open-mindedness and curiosity. And we encourage inter-disciplinary collaborations for the very reason that people with different backgrounds and outlooks can achieve more by learning from working with one another. As well, Josh's messages of peace and goodwill, now as much as ever, need to be heard and taken to heart around the world.

So for all of these reasons, it's a special honor for us to hold this International Conference here at the University of Calgary. On behalf of President Weingartner and the University of Calgary Community, I want to welcome you, and wish you a stimulating and rewarding conference.

Thank you

Dr. Saleem Qureshi

Dr. Regula Qureshi

* Dr. Saleem Qureshi

Dr. Saleem Qureshi is Professor Emeritus of Political Science at the University of Alberta. He has acted as Chair of the Departments of Political Science and East Asian Studies; he has also been Associate Dean and Acting Dean of Arts. He continues to teach and publish in the areas or Middle Eastern and Islamic Politics, and his research has involved study and travel in most countries of the Islamic World. Urdu and Persian poetry has always been his love, as he has descended from a long line of poets and Sufis.

- *We decided to print the picture of this lovely and unique couple who not only share their lives together but also the sizzling passion for Fine Arts.*

Josh Malihabadi: A personal reminiscence of the man, the poet and his poetry

Dr. Saleem Qureshi (Prof. Emeritus)
University of Alberta, Edmonton, Alberta, Canada

I might have heard Josh recite his poetry, or I might have read his poetry earlier, however, I distinctly remember the 1947 All India Mushaira on All India Radio where Josh recited his very famous nazm,

Ai jan-e-man, janan-e-man

سر پر دو شالا سرمئی پیکر میں جوڑا اگر ئی
لب سرخ ، پنٹ ، چپی کالی لیں ، گورا بدن
اے جان من ، اے جان من ——— جاناں من ، اے جان من
اس آیت انوار سے اس مہر کے بازار سے
اس رشتے گوہر بار سے بر خیز و برق برنگ شن
اے جان من ، اے جان من ——— جاناں من ، اے جان من
جو ہے مجھے ، اُن مول ہے تا دُر موتی دل ہے
شانوں پر اب تو کھول ہے زلف شکن اندر شکن
اے جان من ، اے جان من ——— جاناں من ، اے جان من

Praising the beloved, Josh is able to call upon a fantastic variety of metaphors to create a picture, presumably of a woman, that would correspond to what a man may dream. I was thoroughly impressed by the similes and analogies, by the wealth of vocabulary, by the images and by the cadence in Josh's inimitable thunderous voice.

Urdu poetry is blessed with an oral tradition going back to Arabian antiquity and with a style developed in India, a style of reading or recitation called tarannum. Audiences generally enjoy tarannum more because they can focus on the musicality of the presentation. Poets like Jigar Muradabadi, Nishoor Wahidi, Suroor and Khumar Barabankvi have had special success not only because of the excellence of their poetry but also because that poetry was rendered in beautiful musicality. In contrast, non-tarannum reciters among poets whose style is called taht-ul-lafz, while almost as many as tarannum reciters, have very few whose renditions could be considered memorable. Among them, the two outstanding poets have been Josh Malihabadi and Kaifi Azmi, though one should also mention Firaq Gorakhpuri along with them because the quality of his voice gave luster to his presentation. Josh was perhaps the most powerful orator of poetry. His poetry and his rendition ran parallel, each enhancing the other. Mushaira audiences would eagerly await the turn of Josh which usually came at the end, because he was considered to be the most outstanding poet of his time.

The year 1968-69 I took my sabbatical leave and decided to do research in Pakistan and India. I took three bottles of Scotch to Pakistan-one for Josh, one for Faiz and one for Aali- then it was not illegal in Pakistan to own or consume the nectar of the Scots. I mentioned one day to my friend Professor Abul Khair Kashfi of the Urdu Department at the University of Karachi, how wonderful it would be to listen to Josh and share a glass of Scotch with him. Kashfi said that his friend Mujtaba Saheb was very close to Josh and would arrange a private mushaira at our residence. So, on a fixed day Mujtaba Saheb and I drove to Josh Saheb's residence and it was arranged that I would come the next day at six in the evening--Josh Saheb used to start drinking at exactly 6:21PM.

At my place on the dais sat Josh facing a ticking clock, a tray of incense, a bottle of Scotch and a jug of water, and exactly at 6:21 Josh Saheb raised his glass. I joined him while others were bashful to be seen drinking whisky. After dinner Mujtaba Saheb and Tabish Dehlavi recited their poetry. And then Josh Saheb recited his memorable nazm:

Meri Jan, ham na kahte the
My dear, didn't we tell you

God creates Adam and commands the angels to prostrate before him. The angels are reluctant and one of them flatly refuses to do as commanded. This angel tells God about all the evil that Adam and his progeny will spread, but God tells the angel that the angel does not know what God knows. God creates Adam who spreads murder and mayhem. That is when the angels say to God:

Didn't we tell you what Adam would do!

"Yeh Aal E Tegh hey Aulad E Paekan Hum na Khete theh!"

The nazm genre of narrative poetry was not new to Urdu and certainly not new to Josh. While Josh created a lot of memorable poetry on a lot of subjects, the theme which animates Josh's works is azadi and proclaiming human dignity--whether it is man standing up to God, or a subject person rebelling against the imperial master which was the situation of Josh, most of his life, being ruled by the British imperialists. The essence of Josh's rebellion is captured illuminatingly in his famous couple

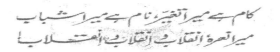

My mission is to change, and my name is Youth
My battle cry is Revolution, Revolution, Revolution!

It was in this context that during World War II Josh considered Germany to be a natural ally of India--how unfortunately erroneously--and wrote his famous ode to Hitler which earned Josh a jail sentence.

Salam Ai tajdar-e-Germany-e-Hitler-e-Azam
We salute you, oh Ruler of Germany, oh Great Hitler

In their common opposition to British rule Josh was a companion to the Nehru family with whom Josh had a very close relationship. He was patronized by the Nehrus receiving a monthly stipend of Rs 200 already in the 1920s. Later, on Independence and with the founding of India's official magazine Aaj Kal, Josh was appointed its editor. In other ways too, it seems, personal closeness with Jawaharlal Nehru continued. Josh told the story that as editor of Aaj Kal he would receive visitors from all parts of India and those he thought important enough, he would let Nehru know of their presence and Nehru would invite them for a meal. After some time, Nehru one day said to Josh: Look Josh Sahib, if he is a gentleman ((i.e. if he drinks alcohol) invite him to dinner (with Nehru) , otherwise, just fop him off at lunch. (lunch peh tarkha do)

In his poetry, Josh was courageous, fearless and thoroughly irreverent, qualities greatly admired by Urdu audiences. Some of these qualities he shared with another great Urdu poet of the 20th century, Muhammad Iqbal. But while Iqbal idolized an imaginary Mard-e-Momin (a perfect Muslim) and his own ideal version of Islam, Josh had his feet more firmly on the ground and was more in tune with those who saw and scorned the hypocrisy of pretensions. Iqbal earned the appreciation of the British who knighted him for his poetry--Dr.Sir Muhammad Iqbal--, whereas Josh took on the British and ended up in prison. Josh's scorn at the pretense of the religious is so powerfully rendered that there will be few competitors to it--just read his long nazm entitled Fitna-e-Khanqah.

Ek din jo bahr-e-Fateha ek bint-e-mehr-o-mah

Pahonchi nazar jhukae hue su-e-khanqah
Zohad ne uthai jhijhakte hue nigah

Honton pe dab ke tut gayi zarb-e-LaIlah

Barpa zamir-e-zohd men kohram hogaya

Iman dilon men larza par andam ho gaya

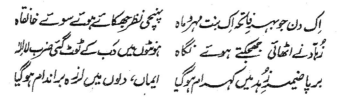

One day, with the intention to offer Fateha, a daughter of the sun and the moon (a beauty) Arrived at a monastery with downcast eyes (humility and modesty).

The pious raised a hesitant glance,

And their chant of "Oh God" died down on their lips.
The conscience of piety got convulsed

And faith in the hearts became shaken....

Here you find a naughty smile at the foolishness of those one is taught from childhood to respect, but one sees that the apparently respectable are just as vulnerable to human frailties as anybody else.

Now read in comparison Iqbal's dialogue between Jibril and Iblis (Gabriel and Satan):
Hamdam-e- dairina kaisa hai jahan-e-rang-o bu
[Insert a few lines in Urdu and English translation]
It is beautiful, profound and very moving but also clearly rebellious, with Iblis scoring a resounding victory over Jibril in the poem's conclusion:

> Main khatakta hun dil-e-yazdan men kante ki tarha
> Tu faqat Allahu, Allahu, Allahu, Allahu.

I prick the heart of the Almighty like a pointed thorn

And you just keep on muttering "God Is, God Is, God Is"

Josh, however, uses his mastery of satire to carry further the concept of human greatness in his Rubais, not to be forgotten even in the enjoyment of pleasure. And he even goes beyond challenging God, as if addressing the universe.

یہ رات گئے عین عیش کے ہنگام
پر تو یہ پڑا پشت سے کس کا سر جام؟
"یہ کون ہے؟" "جبریل ہوں" "کیوں آئے ہو؟"
"سرکار! فلک کے نام کوئی پیام؟"

> Last night, during mirth making,
> Whose shadow fell on the goblet from behind?
> Who are you? "I am Gabriel", Why have you come?
> "Majesty, would you like to send any message to the

یہ اوج، یہ اجلال، یہ اعزاز، یہ جاہ!
شانوں پہ مرے مہر، تمیتیلی پہ سے ماہ
"دیکھو دستک پہ دے رہا ہے جبریل
"جبریل نہیں، قبلۂ عالم — اللہ"

Behold, what loftiness, what distinction, what elevated rank
The sun on my shoulders, the moon in my palm

Is it Gabriel knocking on the door?

No, your Greatess, it is God.

Josh's vocabulary--which seemed unlimited, his compositions and rendition, all had a crispness that is rare in most other Urdu poets. It was always a sheer delight to listen to Josh reading his rubaiyat and nazms (he wrote not many ghazals) and one could spend an evening, listening to Josh while being soaked in the dew of spiritual refinement. There was a kind of delight, beyond a religious experience and beyond what intellect could conjure. Perhaps Wordsworth could express that feeling in two lines:

And my heart leaps up
When I behold a rainbow in the sky

Something I remember feeling when half a century ago, on a bus from New York to Montreal, when I woke up very early in the morning to see dawn breaking over the Adirondack Mountains. The views appeared to be divine. In that feeling of ecstasy this couplet of Josh came to my mind like a revelation:

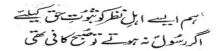

For insightful beings like us, the existence of the Divine,
If the Prophet had not asserted it, morning would have been proof
enough.

Josh in his later years perhaps did not feel good about his decision to migrate to Pakistan. The political and social climate in India was more in tune with Josh's way of thinking and he was valued there. In Pakistan the bigotry and narrowness of mind had space only for those whose minds were full of conformity and the marrow in whose bones reeked of abject submission. Such a climate had no space for a Josh or someone like Faiz. The poets who should have been valued like national treasures were hounded like some infectious disease, and Faiz was essentially exiled and forced out by the minions of a saw-dust Caesar. The only ruler of Pakistan who showed any appreciation of culture was Zulfikar Ali Bhutto who appointed Faiz as his cultural adviser. However, for all his worldly tries Bhutto met the fate of regicide at the hands of another tin-dictator who masqueraded as a defender and promoter of religion. Josh escaped this fate, partly because he was not very actively involved in political issues.

On matters of this world and the next, Josh held rather eclectic views. Perhaps life experiences had made him a pessimist regarding human existence, and he did see life as a struggle and rather full of suffering:

> *Keh yeh dunya sarasar khwab aur khwab-e-parishan hai*
>
> *Khushi ati nahin sine mein jab tak sans ati hai*
>
> *This world is nothing but an illusion , and a confusing one at that*
> *Happiness eludes as long as one has the breath of life.*

Further on, in another ghazal, Josh said it even more succinctly:

> Kaha jata hai mujh se zindagi inam-e-qudrat hai
> Saza kya hogi us ki jis ka yeh inam hai saqi

I am told that life is a reward from nature
What, I wonder, would be a punishment, if this is a reward

But in this very ghazal he goes on to express a Socratic view of life and death:
> *Na jane nau-e-insan kyun ajal se khauf khati hai*

Ajal kahte hain jis ko zahmat-e-yak gam hai saqi

Why, I wonder, are humans so afraid of death?
Because what is called death, is but one step in the journey of life.

This essay does not pretend to be a literary critique of Josh's poetry; it is only a personal and individual appreciation of what Josh as a person and as a poet contributed to the culture and cultural enjoyment of Urdu-walas. Therefore let me end by paying my own tribute to Josh's unique qualities: His poetry had intensity, humor, even sarcasm. It gave voice to the feelings of those who yearned for independence and who rejected conventional metaphors for self expression. Josh Malihabadi was a most distinguished bearer of a literary tradition, and his poetry made him a hero of the Independence Movement. Most of all, Josh was a beacon of freedom and individual assertion against unthinking conformity. His poetry will go on giving lustre to Urdu literature and he will continue to be one among a few truly great Urdu poets. Josh said it best himself:

Adab kar us kharabati ka jis ko Josh kahte hain
Keh yeh apni sadi ka Hafiz-o-Khayyam hai Saqi

Pay homage to that Baddie who is called Josh

Because he is equal to Hafiz and Khayyam in his century

Josh Malihabadi-Living through Communalization and Partition of India

By

S Irfan Habib

Maulana Abul Kalam Azad Chair

National University of Educational Planning and Administration

New Delhi

Josh Malihabadi lived through a period which was witness to massive political and social turmoil. He was around when freedom struggle made huge strides towards the attainment of independence. And he also went through the agony and pain of the tragic partition of India. He remained steadfastly committed to Hindu-Muslim unity and composite nationalism in his personal life as well as in his poetry. Though he later crossed the border, he was not able reconcile with the two nation theory which was the basis of this division. There were several other celebrated writers and poets during this period who confronted the divisive politics of all hues with their combative and creative prose or verse. And this was not true of Urdu language alone; there were Hindi and Bengali writers who remained resolutely devoted to pluralist ethos and composite nationalism. Josh was one of the prime actors in this battle for sanity through not so infrequent spurts of madness during the last three decades before independence and partition.

I do not formally belong to the community of Urdu scholars, who understand the nuances of Urdu literature. Being a student of modern Indian history, I have been a user of Urdu language material for my researches in history of science as well as political history. With this confession in place, I shall attempt to briefly locate our poet of revolution, one of the most apt sobriquets with which we know him in the Indo-Pak sub-continent, in the context of the three crucial decades of the 1920s, 30s and the 40s. I will particularly attempt to locate him in the context of the revolutionary politics and the ideals of composite nationalism, which he shared with Bhagat Singh and his comrades.

The communalization of Indian polity and society got institutionalized in the 1920s with the founding of the RSS and also the Tablighi Jamaat. The abrupt withdrawal of non-cooperation movement in 1922, which also had Khilafat issue tagged with it, added to the troubles of the beleaguered Congress leadership. The Indian polity was communally vitiated like never before and many were swayed from one spectrum of politics to another. The aftermath of the withdrawal after Chauri Chaura incident led to serious rethinking within the Congress party itself. The leaders like Jawaharlal Nehru and Subhas Bose expressed their skepticism about the Gandhian methods and his faith in non-violence as the only means to fight for India's freedom. A large number of revolutionary youngmen, who had agreed to give the Mahatma a chance and had enthusiastically participated in the non-cooperation movement, were disenchanted with the sudden call to give up the battle in the mid way. The country was plunged into the deepest gloom; the mountain, many felt, had brought forth a mouse. Subhas Bose believed that it "was nothing short of a national calamity."[1] Jawaharlal Nehru went to the extent of saying that if it was the inevitable consequence of a sporadic act of violence, then there was something lacking in the philosophy and technique of non-violent struggle.[2] Many young men like Chandra Shekhar Azad, Bhagat Singh and Manmathnath Gupta could not appreciate Gandhi's concept of combining politics with morality which had dealt a fatal blow to the popular movement.

They felt the national bourgeois leadership was terrified at the revolutionary outbreak of the peasantry and that it has betrayed the workers, the peasants and the youth. The impact of the Bolshevik revolution was being increasingly felt and this led to their outlook becoming broader. It was not only the young generation of revolutionaries that was exposed to the new ideas but the elders 'have also started discussing Soviet Revolution and Communism in 1924.'[3] The upsurge of the working class after the First World War greatly influenced all of them. They watched this new social force carefully. They could see the revolutionary potentialities of the new class and desired to harness it to the nationalist revolution.[4] 'Socialism, though not clearly understood, was attracting their minds and the ideals of

S C Bose, *op.cit*, p.90.

[2] M N Gupta, *They Lived Dangerously*, Delhi, 1969, p.56.

[3] Jogesh Chandra Chatterji, *In Search of Freedom*, Calcutta, 1967.

[4] S.N. Sanyal, *Bandi Jeewan*, Two Volumes, Allahabad, n.d, pp. 237-9. V. Sandhu, *Yugdrastha Bhagat Singh*, in Hindi (Delhi, 1968). p. 138; Yashpal, *Sinhavalocan*, in Hindi (Lucknow, 1951), Vol. I, p. 138; Ajoy Ghosh, *Articles and Speeches* (Moscow, 1962), p. 15.

social justice which were in a nebulous form in the earlier period were turning towards taking a distinct shape.' The Hindustan Republican Association, a revolutionary group, was reorganized and also renamed by Bhagat Singh and his associates as Hindustan Socialist Republican Association in 1928. Revolution or Inquilab was proclaimed as their objective and Inquilab Zindabad became their battle cry to fight against both-colonial as well native oppression. It was during these tumultuous times that Josh proclaimed:

> *Kaam hai mera taghayyur, naam hai mera shabab*
>
> *Mera nara hai inquilabo-inquilabo- inquilab.*

Josh was sensitive enough to understand the pulse of the times and was himself convinced that mere freedom from the British will not serve the cause of the poor. Revolution or Inquilab was necessary to facilitate the building of new India where exploitation of man by man will not be possible. The revolutionaries, with whom Josh shared his vision of India, were committed to Hindu-Muslim unity and had an inclusive image of an independent India.

Till the late 1920s, the Congress party was not clear in its demand for independence; it rather wavered between Self-government and Dominion Status and finally proclaimed complete independence as its goal in the 1929 Lahore session. This was again one of the major differences between the revolutionary groups like HSRA and the Congress. The revolutionaries stood for complete independence and had no ambiguity in pressing for such a demand. Our poet of revolution is also categorical in his faith in total freedom, where even a minute of subservience was intolerable. He wrote:

> *Suno aye bastagaan-e-zulf-e-geti*
>
> *Nida yeh aa rahi hai aasman se*
>
> *Ke aazadi ka eik lamhaa hai behtar*
>
> *Ghulami ki hayat-e-jawidan se*

One can see the commitment of Josh to India's freedom and how it matched with the ideals of the revolutionary groups in the 1920s and 30s. It was during the 1920s that Josh began his subversion of the prevalent and widely accepted beliefs. It all began from home, rebelling against his father, questioning the institutionalized religion and virtually becoming an agnostic.[5] It was during this crucial decade, crucial for the future Hindu-Muslim relations and the ultimate division of the country, that Bhagat Singh and his associates were articulating for composite nationalism. There is no evidence to prove that Josh was familiar with these developments, however they were independently moving towards a common objective of bringing in rational and revolutionary methods to transform India. It was during the 1920s that several writers began talking about secular nationalism, which was the main inspiration behind much of liberal-left activism from this decade onwards.[6] The following couplet from Josh aptly describes the thinking during the period:

Dil milte hain jis main se, maabood who main tapka

Paymana-i-Hindu mein, mina-i- musalman mein

The 1930s saw an increase in the bitterness of relationship between the two communities and violence around sectarian issues became rampant. One of the major riots took place in Kanpur where Ganesh Shankar Vidyarthi, the well known journalist and Congress leader was hacked to death. Bhagat Singh also worked with him in his paper Pratap while in exile from home. Josh expressed his pain and anguish in the following lines:

Tujh pe laanat aye firangi ke ghulam-e-besha-ur

Yeh fiza-I sulah parwar, yeh qataal-i-Kanpur

Dil mein khotapan, iradon mein badi niyat kharab

Aur siyah baatein! Yeh aalam aur aazadi ka khwaab

---

[5] Josh Number, *Afkaar*, Oct-Nov 1961, Karachi.
[6] Mushirul Hasan, Memories of a Fragmented Nation: Rewriting the Histories of India's Partition, The Annual of Urdu Studies,

He castigated the British for their nefarious role in dividing the society and also mocked at those who dreamt of freedom while simultaneously fell prey to the divisive colonial politics.

One of the most sensitive issues, which played a significant role in defining Hindu-Muslim relations during these decades, was the fate of Urdu. The fears were generated during the times of Syed Ahmad Khan, who had to confront bitter hostility from the Hindi protagonists during the late 19th century. There was almost a division of the elite into Hindu/Hindi and Muslim/Urdu binaries, despite attempts by several progressive thinkers and writers in both the languages to look beyond such sectarian compartmentalization. When partition became inevitable, one of the main factors for Josh to make a choice was the fate of Urdu in India and Pakistan. Josh, who declared along with a host of other progressive writers that 'we cannot partition Urdu'[7], went and came back and went again several times over, unhappy in that he had no nation, no home now, and probably unclear to the end whether Urdu had been partitioned and what its fate would be in the two countries.[8] The language issue remained central concern for several others like Begum Anis Kidwai, who wrote soon after partition and independence that the language she heard being spoken in the Government House led to a depression. "A language was being spoken there which was stranger to us than English, a language in the words of Josh Malihabadi:

Jis ko dewon ke siwa koi samajh na sake

Zayr mashq hai woh andaze bayan ay saqi.[9]

Jawaharlal Nehru was committed to hold back Josh from crossing over to Pakistan and he soon gave him the task of editing the Urdu magazine Aaj Kal in 1948 and also appointed him advisor in the All India Radio. However, Josh remained skeptical about the fate of Urdu in independent and Hindu majoritarian India. Whenever he went

---

[7] *People's Age,* September 7 1947.
[8] Gyanendra Pandey, *Remembering Partition*, Cambridge, 1989, p.171.
[9] Begum Anis Kidwai, 'In the shadow of Freedom', in Mushirul Hasan, ed, *India Partitioned-The other face of Freedom*, Roli Books, New Delhi, 2005, p.162.

across to Pakistan to participate in mushairas, he was approached by several highly placed friends there to shift for the future of his family and his language. Jawaharlal won't be there forever to look after him, he was told, and the prospect of Nehru's death during his lifetime shook him emotionally. While living through the trauma of partition and communalization of Indian polity, Josh also used to comfort himself with the thought that "mutual hatred and prejudices would be overcome. A socialist government would be formed, one that would put an end to the divisive forces. That is when religious collectivities would be replaced with universal brotherhood:

Ye ek shab ki tarap hai sehar to hone do

Behisht sar pe liye rozgaar guzrega

Faza ke dil mein purafshaan hai aarzooai ghubaar

Zaroor idher se koi shehsawaar guzre ga."[10]

Josh ultimately decided to move over to Pakistan in 1956, which of course angered and shocked Nehru no end. Even the granting of citizenship in Pakistan raised hue and cry, and both Urdu and English newspapers went after him. He wrote that "My going to Pakistan was like a dreadful dacoit ransacking the treasures of Qarun. Or Abraha laying siege to the Ka'aba." Josh was one of those many, who found discomfort in Hindu majoritarian India; while at the same time could not conform to the ideals and inspirations of the new state of Pakistan.

---

[10] Mushirul Hasan, op.cit, 'My Ordeal as a Citizen of Pakistan', p.199, originally published as Pakistan Shriat, *Yadon ki Baraat*, Delhi, 1992, pp284-298.

Dr. Pervez Hoodbhoy

Chairman, Department of Physics

University Quaid-e-Azam
Islamabad 45320, Pakistan

Profile: Pervez Amir Ali Hoodbhoy is professor of nuclear and high energy physics, as well as chairman, at the department of physics, Quaid-e-Azam University, Islamabad. He is an active physicist and often lectures at US and European research laboratories and universities. He is the author of "Islam and Science - Religious Orthodoxy and the Battle for Rationality", now in 7 languages.

Dr. Hoodbhoy received the Baker Award for Electronics and the Abdus Salam Prize for Mathematics. Over a period of 25 years, he created and anchored a series of television programs that dissected the problems of Pakistan's education system, and two other series that aimed at bringing scientific concepts to ordinary members of the public.

In 2003 he was awarded UNESCO's Kalinga Prize for the popularization of science.

Dr. Hoodbhoy received his BS, MS, and PhD degrees from the Massachusetts Institute of Technology

South Asia's Apostle of Secular Humanism – Josh Malihabadi

By

Pervez Hoodbhoy - Keynote Speaker

Shabbir Hasan Khan (December 5, 1898 - February 22, 1982) of Malihabad, known by his nom de plume as Josh Malihabadi, was not a particularly popular poet in his native land, India. For reasons that are not entirely clear, a decade after Partition – against the advice of his friend Prime Minister Jawaharlal Nehru – he chose to migrate to Pakistan. But Pakistan, where he lived his final years, turned out to be even less enamored with him than India. The man on the street today, assuming he has heard of Josh, would probably associate the name with the lyrics of certain popular film songs, or perhaps with his somewhat raunchy autobiography yaadon ki baraat. Apart from this, looking around in bookstores in Islamabad, one finds that other his works are unavailable.

Those steeped in the high culture of Urdu poetry do not really care. They know well the power and exhilarating beauty of Josh's literary creations. His dexterity and genius in transposing thoughts into words created new thoughts and expressions. Poetry flowed from his pen like water from a bubbling spring – he is said to have authored well over 100,000 shairs (couplets) and more than one thousand rubayaats. Some among them represent the finest that Urdu poetry has to offer. This puts him into the pantheon of Urdu poets alongside giants like Ghalib and Iqbal.

But it still bothers one as to why this prodigiously prolific poet has not received, to date, recognition commensurate with his literary achievements. Perhaps one should not be surprised. Almost by definition, an iconoclast is not supposed to be popular in his own culture or country. Indeed, those who dare expose deep dark truths are likely to be reviled rather than praised. Josh the secularist, deeply unhappy about the partitioning of his country on the basis of religion, should not have expected to find recognition in the Islamic Republic of Pakistan. And he did not! It is said that at his funeral there were only seventeen persons present – this in a country where oftentimes many hundreds, or even many thousands, turn out to mourn the departed.

Does iconoclasm explain away Josh's lack of popularity? Perhaps this is being a bit too glib. After all there are Urdu poets who also belonged to the genre of ideological and political dissidents. Some eventually did attain fame and acclaim during their lifetimes. Among Josh's most celebrated dissident contemporaries were Faiz Ahmad Faiz, Habib Jalib, and Ahmad Faraz. Now that there is no squint-eyed General Zia-ul-Haq and his goons to muzzle them, their verses have found their way into rather staid drawing rooms, and are even sung and recited on television. So why is Josh, who passed away even earlier, mysteriously absent?

Perhaps there are other answers as well. Josh's poetry is complex in thought, rich in structure, and uses alliterations and allusions that are subtle. The language is oftentimes difficult: its comprehension requires a vocabulary wider than possessed by the average reader of Urdu. Although a century ago they would have been easily understood, many of the words he casually uses have become arcane and unfamiliar. This is still truer in the birthplace of Urdu – India – where the language is increasingly marginalized, vulgarized, and stripped of its grace and finery. Moreover, contrary to later trends of Urdu poetry, azad sha'aree or free verse was always anathema for Josh. As a stickler for rules, he insisted upon purity of form and adhered to its rules as though he was composing some deeply classical musical raga. So, another possible answer could be: Josh is for the connoisseur, not the masses.

In this short essay I shall draw from Josh's poetry examples that reflect his weltanschauung. His rebellious pen directs withering criticism upon the existing order, challenges those who draw boundaries between peoples, and advocates rational thought over dogmas of the Marxist left or the religious right. His libertarian views and contrarian lifestyle set him apart from the crowd. The conclusion is that this remarkable poet was shunned because his message was too radical for those times, and is even more so today.

A Quintessential Libertarian

Three hundred years ago, philosophers of the European Enlightenment period struggled to define the limits and meaning of individual freedom and liberty. Are these always good things, or only in particular situations and circumstances? When should liberties be curtailed, if they must? The classic libertarian, John Stuart Mill, said:

The sole end for which mankind is warranted, individually or collectively, in interfering with the liberty of action of any of their number, is self-protection. That the only purpose for which power can be rightfully exercised over any member of a civilized community, against his will, is to prevent harm to others....Over himself, over his own body and mind, the individual is sovereign.

Note the key phrase – the individual is sovereign! It runs smack against ideologies of collectivism, as well as the norms of a traditional, religious society. Josh Malihabadi had not studied philosophy or its history. Nor did he have a university degree. Quite probably, he had not read Mill. But being instinctively a rebel, Josh rediscovered and re-expressed in his own idiom the fundamental yearning of all humans to be free:

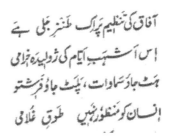

(Rough translation: Written across the cosmos is a line in bold letters. It says that the dance of time has brought to us a new age. So worship no more the graves of ancestors nor supplicate the angels for they cannot give us wisdom. Man can no longer accept the chains of slavery.)[11]

---

[11] NOTE: A worthwhile translation of Josh's works appears not to exist. The reader is warned that my attempts in the remainder of this essay inadequately convey the beauty of his verse.

For Josh as a libertarian, what one eats, drinks, wears, or does in private is a matter of personal freedom and not for any state or society to decide or regulate. This is opposite to how our world actually works: heinous crimes frequently go unpunished but an individual may be pillorized, publicly humiliated, and stripped of dignity for actions that have harmed no other. Josh lashes out against this hypocrisy:

وحشت رَوا ، جَفا و رَوا ، دُشمَنی رَوا

بَل بَحُل رَوا ، خَر وكشش رَوا بَنتِنی رَوا

بِشوَت رَوا ، فَسا و رَوا ، رَه زَ نی رَوا

اَنقَط ِبُرَ د ه سے شَے کہ سے ہَکَر دنی رَوا

اِنسان کے لہُو کو پِیو ، دُنیا عام ہے

اَنگُور کی سے شَراب کا پِینا حَرام ہے

(A rough translation: Insanity thrives, ill-will thrives, enmity thrives, chaos thrives, disorder thrives, rumoring thrives, bribery thrives, conflict thrives, theft thrives. In short, all that is bad does so splendidly well. Drink the blood of man and it matters but little. Drink wine from the grape and you are damned till eternity.)

What a brilliant encapsulation of our collective experiences! On the one hand, Pakistanis find themselves trapped with venal and kleptocratic political leaders who empty the public treasury again and again, and public servants and policemen who stuff their pockets. On the other side are hate-filled ideologues who stoke uncontrollable fires of faith that lead to murders and massacres. Nevertheless, state and society pardon criminals but reserve their harshest punishments for innocents who merely exercise their right to personal choice.

The victims of this vile hypocrisy: the daughter who dares choose her mate instead of obeying her parents, the woman who seeks refuge from a brutal husband, the student who points out his teacher's mistake in class, the young man who breaks from the stupefying traditions of his village, the university girl who dares to hold hands with her boyfriend, and the thinking person who sets aside the faith of his ancestors. They are hounded, beaten, defaced with sulphuric acid, whipped and paraded naked, jailed, and some have been thrown before ferocious dogs that ripped apart their flesh. An unending deluge of horrors flows whenever one opens the daily newspaper. Yet, while moralizers on television, and in places of worship, prattle endlessly about "sinful behavior", they are silent about human suffering. In fact, they often willfully contribute to it.

The ongoing Talibanization of Pakistan is surely the antithesis of freedom, a crushing blow to the human spirit and a re-tribalization of society. Threatened more than all else is freedom for Pakistani women. In just one year there were 1400 reported honor killings. In much of rural Pakistan a woman is likely to be spat upon, beaten, or killed for being friendly to a man or even showing to him her face. Newspaper readers expect – and get – a steady daily diet of stories about women raped, mutilated, or strangled to death by their fathers, husbands, and brothers. Energetic proselytizers like Farhat Hashmi have made deep inroads even into the urban middle and upper classes. Their emphasis is on covering women's faces, putting women back into the home and kitchen, excluding them from public life, and destroying ideas of women's equality with men. Female state officials have been shot and killed, and fatwas issued against others. A hypocritical society sinks to ever lower depths even as the collective piety increases by the day, and the faithful teem into mosques.

Oppression by tradition, custom, and religion is nothing new. But once upon a time, defiant messages of freedom – like Josh's – could strongly resonate with the Pakistani public. Many will remember that powerful speech of Zulfiqar Ali Bhutto – which bears an eerie similarity to the poem quoted earlier. Bhutto had lashed out against his mullah detractors in the 1970 elections saying: ha'an main sharab peeta hoon, logon ka khoon nahin peeta [Yes, I drink wine but not the blood of innocents]. The crowd roared approval. Bhutto won the first – and perhaps the only genuinely significant election – in Pakistan's history. Tragically, he betrayed his electorate and reneged later on much of what he said he stood for. But, in the end, his capitulation to the mullahs and instituting Islamic laws did not save his neck. He died writhing at the end of a noose that he fashioned for himself.

Would Bhutto's boldly defiant message – or something similar that violates today's social norms – have the same effect today? Could it even be voiced? Unlikely! On the contrary, such a frank public admission would be suicide for any whisky-drinking military general or political leader. Unlike Bhutto, the new crop of leaders cannot take chances, being aware that within the Pakistani lower-middle and middle classes there now lurks a grim and humourless Saudi-inspired revivalist movement that cannot tolerate even a whiff of irreligiousity. Everyone knows that public figures – including Pakistan's present and past presidents – cheat on their wealth declarations, do not pay their due share of taxes, rig elections, bribe judges, eliminate rivals, and place unqualified favorites into positions of power. But all is washed clean as they rush to perform Umrah several times a year in Saudi Arabia. Their unctuous piety is displayed in Ramzan with lavish fast-breaking iftar parties and taraveeh prayers. If any blemishes remain, they can always be wiped off with an extra Haj pilgrimage.

Who can deny that the times have changed? A transformed Pakistani culture now frowns upon every form of joyous expression, including the dance and music that had been a part of traditional Muslim life for centuries. Kathak dancing, once popular among the Muslim elite of India, has no teachers left in Pakistan. In Taliban controlled areas of the Frontier province, even the entirely male-performed Khattak dance has disappeared. Thousand year old statues are blown up, and education for girls declared haram. Lacking any positive connection to culture and knowledge, this new revivalism seeks to eliminate "corruption" by strictly regulating individual freedoms. Meanwhile Pakistani urban elites, disconnected from the rest of the population, comfortably live their lives through their vicarious proximity to the West. Even the bearded ones lust for the "Green Card". But on Fridays they don their prayer caps and drive their shiny new imported cars to their neighbourhood mosque. Rich but bored middle-aged housewives, whose only job is to manage a fleet of servants, go to Al-Huda centres and return clad in burqas. Their conversion to the Faith has been quick and expedient.

Those Pakistanis who consider their country morally superior to the West should be deeply ashamed that, while they burn churches and temples in their country, mosques and Islamic Centers flourish in America. There is no church in Saudi Arabia but new mosques are perennially under construction in the US and Britain. Do those who fulminate day and night in Pakistan against religious persecution of Muslims in the West ever reflect on this fact?

Words fail to describe recent horrors. In 2009 a frenzied mob of 20,000 Muslims went on a rampage against Christians in the town of Gojra in Punjab. They had been put into a state of madness by mullahs in madrassas and mosques, who fired them with the notion that a Christian man had destroyed a page of the Quran. The mob destroyed dozens of houses and houses and burnt several Christians to death, including women and children. Of course, there is long history of attacks against minorities in Pakistan and this was just one of very many. The entire village of Shantinagar had been destroyed by another Muslim crowd in 1997. Then there is the tragic story of a mill-worker who had been beaten to death near Gujranwala for eating at a restaurant in spite of a prominently displayed notice "No Christians Allowed". Perhaps he thought that he could sneak in unnoticed. What is especially sad is that, in a protest demonstration by Christians in Islamabad against the Gojra massacre, there were no Muslims. The Pakistani media, knowing full well that it was lying, passed off the massacre as a "clash between two groups".

Secular honesty has few followers in an age where hypocrisy is an accepted way of life. Deceit and theft are guarantors of prosperity in today's Pakistan. Josh, the poet, cries out in a moral wilderness.

Josh Was Anti-Imperialist Yet Pro-Modern

At the crack of dawn on 23 March 1931, the twenty four year old revolutionary Bhagat Singh, together with his two colleagues Sukh Dev and Raj Guru, were hanged until pronounced dead. They had courted arrest after throwing bombs – which did not cause casualties – to protest the British occupation of India. Specifically, they had expressed their opposition to the visit of the Simons Commission.

Charged with determining the quantum of freedom allowable to the natives, the Commission had no Indian members. Widespread public protests had had no effect upon the court's decision to award capital punishment to the three revolutionaries.

A sorrowing Josh composed a poem which he read out in the same city, not far from where the three young men had been executed:

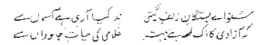

(A rough translation: Hear this all who care for life and love in this world. A voice speaks from the sky. That a moment of freedom is better than a life of slavery.)

Josh's admiration for Bhagat Singh was not merely because this young man was a fighter, but also because he was a free-thinker and atheist. With a keen sense of history and commitment to his goals, Bhagat Singh had educated himself in matters of society and politics before picking up the gun. In this he differed from most others engaged in fighting the British who had thought little about the likely contours of a post-independence society.

For Josh, a Muslim, the fact that Bhagat Singh was a Sikh was irrelevant. What mattered was the inherent injustice of being ruled from afar, and the violent oppression of the colonizers. Even as they prepared for an eventual exit, a class of sycophants was assiduously cultivated by the British. They would remain as instruments for colonial domination, rule from afar. Josh thunders against this elite, who had donned the mantle of their former masters:

برطانیہ کے خاص غلام ان خانہ زاد

دیتے تھے لاٹھیوں سے جو ضربت دتن کی یاد

جن کی ہر ایک ضرب ہے اب تک سر کی یاد

وہ آئی کشی، اس اسی ہیں خوش قسمت ہامراد

شیطان ایک رات میں انسان بن گئے!

جتنے تھے حرام تھے کیسے ان بن سے گئے!!

(Rough translation: These special friends of the British. Whose cudgels had rained upon us blow after blow. Blows, that our still-aching heads cannot forget. Yet today they thrive and thrive. In a flash, devils have turned into angels. They are now the captains of our ship of destiny)

Josh's clear-headed, secular thinking was not shared by most Indians, Muslim or Hindu. Religious reasons competed with secular ones for fighting the British. The "Sepoy Mutiny" of 1857 was triggered when the British introduced new rifle cartridges rumored to be greased with oil made from the fat of animals. The fat of cows was taboo to Hindus while Muslims protested the pig fat. Although Muslims had suffered more than Hindus, they tended to oppose the British for religious reasons more than Hindus.

The reason goes back into history. Although colonization had hit all native peoples hard, it left Muslims in India relatively more disoriented and confused than Hindus or Sikhs. Three hundred years earlier, the development of modern science in the West had led to the emergence of a capitalist order that provided the impetus to forcibly expand Western access to markets and sources of raw materials. Conquest by forces from across the oceans changed forever the comfortable world of India's Muslims who had dominated India for a thousand years. The establishment of British dominion during the 18th and 19th centuries dealt a death blow to the Moghul empire. Elsewhere, Napoleon's invasion of Egypt in 1798 led to a series of changes that ended with the break-up of the Ottoman empire, the last of the great Muslim empires.

European countries colonized virtually all the Muslim world from East Asia to West Africa. A mercantilist and industrializing Western metropolis was on the ascendancy. The old Indian order gasped and then died, unable to withstand the forces unleashed by Scientific Revolution. Bahadur Shah Zafar, the last Moghul emperor, vengefully blinded by the British, spent his last days in captivity. He wrote beautiful Urdu poetry which many people have on their lips even today. But he stood for little besides a decadent monarchy and an order of things that could offer little to the people of India.

The brutalization of a pre-scientific native people by scientifically minded colonists drew a variety of responses ranging from cooptation and despair, to non-cooperation and resistance. Humiliation and helplessness, and a deep sense of resentment, made it difficult for most to see the diversity of the West and its great achievements of the Enlightenment. In any case, the orthodoxy had little use for scientific rationality and democratic pluralism. For them, the farangees (foreigners) were simply kafirs.

The anti-farangee movement amidst the Muslim religious orthodoxy was centred around Deoband, a town in northern India. The Deoband madrassa operated under the slogan that Islam was in danger. Established nine years after the 1857 uprising, it set itself the task of training Islamic revolutionaries who would fight the British; today Pakistani Deoband ulema provide the ideological basis for the Taliban in Pakistan and Afghanistan. The Deoband school became particularly active in demanding the restoration of the caliphate, which had been eliminated by Kamal Ataturk in 1924. Under Maulana Mahmud ul-Hasan and Maulana Husain Ahmad Madni, Deobandis were politically radical, but the movement was socially conservative. Their goal mission was to preserve traditional Islamic learning and culture.

Although it was strongly opposed by the Deobandis, a movement of Muslim modernists emerged in the middle of the nineteenth century. Centering around Syed Ahmad Khan, it sought acceptability for an interpretation of Islam consistent with science and reason. The Muslim elite expanded its educational horizon by allowing its children to study the English language, science, and other secular subjects. Nevertheless, the bulk of Indian Muslims remained rooted in the past and education remained confined to religious subjects for the Muslim masses. The maulanas of Bengal, like the Deobandis of Uttar Pradesh, were adamantly opposed to secular education. In 1835 they collected 8000 signatures against the education reforms proposed by Lord Macaulay, a member of the Supreme Council of India. But these very reforms had been welcomed by the Hindus of Bengal who earnestly supplicated the British for still more schools and colleges. These supplications earned them the contempt of Muslim leaders, who charged that they were sucking up to the rulers.

Muslim conservatism in education had grave consequences for the future. In the 21st century the results of this resistance are evident: India stands at the threshold of being a major technological and economic power while Pakistan remains mired in the backwaters. Pakistan's is being devastated by an Islamic resurgence in the form of Talibanization which, as it gains further ground, threatens to send its people back to the darkest of ages.

In those times, could one have been for progress and yet have been fighting against colonialism? Josh Malihabadi, like other secular Muslim Indian nationalists, thought this was certainly possible. British rule had to be resisted because it was coercive, unequal, and discriminatory even if it had brought elements of the Enlightenment with it. He therefore hated using the English language. But, a half-century before Josh was born; Muslim progressives had already been deeply divided on these questions. For example, Jamaluddin Afghani had sought to bring scientific enlightenment to Muslims while also energetically seeking to overthrow colonial rule across the Muslim world. But he was at loggerheads with another forward-looking contemporary, Syed Ahmad Khan, who had firmly allied himself and his Muslim followers with India's masters, and wanted Muslims to learn science and English. Nevertheless, Afghani and Syed Ahmad agreed on one central point – they both saw traditional cultures as having run their course and now out of steam. They knew that the obstacle to social, cultural, and economic progress was not imperial occupation alone, but also fossilized thought rooted in ancient times.

Josh's position is probably closer to Afghani's rather than Syed Ahmad Khan's. He was against the British – and the English language – but he reserved his strongest attacks against tradition and culture as instruments of mental enslavement. His rhythmically fascinating poem, murdo'on ki dhoom , or, "The Cacophony of the Dead" is a powerful blow against the fossilization of thought:

خلوق کو ، دیوانہ بناتے ہوئے مردے
یاروں کے دماغوں کو چراتے ہوئے مردے
اوہام کے طوفان اٹھاتے ہوئے مردے
عقلوں کو مزاروں پہ بچھاتے ہوئے مردے

آفاق کو سر پر یں اٹھاتے ہوئے مردے
دیکھو اک یہں کیا دھوم مچاتے ہوئے مردے

(A rough translation: The dead drive our people mad. The dead steal the minds of the living. The dead unleash the mighty storms of superstitions. Our minds are trapped in tombs and morgues. The sky too belongs to the dead. Look! Listen to the cacophony of the dead!)

In this poem, Josh speaks equally to Hindus and Muslims, city elites and rural poor, educated and illiterate. Held down firmly by the dead hand of belief and tradition, they drown in superstition and illogic. They pray for rain, attribute earthquakes to the wrath of god, think supplications to heaven will cure the sick, seek holy waters that will absolve sin, look to the stars for a propitious time to marry, sacrifice black goats in the hope that the life of a loved one will be spared, recite certain religious verses as a cure for insanity, think airliners can be prevented from crashing by a special prayer, and believe that mysterious supernatural beings stalk the earth. These superstitions hold as much today as they did decades ago.

The bizarre illogic sometimes boggles the mind. For example, India's 1998 nuclear tests were preceded by serious concern over the safety of cattle at the Pokharan test site. Former Indian foreign minister Jaswant Singh writes "For the team at the test site – which included A. P. J. Kalam, then the head of the Defence Research and Development Organisation – possibly death or injury to cattle was just not acceptable."

India aspires to being a world power, but no Indian politician today can suggest that cows can be eaten. No politician in Pakistan dare suggest that praying for rain won't work. Yet, these neoliths have nuclear science and both countries can annihilate each other in a matter of minutes.

The Cacophony of the Dead continues:

لیلائے تفکر کو سنورنے نہیں دیں گے
ذہنائے تو ہم کو اترنے نہیں دیں گے
تحقیق کی نبضوں کو ابھرنے نہیں دیں گے
تقلید کا شیرازہ بکھرنے نہیں دیں گے

دیکھو کہیں کیا دھوم مچائے ہوئے مردے
اس بات کا ہیزائیں اٹھائے ہوئے مردے

(A rough translation: The dead will not let reason flower. They will not block flowing rivers of superstitions. They will not let minds question and research. They will not allow blind belief to be disobeyed. But they certainly ensure that nothing changes. Look! Listen to the cacophony of the dead!)

Deeply conscious of the calamitous decline in the intellectual energy of Muslims since the Golden Age of Islam, Josh wondered aloud at the causes. What caused a wonderfully alive and intellectually productive civilization to falter, then collapse? Allama Muhammad Iqbal, who is Pakistan's national poet, in his epic dialogue with God (shikwa and jawab-e-shikwa) saw the straying of Muslims from the True Path of the Quran as the reason. But Josh adopts the diametrically opposite path of the "Muatizilla" tradition of Muslim rationalist philosophers.

The dominance of the Muatizilla over long periods of time between the 9th and 13th centuries accounts for practically all of Islamic scientific progress in those times. Their ultimate defeat – marked by bloodshed and persecution – marked the end of Islam's Golden Age. The Muatizilla, who battled their Ashari adversaries on the central issue of freewill versus pre-destiny, believed that Allah had empowered man with the power of reason, the use of which could lead him to choose between alternatives.

The contrary opinion – that of the traditionalists – was that Man was a mere creature of fate, an irrelevance in the greater scheme of things. A straw in the wind, he could be blown hither and thither. All had been predetermined; it was useless to struggle against destiny. Therefore, supplicate Allah and heed his Book; that is the best that can be done.

Striking hard against this notion of helplessness, Josh's Aadmi Nama (In the Name of Man) is a paean of extraordinary eloquence to the powers of Man:

اَے نِگاہ مَولُوئی مَعنَوی
دیکھ سے عِزَّ دِجاہِ آدمی
آدمی ہے، یُوئے گل، رَنگِ حنا
مَوجِ کوثَر، مَوجِ جَے، مَوجِ غِنا

(Rough translation: Look and listen, o' revered mullah. Look at Man's dignity and grace. Man is the flower of life's essence. Man gives color to this world, meaning to its existence, waters the arid desert, and creates the wealth of the universe.)

Josh's attack is head-on, without hesitation or apology. His poetic eloquence pushes him deep into dangerous territory. Perhaps, some might argue, a bit too far. Aadmi Nama continues:

دَسَتِ آدم ، بُت تَراش دُبُت نُما
نُطقِ انسِاں ، مُوجِدِ حَرْفِ خُدَا
وَہم انسِاں ، بانّیُ لاتَ وَمَنات
فَہم انسِاں ، شارِحِ ذاتَ وصِفات
ذِہنِ انسِاں ، پاِبَجُولاں سُوئے ذات
دَرکِ انسِاں ، باِدم قصرِ صِفات
آدمی ، کبُہارِظَن ، قُطُبِ یَقیں
آدمی ، پَرَورِدگارِ کُفرِ ودیں
آدمی ، دانائے اِسِباب وعِلَل
فاتِحِ مُسِتَقبِل دیرِ اَجَل

(A rough translation: With his hand he fashions idols and images. With the power of words he creates the gods. With his superstition he makes the angels. With his intelligence he discovers qualities of the mind. With his mind he walks towards understanding himself. With his understanding he finds the house of knowledge. Man, source of knowledge and worthy of knowing. Man, creator of belief and disbelief. Man, who knows of cause and effect. Man, who shall one day win over death.)

But where did Man come from? Josh was an unabashed believer in the processes of physical law which have produced the wonders of nature culminating in the most wonderful of them all – the human race:

زِندَگی ، سَعئُ بَلیِغ اِرتِقا، کا نازِہَے
آب و آتِش کی کرَامَت ، خاک کا اِعجازِہَے

A Rough translation: Life is the proud result of Evolution. Life is a gift of water and fire, the miracle of earth and dust.)

While other poets – Ghalib, most notably – have sniped from the sides, Josh declares open war on blind belief. His opponents screamed: Idolator! Worshipper of man! But little happened because Josh was an old man when died, his poems were little understood, and he had certainly lived in better times. One wonders: were he alive today, would he still be able or willing to write these lines? Most probably this poet would have been ripped to shreds by a shrieking mob, perhaps like the ones which burnt churches in Shantinagar and Gojra, or that in Shabqadar which had chased a terrified Ahmadi up a tree and shot him as he pleaded for his life.

Nationalism, Religion, Language: Josh's Deadly Triangle

Every reader of this essay almost certainly carries a passport: Pakistani, Indian, Canadian, American, or whatever. Our world is presently divided into nations, which we tend to think of as permanent entities while forgetting how utterly recent they are. The League of Nations in the 1930's had a maximum of 58 members. This is less than one third of the current 192 members of the United Nations. In other words, about 80 years ago, two thirds of the world's current nation-states did not exist.

Even the oldest nation-state is but a few centuries old. I will not take sides in the academic debate of whether Peace in Westphalia, signed in 1648, actually marked the beginning of the first sovereign state. But much before that – fifty thousand years ago or more – our hunter-gatherer ancestors lived in tribes. Loyalty to the tribe was natural, a necessary condition for collective survival. Tribal markers – tattoos, piercings, bones through the nose or ears, binding of feet, dances and songs, giving particular names to children, festivals, marriage rules – were bonding elements because they identified who belonged to which tribe. Attachment to one's tribe was unequivocal and total: the tribe could never be wrong. The individual did not matter, and must be ready to kill or die for the tribe.

Nationalism emerged as an advanced form of tribalism. In Europe, the invention of cannons, roads, and printing presses had made domains of control larger. Coalescing tribes, and larger tribes, could do better than fragmented ones. The notion of a nation slowly emerged. It built upon the myth of a common ancestry, reinforced by similarities of physiognomy, language, culture, or religion. The nation was seen as marching together towards some shared future destiny, and hence that it must work together. This strengthened its capacity to cope with the challenges of a hostile environment, and to compete successfully with other groups animated by similar beliefs.

But there is a downside to nationalism. Wired for "group think", humans tend to assume that their particular group or nation has no peer or rival. However, since obviously not every nation can be the best of nations, this assumption simply has to be wrong. If it was just a harmless assumption who would care? On the other hand, when one group insists on its absolute superiority, there is high risk because the other is automatically reduced to an inferior position. My nation, the true patriot asserts, is better than your nation. We are spiritually pure, you are intrinsically corrupt. Nationalism can then become the justification for mass murder and genocide.

This is why Einstein called "nationalism an infantile disease, the measles of humanity", and Erich Fromm declared that "nationalism is our form of incest, is our idolatry, is our insanity", and that, "patriotism is its cult". Einstein and Fromm both, of course, were Europeans.

Europe, which invented nationalism in the Age of Enlightenment, has suffered more than any other part of the world from nationalism, which soon spun out of control. The two world wars left 70-80 million dead and many times more permanently disabled. The lessons of Europe must, therefore, be carefully studied by people from Pakistan and India.

It is interesting to see how nationalism laid out its roots in Europe. For example, in the 17th and 18th centuries, French culture had imposed itself on many parts of continent. Frederick the Great of Prussia and his court spoke and wrote in French, but they really thought of themselves as Germans. Indeed, a nascent German nationalism was beginning to stir. Even before the establishment of a German national state, the romantic German nationalist, J.D. Herder, wrote a poem in protest against the French culture of Frederick's court in Prussia:

Look at other nationalities!

Do they wander about

So that nowhere in the world they are strangers

Except to themselves?

They regard foreign countries with proud disdain.

And you, German, alone, returning from abroad,

Wouldst greet your mother in French?

Oh spew it out before your door!

Spew out the ugly slime of the Seine!

Speak German, O you German!

About two hundred years later, Konrad Lorenz, the Austrian Nobel-Prize winning zoologist and ornithologist, studied animal traits. But he also explored the biological roots of human aggression. Living in pre-WW II times, he warned against the growing German nationalism:

"We have seen on the screen the radiant love of the Fuhrer on the faces of the Hitler Youth... They are transfixed with love, like monks in ecstasy on religious paintings. The sound of the nation's anthem, the sight of its proud flag, makes you feel part of a wonderfully loving community. The fanatic is prepared to lay down his life for the object of his worship, as the lover is prepared to die for his idol."

Konrad observed that men may enjoy the feeling of absolute righteousness even while they commit the worst atrocities. Indeed, in situations of war, conceptual thought and moral responsibility descend to their lowest ebb. My revered physicist colleague from Denmark, Dr. John Avery, in his remarkable book "Space-Age Science and Stone-Age Politics", (translated into Urdu and freely available at www.mashalbooks.com) quotes a Ukranian proverb that says: "When the banner is unfurled, all reason is in the trumpet". Thereafter, men stop being human and turn into killing machines.

In South Asia, as in Europe, tribalism is generally considered to be on the retreat. But, perhaps paradoxically, in large parts of Pakistan it has been enhanced by technology and protected by modern weapons which tribal people can easily acquire from the developed world. Whether urbanization will create a melting pot, or temporarily lead to a re-solidification of ethnic and linguistic boundaries that will re-tribalize society, is an open question. But the appeal to a larger entity will surely win here too at some point in the future.

The enormous power latent in nationalism was revealed in 1947 yet again. Nationalism dovetailed with religion to create ab-initio the first Islamic nation-state in history, Pakistan. This world-shaking event posed a fascinating paradox: major Muslim political parties, such as the Jamaat-e-Islami and the Jamiat-e-Ulama-e-Hind, fiercely opposed the creation of Muslim nation state. Nevertheless, the personally secular Mohammed Ali Jinnah captured the Muslim mood with his "Two-Nation Theory".

In his 1940 presidential address delivered in Lahore, Mr. Jinnah asserted that Muslims and Hindus were two separate peoples who had separate customs, histories, heroes, and outlooks. Thus they belonged to two separate streams of humanity that could never intermingle nor live in peace together. Without this core belief, there would not have been a Pakistan. Mr. Jinnah assumed as a matter of course that Muslims – by virtue of sharing a common faith – could live together harmoniously and they naturally constituted a nation.

The strength of Mr. Jinnah's Muslim League in the Muslim-majority provinces of India was put to the test during the 1945-46 election campaign. Consequently in the public meetings and mass contact campaigns the Muslim League openly employed Islamic sentiments, slogans and heroic themes to rouse the masses. This is stated in the fortnightly confidential report of 22 February 1946 sent to Viceroy Wavell by the Punjab Governor Sir Bertrand Glancy:

The ML (Muslim League) orators are becoming increasingly fanatical in their speeches. Maulvis (clerics) and Pirs (spiritual masters) and students travel all round the Province and preach that those who fail to vote for the League candidates will cease to be Muslims; their marriages will no longer be valid and they will be entirely excommunicated... It is not easy to foresee what the results of the elections will be. But there seems little doubt the Muslim League, thanks to the ruthless methods by which they have pursued their campaign of "Islam in danger" will considerably increase the number of their seats....

When Mr. Jinnah finally succeeded in creating Pakistan, Josh's reaction to the partition of India was one of dismay. His rubayi "Mourning Independence" (Matam-e-Azadi) was

written in India in 1948 and Josh recited it to a public gathering in front of Delhi's Red Fort on India's first Independence Day:

(A rough translation: Blame me not for the sorry tale of Hindustan. Blame not the seller of wine if it produced no joy. Nor blame the musical instrument for producing mere discordant noise. A cold autumn rain falls on the garden. Those beautiful roses that could have grown will grow no more. Thorns there shall now be many, flowers no more.)

By now the carnage of Partition had already occurred. Neighbor turned against neighbor, friend against friend. A frenzy of blood letting, murder, arson and rape enveloped the cities, towns, and villages of India. Hindus and Sikhs slaughtered Muslims, and

Muslims slaughtered Hindus and Sikhs. Trains filled with corpses arrived at railway stations in Lahore and Amritsar, on opposite sides of the newly established border. A mass transfer of population left a million people died in one of the most catastrophic events of the 20th century. Even today that bitterness is far from gone.

Josh could find no reason to be joyful:

أُبھرے تو جوشش با وہ گلسلدانٌ نہیں ہا

باوَل گِھرے تو رَنگ بَہـارانٌ نہیں ہا

راتیں کِھلیں تو رَقصٍ بگا راں نہیں رہا

بوتَل کُھلی تو جمٍ یا راں نہیـیں رہا

کوئی سَـبیل باوَہ پرَسـتی نہـبیں رَہی!

مَسـتی کی رات آئی تو ہسـتی نہسـیں رہی!!

(A rough translation: Little good does this wine bring. Spring comes without its bright colors. Conversations are limp and lifeless. Even the wine brings little cheer. Drink as much as you want but it still does not help. The night of our celebration is dark and joyless.)

Jawaharlal Nehru, Prime Minister of India, who was present in the audience, was visibly unhappy with the poem, but then listened to it again in a private gathering. He is said to have protested that Josh should not have read it in front of the general public, to which Josh curtly retorted "but it was meant for them"[12].

Among Josh's most brilliant and hard-hitting poems, one must certainly include Zindaan-e-Musulus: Lasaan, Adyan, Autan (The Triangular Prison: Language, Religion, Nation). Some excerpts follow:

---

[12] I am grateful to Iqbal Haider for this anecdote.

کب تک رہیں گے آخرِ یہ طنطنے، یہ تیور
یہ تِیر، یہ کمانیں، یہ نیچے، یہ نِشتَر
یہ آدمی، یہ سالارِ آفاق دمیرِ دوراں
نکلے گا کب جہاں جغرافیے سے باہر

(A rough translation: How long shall this pomp and façade last?
These bows and arrows, these knives and daggers? Man, who presides
over the universe, the king of our times. When shall he escape the
narrow confines of geography?)

The essence of the last line above is the concept of territoriality.
This is so universal and commonplace that it is simply taken for
granted. Individuals internalize territorial dominance as part of the
formation of a personal identity. Now an established concept in social
ethology, territoriality was once a survival imperative. Like their ape
ancestors, humans had to compete for resources necessary for the
individual or group. Boundaries had to be defined. Some territorial
mammals use scents secreted from special glands, to create their
demarcations. Dogs and cats also establish their territories also using
scent-marks, but through urination or defecation. Humans draw maps.

Shall these boundaries remain until eternity? Josh answers:

کب تک بنے رہیں گے اے دارِثانِ آدم
اپنوں میں آب کوثر، غیروں میں تاب خنجر
یہ غیر یہ تصوّر، افلاس یہ آگہی ہے
رشتے نہیں بندھتے، اغیار اس زمیں پر
مشترق سے تا مغرب، آ کر نئل، اک نسب ہے
اس آسماں کے نیچے، اور اس زمیں کے اندر
قوموں میں بانٹتا ہے جو نسل آدمی کو
مشترک ہے اور کا فر کا فر ہے بلکہ اکفر

(A rough translation: O' descendant and inheritor of Adam. Until when shall you want peace for yourself and a dagger for others? This notion of the "other" is so primitive. Remember, my friend, there are no "others" on this earth. From east to west we are all one species, one race. All under this sky and upon this earth are the same. Some work to split us into nations. They play God and are kafirs. Nay! They are not kafirs but the most sinful of kafirs!)

In decrying nationalism, Josh could be equally speaking to Americans who have waged dozens of wars in the last century, invaded countries, dropped atom bombs, leveled cities, starved populations and tortured prisoners. Or he could be addressing the Japanese who today are a peaceful nation. But in 1937 they murdered hundreds of thousands of Chinese and raped between 20,000-80,000 women in one of the worst episodes of human brutality. It is hard to imagine that the Turks, who are almost integrated into Europe, could have slaughtered 100,000-200,000 Armenians. The list goes on.

It is a depressing fact that today, in a world shrunk by internet and mass communication; we still live in nation-states for which people feel intense emotions of loyalty very similar to the tribal emotions of our cave-dwelling ancestors. Tsunamis of patriotism have again and again brought forth millions of patriots anxious to slaughter those on the other side. Somehow the ape within us refuses to go away.

So should one love the country one was born in? Hate it and love another? George Monbiot, a British citizen and columnist for the Guardian, states his position:

I don't hate Britain, and I am not ashamed of my nationality, but I have no idea why I should love this country more than any other. There are some things I like about it and some things I don't, and the same goes for everywhere else I've visited. To become a patriot is to lie to yourself, to tell yourself that whatever good you might perceive abroad, your own country is, on balance, better than the others. It is impossible to reconcile this with either the evidence of your own eyes or a belief in the equality of humankind. Patriotism of the kind Orwell demanded in 1940 is necessary only to confront the patriotism of other people: the Second World War, which demanded that the British close ranks, could not have happened if Hitler hadn't exploited the national allegiance of the Germans. The world will be a happier and safer place when we stop putting our own countries first.

The Lessons for Pakistan

This has been a long essay. What should right-minded Pakistanis conclude from the many themes of Josh's radical, progressive, secular poetry?

At the outset, the reader must recognize that, contrary to what the doomsayers have announced many times in recent months, Pakistan is a nation-state that is not going to go away. But, if it is to a happy nation, it needs a positive vision. What should that new vision be?

Certainly, Pakistan would not have come into existence but for the fear of Hindu domination. Fortunately, there is no reasonable basis for this fear. Hence, there is no need for any further two-nation, three-nation, or multi-nation hypotheses. Pakistan and India are not going to become one country any time in the foreseeable future. Except for a few Shiv Sena crackpots in India, no Indian wants re-unification while Pakistanis would be even more allergic to the idea. Therefore one must get the notion of unification firmly out of the way. Instead, Pakistan must aim towards becoming a normal civilized country, where people live normal, happy lives free of needless prejudice. How should it go about seeking this?

A pluralist democracy is the answer. For sixty years we have feared diversity and insisted on unity. But Pakistan paid a very heavy price because our leaders could not understand that a heterogeneous population can live together only if differences are respected. The imposition of Urdu upon Bengal in 1948 was a tragic mistake, and the first of a sequence of missteps that led up to 1971 – which left the Two-Nation theory in tatters. The faith-based Objectives Resolution of March 12, 1949 had been just as big a disaster for Pakistan because it led to the disenfranchisement of its citizens, and ignored the principle of respecting diversity.

Pakistan is a multi-ethnic, multi-national state – and it must be recognized as such. Its four provinces have different histories, class and societal structures, climates, and natural resources. Within them live Sunnis, Shias, Bohris, Ismailis, Ahmadis, Zikris, Hindus, Christians, and Parsis. Then there are tribal and caste divisions which are far too numerous to mention. These cannot be wished away. Add to this all the different languages and customs as well as different modes of worship, rituals, and holy figures. Given this enormous diversity, Pakistani liberals like to speak for "tolerance". But this a bad choice of words. Tolerance merely says that you are nice enough to put up with a bad thing. Instead, let us accept and even celebrate the differences! Inclusion, not exclusion, must be the new principle. We must learn to accept, and even celebrate, our differences and diversity. Other countries that are even more diverse than Pakistan have learned how to deal with this successfully. So can Pakistan.

Pakistan must – and can – find a new identity without insisting that every Pakistani be a Muslim. Today almost every Pakistani understands Urdu, which was not true 60 years ago. This is a hint that a new Pakistani identity is in the process of formation. Even if they don't always like each other, Pakistanis are learning to understand and deal with each other simply by virtue of having had to live together long enough. And so, unless things fall apart because of the irresponsibility of its rulers, Pakistan will surely become a nation one day – even if it wasn't one to start with.

The future: much depends upon how we deal with Baluchistan. I definitely do not approve of the desire of some Baluchis who want to secede from Pakistan. It is not practical, nor realistic, nor in the interests of the Baluch. Remember, Baluchistan is not East Pakistan; it is part of the same land mass. Baluch, Sindhis, Punjabis, and Pathans must somehow learn to live together. Baluch anger at being cut away from the riches that lie beneath their ground is perfectly justifiable. They are the poorest in Pakistan in spite of being hugely rich in terms of mineral deposits and oil. A formula must be worked out that will appropriately benefit the people of Baluchistan rather than their tribal sardars. Those in Islamabad need to do more.

Still more depends on how we plan to deal with economic inequity. Pakistan has never had land reform, imposes no agricultural tax, rewards feudal lords with seats in parliament, and its institutions empower the rich at the expense of the poor. The landscape is that of conspicuous consumption and abject poverty.

Finally, and perhaps most importantly, the new vision of Pakistan demands that it renounce religious discrimination and care equally and deeply for all citizens. All the myriad sects of Sunni and Shia Islam must be considered equals. The state must care just as much for its Hindus, Christians, or Ahmadis. This must hold even for the odd Pakistani Jew – although I don't think there is any left (there were a few Jews during my school days in Karachi but they all left).

Resting all matters of the state upon religion is a prescription for unending fratricidal struggles. This will continue to pit faithful Muslims against other faithful Muslims. Parachinar and Hangu have been ablaze for years, car bombs still continue to explode in Baghdad even after the Americans have announced their withdrawal, and similar slaughters happen around the globe. The very fact that there is serious disagreement even among believers of the same faith – not to speak of faiths hostile to each other – means that there cannot be only one single truth in any religion, or agreement on how to run a religious state.

For this reason, Pakistan, as a country with many Muslim sects cannot be run by the sharia because, even for Muslims, the obvious question is: whose sharia? Shafi'i, Hanafi, Maliki? Hanbali? And what about the Shias who accept none of these? These questions cannot be pretended away. They have not been resolved in a thousand years. Nor can they be resolved in the next thousand. It is time to move religion out of politics.

This calls for constitutional reform. Pakistan cannot afford a constitution that discriminates between Muslim and non-Muslim. Therefore every law that discriminates between the citizens of this land must be annulled. Every citizen of Pakistan needs to be declared exactly equal to any other irrespective of religion, ethnicity, or class. We clearly cannot impose jizya on non-Muslims and expect loyalty from them. Thus the law must be secular to be uniform.

Further, if we want unity in the face of diversity, then the majority must stop trying to force itself upon the minorities. Most crucially, the state must stop acting on behalf of the majority.

To conclude, sixty years is not a long time in the life of a nation, but it is time enough to learn from grievous mistakes. As times change, needs change. Slogans and mottos, and the avowed national purpose, should also change. Surely, every nation-state in the world stands somewhere along a learning curve.

Time is running out for Pakistan so the learning will have to be quick. Narrowness of vision has made this into a land of suicide bombers. Shredded bodies and twisted limbs lie all around. So let us harken back to Josh Malihabadi's clarion call as he pleads for a new global consciousness welding all humans together. His message rings loud and clear:

کس کھوہ میں ہے آخر تیرا خطیبِ اعظم
اے راستی کی محراب، اے روشنی کے منبر
ہاں وحدتِ خدا کا اعلان ہو چکا ہے
اب، وحدتِ بشر کا، دنیا، کوئی پیمبر!

(A rough translation: Why are our great preachers silent? They speak of righteousness and illumination by faith. They have announced that God is one. But shall they now announce a new prophet who says humanity is one?)

Acknowledgement:

My interest in the poetry of Josh Malihabadi was stimulated by my participation as a speaker in a symposium organized in Calgary, Canada by Iqbal Haider, founder of the Josh Literary Society. In listening to the other speakers, I found myself entranced by the richness and beauty of the poetry which hitherto I had only been casually aware of. I am also grateful for various pieces of information about Josh's life and work that I received from Mr.Haider. These were important in giving this essay its final form.

Dr. Anis Alam

Born on 20th October 1943, educated in Karachi, Chittagong, Islamia College, and Punjab University Lahore, Imperial College of Science London, and Durham University (UK). Returned to Lahore as the youngest PhD in physics in Oct. 1967 to join the University of the Punjab, Lahore. On leave from the Punjab University has worked in Iran (1970-71) as Professor of Physics, in UK as Visiting Fellow History and Social Studies of science (Sussex University 1977), Visiting Scholar (London University Institute of Education 1978-79), in Italy as Visiting Scientist (International Center for Theoretical Physics, 1984-85).. Retired from University of the Punjab, Lahore as Professor in 2004. Worked as Director- Dean of the Ali Institute of Education, Lahore. (March 2004- June 2005) before joining the Lahore School of Economics as Professor of Mathematical Sciences.

Has traveled extensively round the world participating and presenting papers in International Conferences in Norway, France, UK, Italy, Egypt, India, Malaysia and China. Was Associate of the International

Center for Theoretical Physics, Trieste, Italy visiting the Center for short and long periods frequently from 1970 to 1997.

Avid hiker and trekker in mountains, having climbed a peak of over 18000 feet in the Nanga Parbat region with Korakaram Club expedition in 1963.

Deeply interested in history, philosophy, sociology and problems of development especially in post-colonial societies.

Has published 19 research papers in most prestigious international journals (Physical Review, Nuclear Physics, IL. Nuovo Cimento, Acta Crystallographica, Physic Stat Solidi, Solid State Communications, International Journal Of Bifurcation & Chaos); and 16 papers on issues related to science and development that have appeared in international journals (Bulletin of Concerned Asian Scholars (USA), Race & Class (UK), Social Scientist, Bulletin of Sciences (India)) and Proceedings in UK, France, Egypt, Italy, India, Malaysia and Pakistan.

Has been active in popularizing science having published translations of books by Nobel Laureate Prof. Abdus Salam, Steven Hawking and George Gamow. Also published three under-graduate physics text books & three popular accounts of science and philosophy.

Has published over hundred articles in Pakistan's leading daily newspapers; DAWN, NEWS, NATION, FRONTIER POST, JANG, NAWA E WAQAT, as well as leading Pakistani Weeklies, Monthlies and Quarterlies. Contribution to books published internationally and nationally.

Dr. Anis Alam

Josh- Celebrator of Life, Reason and Humanity

I am grateful to Josh Literary Society of Canada and especially Mr. Iqbal Haider who persuaded me to participate in the present seminar on the great poet and scholar Josh. I am privileged to be among such a galaxy of scholars, poets and critics from different continents. Among them there are scholars who have known Josh and have studied him in far greater detail and depth than I. They can initiate a far more informed discussion of Josh's literary works. I am neither a poet nor a critic, only a student of science, having been fortunate enough to know Prof Abdus Salam as teacher and mentor for nearly thirty years. I have taught physics at university level for over thirty five years and been privileged to interact with scholars from around the world. Besides my work in my own specialty of theoretical particle physics I have generally been interested in exploring intricate relationships that seem to exist between science and society. Why science develops in one country or region and not in others. How science shapes and frames our ideas, concepts and worldviews.

I developed of books from my mother. From early childhood I developed a habit of reading. From simple children stories I graduated to more serious literature. Besides literature I have studied history, philosophy and sociology of science and scientific ideas. While in college I read voraciously but studies of Urdu literature was mostly confined to fiction. I knew Josh only superficially, more by his reputation as the poet of the revolution and as a great versifier having a command and mastery of language unequalled in any other living poet. I had not read any of his poetry. In later years his name cropped up as the author of Yaadoon Ki Baarat[1] his famous autobiography.

It is only in the last decade that I came to know Josh a little better. This was through the excellent Urdu quarterly Irtiqa[2] that has been published with regularity from Karachi for the last twenty years. Irtiqa is probably the best quarterly of its kind in Urdu as it publishes serious essays on various science and social science issues of current interest beside fiction, poetry, biographies and criticism. Eminent intellectual/activist Vahid Bashir, Rahat Saeed and late poet Hassan Abid have been the leading spirits behind the magazine.

To celebrate the centenary of Josh's birth a seminar was arranged in Karachi. Irtiqa devoted one whole issue to the proceedings of the seminar[3]. It carried extremely informative and incisive essays on Josh's work. After going through the issue I was motivated to read Josh's famous autobiography " Yaadoon Ki Baarat", that completely won me over. Josh was a person that I could identify with. He came out as a rationalist, a monist, a humanist as well as a firm wahdet-ul-Wajoodi and celebrator of life in all its magnificence and diversity. His attitude was completely that of a scientist. In Yaadoon Ki Baarat he writes, "My thinking had a beginning in thinking about the stars…..As I matured my field of inquiry broadened to include the whole cosmos, I got interested in the basic questions of cause and effect. I wanted to explore all aspects of being and properties"[4]. Josh identified twenty different ways[5] that he wished to employ in studying an object. I don't think an experimental scientist could add many more.

Recently I was sent some of his Rubayyats. The more I studied them the more I got convinced that had Josh's work been popularized we might not be facing the obscurantism and irrationalism that clouds not only common thinking but also the writings in mainstream vernacular media and most of our populace in Pakistan.

How one does understand Josh, his work and life? Josh though born in Maleehabad, United Province in colonized India, speaking and writing in Urdu is a fine example of a Universal man. He acknowledges and owns all advances in knowledge everywhere and through times past and present. He takes pride in being human and being alive. He wishes all others to feel the same way. But he is also aware of his particular situation that of a colonized subject. So he becomes the Poet of the Revolution. Once colonial domination gets overthrown, he uses his intellectual weapons against ignorance, obscurantism, ethno-lingual centrism, religious bigotry and debilitating spiritualism[6]. I view Josh as a tragic hero, as his last years were spent in a totally inhospitable intellectual environment. But he used his pen to continue to fight for rationalism and humanist values.

From early adult lie I have been an advocate and believer in the unity of humanity and unity of knowledge. All knowledge in essence is the understanding of the world and all that it contains, animate and inanimate. All knowledge is the result of wonder and curiosity, the quest for answers to what, how and why. Knowledge can not be confined to certain regions and people. Knowledge once gained becomes part of universal human heritage. In Josh I find a confirmation and reiteration of ideas and values I believe in.

Josh Maleehabadi, assumed name of the scion of a family of Afridi Pathan soldier adventurers was born during the days when the possibility of adventure with the sword was non existent unless in the service of the British capital whose rule was overwhelming not only in the sub-continent but in all other continents. Sun never set in those days in the British Empire which extended over thirteen million square miles and contained over three hundred and fifty million Asians, Africans, Carribeans, North Americans and Australoasians[7]. Josh as an Indian was part of these millions of the colonized. But he was also living in a period when anti-imperialist struggles were erupting all over the colonies. The first socialist revolution had triumphed in Russia. Calls of national liberation was everywhere in the air. Josh became a spokesman for this historic movement. For his poetic efforts he he was bestowed the honour of being called the Shaere Inqilab- the Poet of the Revolution. He was uncompromising in his critique of imperialism and exploitation in general be that by the colonial authorities or their local minions[8]. He was among the original signatories of the Progressive Writers movement. He furthered the struggle for independence, was befriended by the leaders of the nationalist struggle, becoming close friend of Jawahar Lal Nehru, the first Prime Minister of Independent India. Josh lived for another thirtyfive years after the end of colonial rule. His attention shifted from imperialism to nation building.

South Asian culture is generally projected as other-wordly, passive and generally contemplative. South Asians are thought to be generally more interested in preparing for life after death rather than celebrating life here on earth. But that was in general the case all over the world in those pre-industrial societies. During the late fifteenth century when the Sultanate period was nearing its end in South Asia, Europe was undergoing a cultural shift. The focus of intellectual and artistic attention which was dominantly religious started shifting to man and man's creation. Instead of painting the holy family and building monumental cathedrals, majestic villas, fountains and parks started being laid. Michelangelo not only painted the roof of the Sistine Chapel but also sculpted the magnificent statue of David that can still be seen proudly displayed in Uffizi gallery in Florence, Italy. The period also witnessed the dethroning of the Aristotelian-Ptolemaic earth centered model of the cosmos. Scholasticism gave way to acquisition of the knowledge of the real world. Galileo introduced the experimental –mathematical method that has revolutionized science since then and laid the basis of the modern world. Galileo asserted that the basis of knowledge is verifiable observational data not some authority however ancient, respectable or holy. He not only overturned Aristotle, accorded the title The First Teacher through the medieval times, but also the ecclesiastical teaching of the holy church. He suffered but his methodology for science not only survived but has thrived. Most of our knowledge of the present world in all its details has been achieved as a result of his scientific methodology[9]. New observational tools the telescope, the microscope, the clock, the thermometer, the electric battery, the vacuum pump, the spectrometer, have extended the knowable world beyond anything imaginable few hundred years ago. In the 1920s, when Josh was in the prime of his life, a new observational tool the radio-telescope was introduced that has extended our observable universe to unimaginable size. Before radio telescope the universe consisted of only the Milky Way galaxy, now there are over 100 billion more galaxies each containing on the average 100 billion stars[10]. It is dynamic world where change is the only constant feature. Stars being formed, maturing and finally dying in spectacular supernovas or ending less spectacularly as white dwarfs.

The power of the five senses has been enhanced beyond all imagination. Humanity is now capable of anything, however outlandish it may be. In 1958, Josh celebrated the flight of Sputnik, the first artificial satellite that the Soviet scientist sent into space defying the pull of the earth in his poem, " Zamin Ka Burraq"[11].

The tragedy of the non European societies specially the South Asian has been that they encountered rationalism and science not as a force that would help them overcome fear of unknown and liberate them from their prejudices, poverty and underdevelopment, but as a force that helped foreign traders exploit, defeat, subjugate, rule and control them[12]. Their elites instead of welcoming the new knowledge and the rationalism that was the basis for it to equip themselves with the tools to resist and overthrow colonial yoke, abandoned enlightenment as a colonial and an alien construct. They grew introvert, and returned to primordial identities of cast, creed and beliefs. The resistance to colonial rule was mostly passive and couched in religious terms[13].

Even after the formal ending of the colonial rule, the governments in general have not introduced policies that would have ended age old illiteracy and empowered the common people to develop their capability to the maximum. Present day Pakistan has almost three times as many illiterates as was her total population at the time of independence. Ignorance Obscurantism, mysticism reigns supreme. What was ignored was the fact knowledge is a common universal heritage. As Prof Salam was fond of pointing out various people, various regions have contributed to this sea of knowledge. It is to be used for enlightenment and progress of humanity as a whole. Knowledge ought to be acquired, developed and cultivated irrespective of its origin. Josh understood this fact, he highlighted it and exhorted his readers to abandon traditions and use reason to understand and solve problems of this world.

Josh understood that what goes in the name of tradition was once new and had to overcome earlier old established tradition. Hence no tradition or system of knowledge and institutions can be accorded the status of sacred and infallible, that can not be tempered with or given up. He understood that institutions and ideas are human constructs and have a historical character. They have been used to further the interest of particular class or tribe/nation/country/region to the detriment of others. He has identified Ethnicity, Religion and Nationhood as the trinity of prisons[14]. The massacres and genocides not only in recent history but over millennia have been perpetrated in their name. They divide humanity. Josh believes in the one-ness of humanity which he highlights and emphasizes again and again in his works[15]. In fact he not only believes in the one–ness of humanity but in the one-ness of all existence animate or otherwise[16].

During his last years, he directed his efforts to spread his rationalism and humanism as his later works testify.

I would like very much that all his works are made available especially in all public school and college libraries.

More than two thousand years ago The Roman poet Lucretius, a disciple of the Atomist Epicurus, composed his long poem Nature of Things/Universe[17] that tried to describe and explain all the known objects and phenomena in atomic terms without the intervention of gods and demons. In the introduction he explained that he composed his work so that the reader will overcome the fear of death. Only ignorance creates fear. The period since then has witnessed centuries of generalized ignorance punctuated by few centuries of rationalism 9th -11th C among Muslim ruled regions, then enlightenment and the dawn of the modern era. Josh acknowledges and owns the advancement in the human knowledge[18] and the understanding of the world. He advocates the whole scale ownership, absorption and cultivation by all the people everywhere in the world. He is a believer in the eventual triumph of humanity and the dismantling of false gods of exceptionalisms. However, Pakistan in particular and Muslim countries and communities in general are regressing.

Josh though dead for over twenty five years is now ever more relevant.

I congratulate the organizers for taking the first steps in that direction.

References

1. Josh. Maleehabadi, Yadoon Ki Baarat, autobiography, Karachi, 1970
2. Irtiqa, Quarterly magazine published from Karachi, Pakistan since 1989.
3. Irtiqa, Josh Centenary Issue, No. 24, Dec. 1999-March 2000, Karachi
4. Yadoon Ki Baarat, p.17, Maktabae Sher-o-Adab, 1970,
5. Yadoon Ki Baarat, ibid., p.17
6. Josh. M, Ilham-o-Afkar, 1966.
7. Hobson. J. A., Imperialism AStudy, J. Nisbet & Co Ltd, 1902
8. Josh. M, East India Ke Farzandoon Se, poem, 1941 in Yadoon Ki Baarat op.cit., pp. 254-258.
9. Bronowski. J ,The Ascent of Man, Little, Brown and Co, Boston, 1973, ,
10. Sagan. Karl,Cosmos, Ballantine Books, NY, 1980,
11. Josh. M, Zameen Kaa Burraq in Ilham-o-Afkar, 195
12. Anis Alam, Science and Imperialism" in Race and Class 19: 239-251, London, 1978
• Deepak Kumar, Science and the Raj 1857-1905, OUP, 1995
• Gyan Prakash, Another Reason: Science and the Imagination of Modern India, Princeton University Press, 1999
• Baber. Zaheer, The Science of Empire, ,State University of New York Press, 1996
13. Kazim. M, Muslim Fikr -o-Falsafa Aahad ba Aahad, Ch. 12, Mashal Books, 2002.
• Fazlur Rahman, Islam & Modernism

- Aziz Ahmad, Islamic Modernism in India and Pakistan

14. Josh. M, Taslees; Lissan, Otan, Adian (Rubaayaaat)
15. Josh. M, Taslees; Lissan, Otan, Adian, no.2,(Rubaee)
16. Josh. M, Taslees; Lissan, Otan, Adian, n0.3, (Rubaee)
17. Lucretius, On The Nature of The Universe, Penguin Classics, London, 1953
18. Josh. M, Arooj-e-Insani, and Aadmi Nama in Ilham-o-Afkar, 1966

Karamatullah K. Ghori

Former Ambassador of Pakistan

Josh Maleehabadi: Quintessential Iconoclast and Humanist

The choice of Calgary for a seminar on Josh, the great bard of 20th century South Asia, may be inadvertent but gels so ideally with the temperament of the man.

Three years ago I'd my first glimpse of the fabulous scenic charms that the province of Alberta in the Banff National Park, perhaps the greatest ecological treasure of Canada. Getting up very early in the morning—uncharacteristic to my nature and life-style of a night-owl—I couldn't help admire nature for the wealth it had given Alberta in spades. But that eerie, almost surrealistic, calm of early dawn instantly made me recall that immortal verse of Josh Maleehabadi that encapsulates his total submission to nature's enchanting and mesmerizing allure:

Hum Aise Ahl-eNazar ko Saboot-e-Haq Ke Liye

AgarRasool na Hotey to Subha Kafi Thee

This roughly translates as the poet's innate sense of aesthetics compelling him to admit that he sees nature's immutable sense of proportion and discipline in the break of dawn to such an extent that he would be ready to believe in the Divinity of God presiding over this world in perfect harmony, even if there was no Holy Prophet (peace be upon him) to vouch for it.

That was Josh, the quintessential humanist and naturist who, with his exquisite sense of proportion and eye for beauty, could admire nature's mastery of the universe and bow to it in submission unquestioningly. Josh's passion for nature remained unflagging all through his 80-plus years. He would've loved to live a life of serenity in Canada's vast panorama of ecological delights from the Atlantic coast to the Pacific coast. I'd also dare add that he would have loved to become a card-carrying member of the Green Party, especially with Elizabeth May at its head; his life-long infatuation with angular faces of the female of the species earned him accolades as well as barbs-a-plenty, with the latter beating the former by many times over.

But Shabbir Hasan Khan Josh Maleehabadi was much more than just an aficionado of nature's scenic splendors or one with a eye for sensuous faces. He was a man of many dimensions and talents; a polymath in the strict sense of the word.

However, before turning my gaze to Josh's myriad facets, I can't help mentioning an obvious irony implicit in the decision to hold these proceedings in the English language, something that Josh simply abhorred. He was an inveterate adversary and enemy of the British Raj in India and committed his entire adult life to oppose it with all the might of his pen and majesty of his eloquent poetry. By the same token, Josh loathed the idea of using English as a medium of communication, even though he finished his schooling in the Cambridge system of education, then the best one available to the wogs of India, and was quite at home in it. But anyone using English to communicate with him was just inviting his wrath upon himself.

One comes across a passage in Josh's celebrated autobiography, Yadon Ki Barat (Cavalcade of Memories) where the bard talks of having written a letter, in Urdu, of course, to an government official who replied to him in English. The poor official was not to blame for daring to write back to Josh in English, which still happens to be the language of everyday business and correspondence with the Government of Pakistan. However his daring was too loathsome for Josh, who promptly wrote back to the unsuspecting official: I had addressed you in my mother tongue, but you have replied to me in the tongue of your father.

But that said, I should hasten to add that Mr. Iqbal Haider has come up with an exquisite initiative to hold this seminar in English. Why is it so is simple to understand: English isn't only the language of modern technology; it is also, in this age of cyber-net and cyber-space the global medium of instant communication. More than anything else, much as we may regret and remonstrate it, the fact must be acknowledged, even if grudgingly, that it's now also the language that our younger generations—those whose parents still pride themselves on their dexterity in Urdu. Our children, let us face the sour truth, feel more comfortable in writing and reading in English than in the language of their parents. Whether one likes it or not, English has, in fairness to its unassailable global status, has become the Lingua Franca of the world.

Writers, poets and other men of letters using the myriad tongues of South Asian Sub-continent, have suffered as far as recognition of their works, some of them monumental, in lands beyond their native shores is concerned. Tagore was exceptionally dexterous and in good command of English; he used it for some of his great works, which then induced English translations of his works to the extent that he became the only man of letters from the great landmass of South Asia to win Literature's Nobel Prize. But tens of other great names from South Asia, especially giants of Urdu literature, haven't been that lucky. Iqbal was an exception. He was widely translated, not only in European languages but also in Arabic—the most prolific language for literature. But even then he couldn't excite the imaginations of the purse-keepers of the Nobel Prize to loosen their tight grips in his favour.

Josh is, perhaps, the most unlucky of those greats among the Urdu literati to have been totally neglected by translators, although he, more than anybody else among his peers and contemporaries, relentlessly carried a message of a universal community of mankind to rise above the narrow confines and divisions of race, language, belief and culture.

This seminar could well serve the purpose of lighting a trail toward understanding Josh by those who have not been exposed to him, his poetry and his vision of humanity because of the language barrier. In that sense, Mr. Iqbal Haider is a trail blazer and deserves to be complimented for his brilliant idea of bringing Josh to the English-speaking Canadians, including our own children of the new generation who are proud to call themselves Canadians or New Canadians.

Not that we are doing any extraordinary service to Josh and his legacy. This, in fact, was long overdue and we are simply repaying the debt we owed to the great bard whose universalism and unrivalled penchant, as far as Urdu literature goes, for the rise of a global community of mankind based on shared humanism, has yet to be fully appreciated and recognized. This, hopefully, is the first step in that direction.

This should also answer the obvious question as to why Mr. Iqbal Haider should be virtually resurrecting a poet who was shunned and ignored and belittled as long as he lived, and has been almost completely and deliberately forgotten in the years since he breathed his last more than a quarter century ago?

It was a question that still agitates my mind and my faculties why this urge to revive the memory and legacy of a man who was without doubt the most controversial literary figure of his generation and hasn't fared any better by the generation that has come of age since he passed away from this world?

For answers to these questions we will have to make an attempt to understand the life and style of Josh—no easy undertaking this, by any means or yardstick.

Josh was a rebel, an iconoclast and a highly unconventional man, according to the known social, historical and political standards of his times. But he was the least likely candidate to fit the role model or the stereotype of a rebel or revolutionary rising from an environment of penury and, because of it, seeking to balance the scales against him.

Josh was born in the lap of wealth and abundance of it. His ancestors had amassed great fortunes in land and grown enormously rich and powerful. Unlike most of his contemporaries from the world of literature, Josh didn't belong to the struggling middle class with economic survival posing the toughest challenge of life. Instead, he was born with a silver spoon, nay a golden spoon, in his mouth in a prominent feudal family in the heartland of undivided India. It was a different matter that by the time he started his own family he was faced with the stark challenge of earning his own living because the spend-thrift life style of his extended family had drained much of the feudal holdings from their hands.

But Josh remained a feudal in his basic instincts, social mores and societal interaction. He was a prince who would never stoop to anyone nor bend before the high and mighty. There was this stubbornness in his persona that he had inherited from his hardy ancestors who had traveled down to the Gangetic plains of India from their mountain fastness in what was later to become, under the British as it is now in independent Pakistan, known as the North West frontier Province. The blood of tenacious Pathans that he inherited from his forefathers fashioned him as much as it is fashioning those Pathans of our day who are still resisting the onslaught of foreign invaders and adventurers with the same ferocity as their forebears did throughout recorded centuries of history. Anyone doubting this statement should only visit the contemporary geo-political reality obtaining in the lands shared by Pakistan and Afghanistan.

Josh, a scion of those valiant Pathans who wouldn't compromise on the values they considered alien to their code of morals as well as their sense of history was thus a natural to fit the classical mould of an iconoclast, particularly when it came to living in an India ruled by an alien power with the stigma of exploiter affixed on its face as evidence of history. No invader in history has fared well with the Pathans. So there was no question of Josh compromising or relenting vis-à-vis the Farangi occupiers of India.

Josh was prepared to pay the price of his hostility to the British presence in India as its rulers and masters. We learn from his memoirs that he had no compunction in turning down the offer of an English commissioner, who happened to be friends with his father and offered to give him a respectable job in the service of the crown—an offer for which any ordinary Indian would have given his right hand. But Josh being Josh dismissed his offer with contempt. How could he even think of serving the colonialists who had enslaved his people; the question just didn't arise with him, no way, not at all.

He was, in that core instinct of non-cooperation with the British colonial power poles apart from several of his peers who, like him, had unfurled the banner of revolt against the colonial power and written extensively on the subject like him. But they, unlike Josh, had no compunction in joining the British war effort against Hitler. A man like Faiz Ahmed Faiz, with impeccable credentials of a poet and writer of resistance became a cog in the British war propaganda machine. Of course he and others of his ilk—all of them masquerading as socialists and committed members of Communist International—justified their actions by insisting that they were co-operating with the colonial power because Britain had entered into an alliance with the Soviet Union—their ideological font and mentor—to face the common evil of Hitler. Little did they seem to realize that Hitler was patronizing Indian nationalists, like Subhash Chandr Bose, for instance, who saw in the Great World War the chance of a lifetime to deal a mortal blow to British colonialism in India.

Expediency of such a kind simply didn't inform Josh, whose opposition to the British Raj brooked no respite or detour. Expediency wasn't in Josh's lexicon. Even pragmatism had scanty presence in his life.

To Josh opposition to British colonial rule was like a red line drawn wherever he stood, upon whatever patch of earth. That principle, when translated into his stirring poetry, earned him the richly-deserved title of Shair-e-Inqilab or 'poet of revolution.'

But Josh over-stretched his red line of opposition to the Raj by including in its pale those native princes of India whom he accused being in the service of the colonial masters. That uncompromising aspect of his persona—a flaw of character to his detractors and critics, and a manifestation of fundamental belief, to his fawning friends and admirers—landed him into hot waters in the princely State of Hyderabad, where he served the longest period, ten years, of his working life. Denouncing the ruler, the Nizam of Hyderabad as an agent of the imperial power, he literally chopped off the hand that had been feeding him for so long. But Josh simply wouldn't contemplate seeking the Nizam's forgiveness or pardon. That's how unbending or, simply put, head-strong he was about what he believed to be the core mettle of his pristine concept of freedom and human dignity. To some, however, it could just be a case of arrogance and narcissism that came with his genes.

One of Josh's grand sons, Siraj Anwer Khan, recalls in an article written after his grand father's death how he didn't lose a minute before virtually scolding the then autocratic ruler of Pakistan, Field Marshal Ayub Khan, for having greeted him as a renowned alam (which means the world, in Urdu) and not alim(which means a scholar). Now any other man in his place would have simply ignored that slip of the tongue by his immediate boss, let alone the man who was the uncrowned king of Pakistan. Ayub Khan was a Pathan like Josh but since his ancestors hadn't settled down in the culturally fertile plains of the United Provinces (U.P.) of India his pronunciation of Urdu remained un-chiseled. It's quite common for people from the northern and even central parts of Pakistan to call an alim alam, in its distorted intonation. But Josh simply couldn't suppress his natural inclination to correct the ruler of Pakistan and put him on the spot just as he'd have done with a lesser mortal. The backlash from Ayub Khan against that public humiliation was Josh losing the license for cement for which he had gone to Ayub. It was quite a price to pay at a time when he was strapped for cash to make end meet for his extended family.

There are innumerable examples that could be culled, from his memoirs, where he suffered and obviously courted trouble because of his narcissism bordering on megalomania.

We learn from his Yadon ki Barat of his stark refusal to visit film producers of Mumbai, who were ready to hire him as a song writer, in their offices and insisted that they must come to his residence to beg for his services.

He mentions, on another page, having torn to shreds the allotment order of land to build a house right there, in front of the officer who had signed that document only because the official insulted him by not rising to his feet to bid him leave. There, in such reflexive riposte to what he considered an affront to his dignity he is in the august company of Mirza Asadullah Khan Ghalib who, like him, turned down the offer to teach Persian at the Delhi College only because its English principal wouldn't come to the front door to greet him.

In both cases it wasn't only egos bruised that they weren't shown respect due to their station in life. Both regarded it as a calculated affront to the glorious legacy of their forebears who, in their esteem, had earned glory on the merit of their heroic services rendered to Muslim rulers resisting the onslaught of the Farangi. Ghalib, like Josh, didn't rest on the laurels his immaculate poetry; he prided as much, if not more, on the martial merits of his ancestors.

Josh drew a sharp line between his feudal moorings and those of other feudals, like the Nizam of Hyderabad, whose patronage he spurned, although he wouldn't shy away from accepting the life-long pension he earned from the court of the Nizam for his one decade of service to Hyderabad State. His forefathers had earned fame and fortune in the service of Muslim rulers of Oudh who had stood up to the British onslaught against their citadel of power. The Nizam of Hyderabad, Josh knew from history, was a scion of those who had sold their souls to the British colonizers, colluded with them and stabbed in the back the likes of Tippu Sultan, the most valiant of Muslim heroes challenging the Farangi conquest of India.

Therefore Josh had no moral qualm in rebutting the critique of Sir Tej Bahadur Saproo, a notable name in the 20th century freedom movement of India, when he pointed out the obvious contradiction in Josh's concurrence in the severance of service pension from the Nizam, and also accepting another pension from the Raja of Patiala, a Sikh princely state of Punjab. History, he argued, was his witness and best defence.

With his Himalayan pride in the nobility of his genes and bloodline intact, Josh, the inveterate cavalier, led on the campaign of resistance to the Farangi colonialism in India mounted by a tribe of Urdu writers and poets inspired by his stirring example in the first half of the 20th century. Names like Ali Sardar Jafri, Akhtar ul Iman, Kaifi Azmi,

Majrooh Sultanpuri, Shair Lakhnavi and even Majaz Lakhnavi, to some extent, come readily to mind among the legions of those progressive writers, poets and thinkers for whom the Pathan from Maleehabad was a role model of sorts, although many of them would be reluctant to acknowledge it.

However, Josh's iconoclasm against the alien colonizers and their Indian cohorts and satraps came to an end when India won its freedom and Josh's bosom friend, Jawahar Lal Nehru, availed of the earliest opportunity to send India's princely and feudal era packing into the dust bin of history. Josh should have also folded his tent and drawn a line under his epic struggle against the British Raj and its local hirelings.

But Josh wasn't quite done with his crusade against tyranny, injustice and inequality of man. With the first chapter of his struggle in India closed, he cast his eye around and found a ready challenge waiting for him in next-door Pakistan.

Josh, in his memoirs, has defended his decision to migrate to Pakistan for purely mundane reasons; it was for the sake of his children and their off-springs that he bade farewell to India. Even that reason could be disputed. He had an unflagging mentor in Nehru who deferred to him and got him well-settled into a dignified job as editor of All India Radio's monthly magazine, Aaj Kal. In fact the whole Nehru clan deferred to him, Indira Gandhi being as respectful as her father. And there was no surety that there would be greener grass on the Pakistani side of the Great Divide for his progeny to flourish there.

Josh himself, or anyone else among legions of his doting fans or groveling detractors, has said it so but I have a sneaking reason to suspect that the real motive for Josh to move to Pakistan was the challenge awaiting him there. The temptation for a life-long warrior was too great to resist.

By the time Josh was impelled, in 1955, by Mr. Abu Talib Naqv, then Chief Commissioner of Karachi and a fawning admirer of Josh—and many others like him—to cast his die in favour of settling down in Karachi, Pakistan had been taken over by the feudals. The conspiracy, hatched and perpetrated by the feudals of Punjab, in particular—with the active connivance of some progressive writers who had their own axes to grind against the founders of Pakistan—had succeeded in side-lining those who had sacrificed with their blood, toil and labour to hammer out a state for the Muslims of India against the most daunting of odds. The feudals were in full thrall and Pakistan was like a bird of prey in their clutches. What could be a more tempting target for Josh to resume the campaign against tyranny, injustice and oppression, this time, unfortunately by the sons and scions of those who had served the Farangi well and had been richly rewarded by their imperialist masters. He was all set for phase II of his career of an iconoclast.

It's true that Josh didn't support the Pakistan Movement in its early phase. He was, in that period, a supporter of the Indian National Congress and promoted the idea of a united India, sans the British imperialists. But once converted to the idea of Pakistan he never opposed it or participated in any effort, once it had become a reality, to unhinge the state. There, he was in marked contrast to those Moscow-inspired and communism-influenced intellectuals and poets, like Faiz Ahmed Faiz, who struck a deal with fortune seekers, in the Pakistan Army and among the feudals, to actively conspire against the fledgling state.

In Pakistan he went through cyclical phases of patronage and disdain. Surprisingly, he received a much cordial reception from the bureaucrats, whom he didn't particularly fancy, than his fellow poets and writers, many of whom regarded him a threat to the niches they had carved out under feudal and political shelters. Top bureaucrats, mostly old I.C.S. breed, co-operated with him a lot and made his transition relatively easy. Men like Mussarat Hussain Zuberi, Mumtaz Hasan and Aftab Ahmed Khan cut corners for him to get government cushions under him. He'd every right to feel bitter about the cold shoulder from many quarters and complain:

Translation:

Mein Karachi maen hoon aise jese Koofe maen Hussain

'I'm stranded in Karachi the way Hussain was in Koofa.'

But it's a fact that those who could be blamed for inviting him to Karachi didn't desert him. Mr. A.T. Naqvi, the force behind his move to Pakistan, remained his mentor to the hilt even though he lost his prime Karachi post because the then Prime Minister, Chaudhry Mohammad Ali, didn't take kindly to his sponsorship of Josh.

Notwithstanding his personal disappointments, perhaps because of his exalted expectations, he received a much better deal from the Pakistani hierarchy of power than any other contemporary man of letters, with only Hafeez Jalandhari, the poet behind the national anthem of Pakistan, getting into his league.

Josh got the best deal possible from the government of Zulfiqar Ali Bhutto, largely because of Maulana Kausar Niazi, Bhutto's Minister of Information and right hand man. Niazi, himself a poet of considerable merit and an eloquent orator, admired Josh immensely and made sure that the umbrella of government patronage was unfurled to the fullest extent possible for Josh. I'd the good fortune of sharing many an evening with Josh Saheb in that period of his sojourn in Islamabad—where I was posted as a Director in the Foreign Office—in the company of a senior Foreign Service colleague and mentor, Ambassador Irtiza Hussain, who hailed from Lucknow and had known Josh from before. Josh Saheb looked totally relaxed and at home in Islamabad and those evenings spent with him were a treat to my aesthetic senses, if not for anything else .Josh Saheb held court at his own, government-endowed, residence as well as at the residence of Ambassador Irtiza Hussain like an emperor holding his audience in total thrall, especially after he had had a sun-downer or two down into his system. Senior bureaucrats in that grade-conscious and highly stratified capital city of Pakistan seemed in awe of Josh because of his connections with Maulana Kausar Niazi and, by implication, with ZAB.

Bhutto's downfall and the rise of General Ziaul Haq on Pakistan's political horizon spelled doom and gloom for Josh. His life style of a totally liberated, if not libertine, man didn't sit well with the new ruling elite; his religious philosophy, of which he spoke freely and held back nothing, became the biggest bone of contention with the Zia brigade of orthodox and highly opinionated men of limited vision and convoluted sense of religion and man.

It was Jamaat-e-Islami that led the charge against Josh and sniped at him to their heart's content. This was the same political party that had openly opposed the idea of Pakistan and campaigned against it. But now its purblind leaders and camp-followers got in the vanguard of those questioning Josh's loyalty and commitment to Pakistan. That makes me wonder if the Jamaat would've behaved the same and gone after Josh with the same fervour and zest had its founder and principal ideologue, Maulana Abul Aala Maudoodi been alive? Maudoodi and Josh were friends since their days together in Hyderabad Deccan and Josh was one of the very few men who addressed the Maulana on first-name basis. That period of decline, in which he was shorn of any vestige of government support, haunted him to his grave.

Curiously, Josh fared much worse at the hands of his peers from the world of literature and intelligentsia in Pakistan than with the denizens of the power corridors. Many of his contemporaries took alarm at his becoming a permanent fixture of the Pakistani literary landscape. They felt threatened of the giant-killer Josh also toppling them off their high perches and pedestals. Even an icon like Baba-e-Urdu Maulvi Abdul Haq campaigned against him. Josh returned the compliment in a no-hold-barred riposte in his memoirs, demolishing the icon. He was equally unsparing of Shan Ul Haq Haqqi, his immediate boss at the Urdu Lughat (Dictionary) Board. I got the honour of knowing Haqqi Saheb much later in Toronto. By then his salad days had long been over and he was a shadow of his past. However, I couldn't muster the courage, ever, to debrief haqqi Saheb on all that Josh wrote about him in Yaddon Ki Barat.

Josh should've known that the cancer of feudalism had struck lethal roots in Pakistan's body politic by the time he appeared on its firmament. But the most worrisome trickle-down effect of the feudal syndrome was that its poisonous nectar had also seeped into the country's literary and intellectual strata. Josh could never rub off the stigma of his years spent in independent India, or Bharat. His closeness with Nehru put a huge question mark on his fidelity to Pakistan in the eyes of myopic pen-pushers masquerading as true nationalists and intellectuals. Their lowly ceilings and tunnel visions couldn't comprehend the cosmic heights of Josh's universalism and humanism that made all of them look like Lilliputians.

On top of it, Josh wasn't a son-of-the-soil and had the misfortune of having been born on the banks of a wrong river. He was an outsider to them and their blinkered sense of intellectual enquiry. Josh stood no chance of bringing down the walls quickly erected around him; what chance could he have when a genius of Olympian heights like Ghalib had already been put on the back burner to simmer there because he was, henceforth, to be remembered as an Indian poet and not a colossus of Urdu literature.

Josh's greatest misfortune was that in the Pakistani pantheon of literature he walked too closely behind the shadow of a giant like Iqbal, the dreamer and undisputed ideologue of Pakistan.

Josh had established his own reputation of a Shaer-e-Inqilab (Poet of Revolution, or revolutionary poet) in Iqbal's life-time. There was a lot in common between the two and Josh remained deferential to Iqbal till his last breath. Both shunned the narrow and suffocating confines of a strictly land-based sense of nationalism. Josh was as much a Universalist as was Iqbal and fully shared his cosmic vision of a global community of men inspired by universal truths of freedom, justice and fairplay.

Iqbal, of course, had an edge over Josh because of the difference of scale in their scholarship. Iqbal had drunk deep at the myriad springs of European philosophy, which enabled him to synthesize his Islamic moorings with them and come up with his immutable intellectual model of Mard-e-Momin. On the other hand, Josh's ideological aversion to everything western barred him from going Iqbal's way.

Iqbal was one icon that Josh wasn't after and never entertained any thought of dislodging or demolishing him from his high and exalted pedestal in the pantheon of South Asia's 'greats.'. But he also lost out to Faiz for reasons that had nothing to do with the caliber or mettle of his poetry vis-à-vis that of Faiz.

Together with Iqbal, both Josh and Faiz make the three-some leading revolutionary poets of Urdu in the 20th century, with Iqbal clearly leading the pack. But Josh also came second-best to Faiz in the esteem of most Pakistani intellectuals not because the majesty of his words and the sheer elegance of his diction seemed much too strident, or even jarring to some, in comparison to Faiz' soft, supple and sensitive diction and the lilting cadence of his sophisticated syntax. Josh lost because the Pakistani literary scene had been infiltrated heavily by special interest groups, lobbies and cartels. Josh had never been known for being a partisan of this or that lobby or special-interest group and despised the feudal intrigues that were becoming a norm of Pakistan's increasingly Byzantine literary milieu. He deemed his persona as being far above such crass shenanigans that smelled of feudal cunning and intrigues. The result of his aristocratic detachment went against his status in the pecking order of a Pakistan rapidly losing its national cohesion and being consumed, instead, by inward looking ethnic and linguistic biases. Josh was very much an outsider to this unfolding spectacle.

Let us be fair, besides, to Faiz in this contest in which neither he nor Josh had any role or interest; both, in fact, were unwitting cohorts to those pygmies of literature—politicised literature, that was—who were seeking to use the Olympian heights of the two to add inches to their own, stymied, stature.

Faiz had broken through the barrier of national boundaries of literature and acquired international stature, perhaps unwittingly. His socialism was entirely home-grown but had been hijacked by communism, especially the one pegged on Moscow's leadership, to serve its own propaganda. It became a handy tool in the tussle for one- upmanship triggered by the Cold War. Faiz became a poster poet for communist war of nerves against the west. And from there he moved on to the Arab world, this time as a willing and ardent supporter of the Palestinian cause against the Israeli oppression and enslavement. This scribe's long exposure to the Arab world witnessed Faiz' ascending popularity graph among the Arab intelligentsia once he became editor of PLO's official magazine from Beirut, Lebanon. He was only the second poet and writer, together with Iqbal, who excited Arab imaginations and became well respected with the Arab intellectual mainstream. Josh wasn't blessed with that kind of supra-South Asian popularity and persona and, apparently, made no effort to take to Faiz' route.

However, Josh was too familiar with reverses and adversities to be put off by them. He took them in his stride, almost stoically, and gave back as well as he took. He tells us in his memoirs, at the writing of which at the start of the 70s he was without a job, that he was living through the 5th cycle of economic reverses in his life. But he was as nonchalant and blaze about that latest turmoil in his life as he'd been about the four earlier ones. The born optimist in him never lost faith in his capacity to rebound and start all over again with a new élan. Like the proverbial phoenix he was accustomed to rising from his own ashes.

Josh's faith in himself and his ability to rejuvenate his role of a universalist pining for the collective good of mankind, especially its oppressed classes, was anchored, deeply, in his perception of an ideal man. The role model that inspired him most was that of Syedna Hussain Ibn-e-Ali, the grand son of the Holy Prophet (Peace be upon him) and the martyr of Kerbala. Josh's stirring poetry, especially that where he talks of human civilization's perennial conflict between good and evil, between right and wrong, is studded at innumerable places with allusions of Kerbala and Hussain, Islamic history's most revered martyr.

The choice of Hussain at once signifies Josh's own commitment to uphold the sanctity of life and position a dignified society on the immutable principles of justice and equity. There can be no place in such a social order for tyranny and oppression. Josh found in the person of Hussain the hero who wouldn't blink in the face of tyranny and would hold back nothing to resist its onslaught with all his might. Hussain's sacrifice of his own blood, and the blood of his whole family for the sake of his crusade against the tyranny of Yazid was, to Josh, the epitome of man's eternal struggle for a just society pegged on equity and dignity.

Josh found a nexus between Hussain standing up to Yazid's reign of terror and his own life-long campaign to rid the world around him of tyranny and injustice and uphold the inalienable right of every man to a life of dignity and liberty. Josh's own universalism and humanism discovered a perfect sync with Hussain's laudable mission to rid the then Muslim world of Yazid's thuggish rule and an order of oppression and injustice it so wantonly epitomized. And he had no doubt that the future belonged to Hussain and his noble mission because it was anchored in progress and evolution of man in a more enlightened world, which would relate mankind ever more closely to Hussain's vision. He summed up his optimism that the future belonged to Hussain and, by inference, to Josh, in this eloquent verse that could be hailed as the distillate of his Universalist ideals:

Translation:

Insan ko Bedar to Holayne do

Her Shaqs Pukare ga hamerey hein Hussain

Let human intellect mature;

Then every man would claim Hussain as his own.

Josh's ideological affinity with Hussain, the most revered martyr in Islamic history, instilled in him an unremitting confidence and faith about the righteousness of his own mission. Notwithstanding all the sniping that went on against him from the hideouts of Ziaul Haq's cold-hearted ruling elite, or his callous lampooning at the hands of some of his puny peers from the literati, Josh wouldn't falter in his determination to pursue his advocacy against oppression and injustice to his dying breath. Like Hussain, he lived what he preached, hardened in the belief that the moving finger of fate had ordained for him, too, the denouement prescribed for Hussain, i.e. his name to serve as a shining example forever. The following verse encapsulates this perception in crystal clarity:

Translation:

Paigham Mila Tha jo Husain Ibn-Ali ko

Khoosh hoon Wohee Paigham-e-Baqa mere liye hai

The message of eternal life bestowed on Hussain;

Is also good for me, I'm so delighted.'

Josh's intellectual and visceral affinity with Hussain also informed his humanism, despite his ancestral roots still firmly planted in a feudal culture. Indeed his inborn poetic dispensation was another cardinal factor moulding his personality. In his memoirs we come across a number of anecdotes from his childhood days where the two extremes of feudal narcissism and poetic humaneness run parallel to each other.

In one anecdote, Josh, the spoiled brat, beats a servant boy black and blue, which makes his aristocratic grand father immensely proud that his progeny had inherited all the right genes from him. But once Josh had given the lad a thorough thrashing he quickly compensated him with money and admonishing him to eat good food with it in order to put some fat on his bony torso, and be ready to face an encore of that experience with greater resilience.

In another peek into his childhood of plenty, we read about an old servant of the family addicted to opium. Josh was a confidant of the old man and plied him with a bowl full of fresh cream—an essential perquisite for opium smokers—every day from the family's kitchen. The lady in charge of the kitchens, a sort of a female major domo, suspected another woman working in the kitchens for spiriting away that prized fresh cream and wanted Josh's mother to fire the woman. But Josh, hearing the baseless accusation against the unsuspecting woman stepped forth, instantly, and confessed to his mother that he was the one to squirrel away the booty of cream to the opium addict because the old man was too poor to afford fresh cream on his meager means.

That was Josh, a born defender of the poor, the indigent and the down-trodden; a crusader on behalf of the wretched of the earth. That was a role that came naturally to him because of the sensitive and caring-for-humanity poet that was born in his persona. Along with this unremitting and unstinted compassion for the disenfranchised people of the world, he also developed, from early childhood the life-long passion to speak the truth and nothing but the truth, no matter how inconvenient that might be for him and embarrassing for his interlocutors, friends or foes. The foundations of Josh, the unflinching warrior and crusader, were laid very early on in his life. The contours of his well-chronicled and reported battles with the privileged and the powerful were shaped almost in his infancy.

No wonder, therefore, that although a relatively late comer to the Pakistani scene, he became quickly attuned to its calls and his prolific pen and ever-alert mind got down to work as a champion of the people of Pakistan—a lot bewildered and out of its wits at the unraveling of the dream of Pakistan at the hands of its inept and uninspiring political masters, most of whom hailed from the feudal elite that Josh so much loathed and despised.

There was a remarkable piece, a commentary on politics of the day, that Josh penned for the then popular and left-leaning weekly, Lail-o-Nahar ('Night and Day')in its 7 to 13 December 1970 edition, dates close to the heels of the then impending general elections in Pakistan. Those were the most historic general elections of Pakistan that, eventually, changed the course of its history, triggered a civil war in East Pakistan and ultimately led to the birth of a sovereign homeland, Bangladesh, for its people.

 Josh's brilliant and incisive analysis of the then Pakistani political scene reads as fresh as if it were written yesterday, because all that he said about the forces of tyranny and social injustice then stalking the political landscape can, very easily, be extrapolated on what's happening in Pakistan of today. It reads like a testament of cold facts and harsh realities that holds good for all times to come in Pakistan unless the demons devouring the ill-starred society were eliminated and the people rid of their baneful hectoring over the land.

Josh laments, in this evocative and enthralling tract, that the people's voice has been silenced by merchants of doom—both from the feudal aristocracy and those from religious orthodoxy. He can't help comparing the lot of the browbeaten people of Pakistan with those who were partisans of Imam Hussain in their hearts but had been crushed and silenced to such an extent by Yazid's oppressive regime that they cared not to stand up for the defence of Hussain.

Josh sounds almost prophetic in his expose of the polarization of the then political forces in the country and warns, in so many words, "*If*

this tempo stays its course then that day is not too distant when a horrendous civil war will be triggered. It will snuff out life from hundreds of thousands of homes and families, corpses will litter the streets of Pakistan and the blood of the Pakistanis would flow freely."
(My translation of his Urdu prose)

And that was precisely what happened in East Pakistan, within months of the bitterly contested elections and the refusal of the West Pakistani ruling elite to abide by the verdict of the people at the polls. We all know of the horrific toll in blood that was exacted by our 'brave' soldiers and generals from the hapless people of East Pakistan.

But who would deny that Josh's perceptive insight into the Pakistani political culture and his prognosis of what afflicted it is as valid today as it was timely then when he wrote his treatise. That should also mollify the angst of those who might think Josh was not relevant to our times.

Josh speaks in his cathartic piece of the need for the voice of that slim minority of enlightened people (He, in his high-flowing diction calls them men endowed with 'ecstasy of enlightenment' or in his chaste words, Inbisat-e-Shaoor).

Like Plato's Republic ruled by the nobility, Josh's ideal society for Pakistan should be inspired, if not actually led, by enlightened men of ecstasy. They should be the ideologues underpinning a just social order in which the rights of what Iqbal hailed as Banda-e-Mazdoor, or the working class, would be protected and guaranteed.

But Pakistan of today is far from any fulfillment of that ideal. Iqbal's dream has morphed into a nightmare of unremitting tragedy. Jinnah's Pakistan is truncated and teetering on the verge of collapse. Josh's ideal republic has yet to be conceived in the womb of the land he loved and pined for.

But the jury may remain out for a long time to come on whether Josh, had he been alive, would still have nursed his great reservoir of optimism for this mass of humanity, inhabiting the confines of Pakistan, rebounding in zest or would he be despairing at its death wish and pulverization?

Josh died a bitter and broken man whose dreams of a humane and egalitarian world had been robbed by rogues and scoundrels stalking the land in his times as they have, indeed, continued to lord over it up until today.

Josh wrote his own epitaph in a verse that is in sync with the despair of so many others like him who still long for the 'ecstasy of enlightenment' to be the order of the day in Pakistan but are devastated seeing robber-barons and scum of the earth ruling the roost.

Josh sounded uncharacteristically morbid in that epitaph but was brutally right in drawing a line under the character of a nation that seems to take a vicarious pleasure in ignoring and humiliating its heroes, and has yet to learn the fine, though in our case elusive, art of honouring them:

Translation:

> *Yeh Murda hein Zindon se Inhe kya Nisbat*
>
> *Jab Murda banogey to yeh Pehchanein gey*
>
> '*They're dead, and have no relation with the living;*
>
> *They will only recognize you when you're dead.*'

The posterity in Pakistan will have a huge task on its hands in proving Josh, the immortal bard, wrong.

Dr. Naweed I. Syed (FRCP Edin.)

Professor, Head

Cell Biology and Anatomy

Research Director

Hotchkiss Brain Institute

Alberta Heritage Medical Research Scientist

Canadian Institute of Health Research Investigator

Parker B. Francis Fellow (USA)

Alfred P. Sloan Fellow (USA)

Faculty of Medicine

**University of Calgary,
Calgary, Alberta
Canada**

Scanning the Brain of an Intellectual: Josh the Immortal

Russian Psychologist Lev Vygotsky once said: "the act of putting spoken words and unspoken thoughts into written words, releases and in the process, changes the thoughts themselves". As humans evolved to use written language more and more precisely to convey their thoughts, their capacity for abstract thoughts and more novel ideas accelerated. Genetics studies on human evolutions have revealed that novel thoughts come easy for those who have mastered the art of languages. Shabbir Hassan (Josh Malhiabadi) – is then the epic of such human intellect as he had an innate propensity for languages and thus could capture an idea, a scene, feelings and emotions in a manner that was inconceivable to others. Myriad brilliant minds have written amply about Josh – who was undoubtedly one of the greatest minds to have ever lived on the Indian subcontinent. These writings have provided us with tremendous insights into Josh's intellectual brilliance that not only empowered Urdu language to acquire its current literary stature but also to unravel the mysteries of nature [1], lessons of history [2], the underpinnings of philosophy [3] and the human conscious [4]. Unfortunately, for someone like myself – Josh's writing is not easy to understand – he creates words the way God created the universe – seamlessly and effortlessly. His vision and wisdom do not conform to the norm [5]– his cognitive [6] and perceptual intricacies [7] have no bound – he sees the unseen [8]– he hears the unheard [9]– he speaks the unspoken [10], he challenges the dogma [11] – incites curiosity [12] and his rebellious nature [13] justifies the very existence of his being. Josh has always denounced the cult of personality [14], backward thinking [15], lethargy [16], ignorance [17], hatred [18], conjecture [19], bias and based desires [20], traditional outlook to the life, cultural and spiritual bounds [21] – all of which short circuit the very spirits of the human intellect. While Josh's magical and spell bounding command over language mesmerizes [21] its readers, his creative instinct is independent of ideas to thoughts that are increasingly autonomous [22], transformative

[23], and ultimately independent of the text [24]. At another time in history, these attributes would have sufficed to earn him the stature of

a saint. Unfortunately, the people of his own tribe not only undermined every aspect of his existence, but they also betrayed his intellectual curiosity, human spirit and independent thinking – only because they did not conform to the so-called traditional cult of that time. Any other nation would have taken tremendous pride in nominating him for a noble prize – whereas his own people continue to ignore his literary and intellectual contributions. Incited by this very spirit of fairness, honesty, freedom of thoughts that Josh Sahib's writing instilled in me, I am gathering courage to devote this article to his legacy – not his memory - as the later is meant for those who are mortal – Josh Sahib in my humble view is immortal [25]. This article is neither a review of his literary work nor a critique of his personality – this I leave to the experts. I will however, attempt to share my thoughts vis-à-vis how a brilliant mind - such as that of Josh Sahib - may have been 'structurally configured' to provide the substratum for his mental energy that has encapsulated and enlightened curious minds for generations.

A memorable scene in Carols Ruiz Zafron's "Shadow of the Wind" depicts a scenario in which, the youngest Protagonist, Daniel, is introduced to his first deep experience with books, as his father takes him to find his own "personal volume", in the mysterious library:

"Welcome to the cemetery of Dead Books Daniel ---- Every book, every volume --- has a soul. "The soul of a person who wrote it and of those who read it and lived and dreamed with it. Every time a book changes hands, every time someone runs his eyes down its pages, its spirit grows and strengthens".

Notwithstanding an early childhood exposure to Josh Sahib's poetry – the person who literally and figuratively presented Josh to many of us as a gentile giant of human spirit is Mr. Iqbal Haider. Iqbal 'Bhai's' love and commitment towards Josh sahib's literary contributions is difficult to measure – even if one were to borrow a few words from Josh's personal dictionary. It does nevertheless speak to the sense of "payback" that Iqbal Bhai felt that he owed not only to Josh Sahib as a decent individual but more importantly, to the fragrance of human values and foresight that he acquired in the company of this mentor. I dare not dedicate this article to Josh Sahib – I have therefore opted to credit this paper to 'Iqbal Bhai' who provided me with all necessary encouragement to peak into the brain of the most beautiful mind of the 19th century.

Physically speaking, Josh is not among us today. To gain insights into his brilliant mind

– one would therefore have to rely upon the intellectual transformations that are brought about in us by reading his published accounts. One would hope that these insights would serve as a remarkable petri dish, which when viewed under a microscope would serve as a scanner – enabling us to examine how he perceived things and then captured both their essence and spirit through words. The immortality of his intellectual contributions has since served him well and he lives in our thoughts vicariously as Josh – the immortal. Such an examination however, requires multiple perspectives – ancient and modern linguistics, archaeology, history, literatures, education, psychology, and neuroscience. The goal of this article is to integrate these disciplines to present new perspective on the working of a marvelous mind that not only created new knowledge but was also pivotal in its dissemination.

Reading enables us to leave our consciousness and pass over, into the consciousness of another person, another age, another culture. "Passing over", a term coined by theologian John Dunne, describes the process through which reading enables us to try to identify with, and ultimately enter - for a brief time - the wholly different perspective of another person's consciousness. When we pass over into how a knight thinks, how a slave feels, how a hero behaves – we never come back quite the same; some time we are inspired and other times saddened but we are always enriched. Through this process, we learn about the commonality and the uniqueness of our own thoughts – that we are individuals but not alone. The moment this happens - we

0are no longer limited to the confines of our thinking. Wherever they were set, our originals boundaries are challenged, teased and gradually placed somewhere else [Maryanne Wolf]. Nowhere else is this more evident than Josh Malhiabadi Yaadon Ki Baraat – whose several earlier versions – he himself first blessed to the trash can - before being "compelled" to publish the edition that is in print today. This supports the notion that Josh's brilliance had reached the evolutionary perfection of human thoughts – as even today, his work remains unchallenged. This article has benefited a great deal from reading Josh Sabhib's biography presented in his book Yaadon Ki Baraat. World-renowned scholar Dr. Kulb-e-Saddiq once told me that while traveling by train to his hometown he was reading Yaadon Ki Baraat. The book had entranced him to an extent that other passengers had to remind him that the train had already arrived at his destination platform and was about to depart onwards. So has been the impact of Josh sahib's work on almost all other intellectuals that I have known. This sense of curiosity must had something to do with the brilliant mind that they were all attempting to peak into.

In instances, where a scientist, physician or a surgeon does not have the luxury of "reading" someone's mind through one's written text – it may help to gain insights into the working marvels of such a beautiful mind by examining the functional working of his/her brain – the Mecca of one's intellectual thoughts. Here, I will attempt to shed some light onto the structural organization that might have formed the basis for the wiring of this marvelous mind.

Marcel Proust once said: "We feel quite truly that our wisdom begins where that of the author's ends, and we would like to have him give us answers, while all he can do is give us desires. And these desires he can arouse in us only by making us contemplate the supreme beauty, which the last effort of his art has permitted him to reach. But by ... a law, which perhaps signifies that, we can receive the truth from nobody, and that we must create it ourselves, that which is the end of their wisdom appears to us as but the beginning of ours". Proust's understanding of the generative nature of reading contains however, a paradox: the goal of reading is to go beyond the author's ideas to thoughts. This is however, not feasible in the case of Josh Sahib – whose vision is infinite [27] and wisdom [28] beyond grasp. In his case, therefore one does not run the risk of interpreting his work beyond the conceptual and intellectual framework in which Josh had initially orchestrated it in his written work.

While writing this article, I would like to offer a disclaimer and caution the audience that although they may get a bird's eye view of this brilliant mind though the 'CT' scan of my limited knowledge in the field of brain research – that is with limited vision - whereas, Josh Sahib's intellectual depth is infinite and beyond my comprehension.

Throughout history, neuroscientists and psychologist have proposed numerous theories to define the biological basis of intelligence and these ranged from larger brain sizes, lateral frontal cortex, larger inferior parietal region to larger size of the white matter. For instance, although Albert Einstein's brain size was average, his Inferior Parietal region, which is thought to be involved in the mathematical reasoning, was 15% wider on both sides than an average person. If his overall brain size did not differ from other men, than the extra 15% growth in his inferior Parietal region would have to have occurred at the expense of other brain regions. Indeed, Albert Einstein's brain was found to have smaller Peri-Sylvian region, which is responsible for linguistic intelligence. Perhaps it was this change, which was responsible for his meager linguistic and communication skills. For instance, he could not speak until the age of 3, whereas most other children start speaking when they are 1-2 years old. Similarly, at the age of 16, he failed language exams for the Swiss Federal Institute of Technology and even as an adult; he was terrified of speaking in public and was a abysmal speaker. While these theories based on either the size of any given brain region, white matter etc could never be tested experimentally, they do nevertheless suggest that there might exist various different forms of intelligence – each unique to an individual. In addition to specific networks of brain cells that are dedicated to select mental faculties, an interplay between various different brain regions is likely required for the "master intelligence" thus enabling one to excel simultaneously in various different disciplines that require an interplay between different brain networks underlying different intelligences. In the case of Josh, while it remains unknown whether any given regions of his brain were significantly larger than normal, we know for sure that he would have to have mastered the art of reading, writing, comprehension, cognition, and verbal communications faculties. While some aspects of his intellect may have been inherited and acquired trough the genetic interplay of his parental gene pool, it is apparent that his environment played a critical role in shaping the final connectivity maps of his brain. He was well versed in several languages (Urdu, Parisian, Hindi, Arabic, English etc) and had masterful command over alphabets [28], which he used to either create new words, or strung the existing vocabulary into sentences and phrases that are still a masterpiece of Urdu poetry [29]. To understand how Josh might have given new meanings to older words [30] and stretched the limits of human cognition thereby opening new windows of novel imaginations [31], it is important to understand how the nurturing environment that he grew up in, might have influenced the wiring of his brain.

All nervous system functions ranging from simple reflexes to complex motor patterns, cognition, learning and memory rely upon networks of brain cells that are orchestrated during early development. The human brain is comprised of ten of billions of excitable cells, termed neurons, which are interconnected with each other through specialized contact points termed synapse. It is through these synapses that most neuronal communications occur in the form of both electrical impulses and chemical signaling. Perturbation of synaptic connectivity between the brain cells results in all brain function disorders such as Parkinson and Alzheimer's and Autism spectrum. Most neurobiologists believe that the basis for all animal intellect is contingent upon the efficacy with which brain cells (not their numbers) communicate with each other. Developmental neurobiologists believe that some aspects of brain wiring is "hardwired' that is genetically determined, whereas a vast majority of the total brain output relies critically upon experience dependent synaptic plasticity which forms the basis for all forms of learning and memory, cognition, linguistic ability, scholastic, social, intellectual etc faculties of the human mind that were displayed by Josh sahib.

As mentioned earlier, some aspects of our brain circuitry are hardwired and rely upon inherited genes and their encoded proteins. For instance, a rat raised in the laboratory for decades may have never "heard" – over several generations - from its ancestors that the furry looking animal - called cat is a potential threat to their lives. And yet, whenever confronted by it, a rat is always scared of a cat. Thus in instances, where an animal's survival depends on some innate instincts that are vital for its existence, the 'nature' builds in its brain a hardwired circuit which functions independent of any prior experience. Similarly, a deer hit by the floodlight would always freeze – independent of prior training or exposure to such stimuli. In many other instances however, parents would need to educate their children that a snake or a grizzly bear are dangerous, and that they should not stick their hands either in an electric socket or play with fire. All humans are nevertheless, intuitively afraid of the unknown and to overcome these fears, one would need to be educated about its potential dangers. In summary, it is evident that some aspects of our brain circuitry are hardwired (i.e. genetically determined), whereas a larger contingent of the neuronal networks requires experience-dependent synaptic plasticity, which is pivotal for the survival of the species. In the context of synaptic plasticity (a change in the synaptic strength between neurons), it is also important to appreciate that if one were to re-direct retinal gangionic cells (projecting from the eye to the visual cortex in the brain and help to establish vision in all animals) towards the auditory cortex (hearing center) during early development – the sensory information carried by these brain cells can completely switch the auditory cortex function to that of visual cortex and the resulting animal would still have a 20-20 vision. Thus during early developmental stages, the nature of sensory signal (visual input) that one is expose to has the ability to completely change the function of various neuronal networks in the brain. These changes however, rely critically upon early sensory experiences, which in turn play essential role in shaping the final connectivity patterns in our brain. On the other hand, if one were to place a patch over an eye of a kitty cat, albeit only for a few days; subsequent to the patch removal, the cat will never see in that eye. These studies, clearly demonstrate that there is a critical stage in ones early life when sensory input plays an essential role in the establishment and the reorganization of the brain circuits. Moreover, no single brain circuit can function independent of its corresponding counterparts; it is therefore imperative that extensive communications must exist between various different brains centers involved in related behavioral programs. A failure to do so would result in "miscommunications" between brain centers thus severely compromising its functional capabilities. For example, a person who could not hear following birth would also not speak, as the neuronal networks controlling these brains functions are intricately interlinked. It therefore suffices to say that although Josh may have inherited some aspects of his intelligent, he owed his brilliance in larger part, to his exposure to reading and learning multiple languages – which when coupled with his real life experiences – created a dynamic combination of intellect and mastery over human conscious, vision and wisdom. As Renae Richardson noted "we can not harvest much intelligence without wisdom but there is very little wisdom in the unintelligent". He further points out that, "Intelligence is the ability to manipulate the knowledge that has been obtained for one's own purpose". It therefore stands to reason that Josh sahib must have taken a very keen, personal interest in every aspect of his life – not from a bird's eye-view – rather with the intent to understand and reflect. This empowered his sensory perception with microscopic ability to see the unseen, whereas his higher learning and memory, and cognitive functions worked to store and retrieve this information in a blink of an eye. To re-paraphrase, we are all born with unique building blocks that form the substratum for our 'personalized intelligence' – all submerged into the pool of sensory input. Our early exposure to such sensory exposure and the ability to retain, organize and manipulate this stored sensory information at a rapid pace, endows our brain to easily manipulate a composition, languages, invention, an idea or a design. This concept is perhaps best personified in Josh Malhiabadi.

Unravel the mysteries of nature

زندگی ، مرتے ہوئے پتّوں پہ، بوندوں کی کھنگ ـــ
صبح سرما کی کرن، شام بہاراں کی دھنگ ـــ
بول۔ تِتلی کی اُڑان، آواز۔ کو ندے کی لپک ـــ
کوکتی بر کھامیں، سارنگی کے تاروں کی لپک

سہر تن میں ، بچپن والوں کی گلی ہے زندگی
گردن آفاق میں ، چمپا گلی ہے زندگی

Lessons of History:

ایمان کو ، لذّاتِ کی خواہش ہے شدید

ہر خیر ہے ، اسبابِ طرب کی تمہید

حوران بہشت و دُخترانِ کفّار

باقی نہ اگر رہیں تو غازی ، نہ شہید

Underpinnings of Philosophy:

انسان ، ازل سے ہے جہُول اور ظلوم

لے دے کے ہے لبس ایک شعورِ موہُوم

طفلِ ناداں ہے ، آئینے کے آگے

کس کا یہ عکس ہے ، اُسے کیا معلوم

Human Conscious:

اے دوست ، دل میں گزر کہ درّت نہ چاہیے

اچھے تو کیا ، بُروں سے بھی نفرت نہ چاہیے

کہتا ہے کون ، پھُول سے رغبت نہ چاہیے

کانٹے سے بھی مگر تجھے دہشت نہ چاہیے

———————————

کانٹے کی رگ میں بھی ہے لہو مرغِ زار کا

پالا ہُوا ہے وہ بھی نسیم بہار کا

Vision and Wisdom does not conform to the norm:

خودبین و خود آگاہ کیا ہے کس نے
ایمان کا بد خواہ کیا ہے کس نے
انسان کو، شیطاں نے کیا ہے گمراہ
شیطان کو گمراہ کیا ہے کس نے؟

Cognitive and perceptual intricacies:

افکار میں جب غوطہ لگایا میں نے
آفاق کو، پلکوں پہ جھلایا میں نے
ادراک کی میزان میں تولا جس وقت
سائے میں بھی، وزن و حجم پایا میں نے

Sees the Un-seen:

مبنی تیرا حدیث و آیات پہ دین
میں، شہرِ تامل و تفکر کا مکین
تو، شیفتۂ نطقِ رسالت ۔ اور میں
حرفِ ناگفتۂ نبوت کا امین

Hears the unheard:

میرے چاروں طرف ہے اک طرفہ خروش
اِک قوس ہے پشت پر، بشکلِ آغوش
آخر، یہ تعاقب ہیں میں نظر کس کی؟
یہ کون مجھے ڈھونڈ رہا ہے لے جوش؟

Speaks the unspoken:

خُود بین و خُود آگاہ کیا ہے کس نے
اِیمان کا بد خواہ کیا ہے کس نے
اِنسان کو، شیطاں نے کیا ہے گم راہ
شیطان کو گم راہ کیا ہے کس نے؟

Challenges the dogma:

پُشتِ اِیماں کا خم نِکالا ہے کبھی؟
اَقوال کو، اَفکار میں ڈھالا ہے کبھی؟
اِقرار کے ساحل پر اکڑنے والو!
اِنکار کا قُلزُم بھی کھنگالا ہے کبھی؟

Incites Curiosity:

ہر بام ہے، اک کشورِ دیگر کا علم
ہر نام ہے، اک رایتِ نو کا پرچم
ہر فرد ہے، اک جدا نظامِ شمسی
عالم میں بسے ہوئے ہیں اربوں عالم

Denounces the Cult of Personality:

بوسیدہ روایات کی حرمت نہ کرو
تحقیق و تجسس کی اہانت نہ کرو
دینِ آبا بھی، تم کو لاحق ہو جائے
ماں باپ سے، اتنی بھی محبت نہ کرو

Backward thinking:

تر دامنی و عصمت و کفر و پیمبری
ابر و شعاع و سایہ و تنویر و تیرگی
خورشید و ماہ و ذرہ و ناہید و مشتری
پُل تو رو سنگ و جوہر و حیوان و آدمی

___

اور یہ جو دشت و کوہ و بیابان و باغ ہیں
سب ایک ہی خاندان کے چشم و چراغ ہیں

Lethargy:

جس رنگ سے جی رہے ہو، یارانِ حرمیں
واللہ کہ جینے کا یہ انداز نہیں
بیدار ہو، اے زمیں پہ سونے والو
اس سے پہلے کہ تم پہ سو جائے زمیں

Ignorance:

جودت کا گوہر، مہرِ مبیں سے بہتر
حکمت کی حلاوت، انگبیں سے بہتر
عالم کا دیا ہوا گمانِ بد کبھی
جاہل کے عطا کردہ یقیں سے بہتر

and Hatred:

بے شک، جو بخشتا ہے، دَھڑکتے دلوں کو چین
اُس کا وجود، بزمِ جہاں کی ہے زیب و زین
لیکن وہ بد شعار، جو ہے ننگِ مشرقین
وہ شخص بھی ہے، آدم و حوّا کا نورِ عین

پُر زے کبھی نہ مہر و وفا کا لباس کر
دل ہے تو، اپنی ماں کے چہیتے کا پاس کر

Lecture Delivered at the
Josh Literary Society Symposium
August 15, 2009
University of Calgary, Alberta, Canada

"Josh's Vision: In Search of Truth and Change; A journey
through his time and beyond"

Dr. Rafat Ansari

Due to Dr. Ansari sudden illness the paper was presented by Mr.
Shakeel Ahsan, an avid admirer of Fine Arts and Josh.

About the speaker:

Dr. Rafat Ansari has been with NASA for the past 20 years. Currently, he is leading the Vision Research & Human Health Diagnostics Laboratory of NASA's Glenn Research Center in Cleveland, Ohio. He has advanced the light scattering technology for space experiments on-board the space-shuttle orbiter, space station, and biomedical applications here on earth. His research thrust is to diagnose diseases non-invasively and quantitatively much before the clinical symptoms appear to monitor health of astronauts in long duration missions. He frequently flies on NASA's zero gravity aircraft where he conducts medical experiments in weightless conditions.

Dr. Ansari is recognized internationally. He is frequently invited to give lectures all over the world and has served on several national and international scientific panels and as invited clinical guest faculty at several prestigious universities in US, Europe, and Asia. He has over 80 featured articles and cover stories in leading scientific & technical magazines, news papers, and interviews on NPR, ABC News, NYT, Washington Post, CNN WebMD, CBS News, NBC News, Europe TV etc.

Dr. Ansari is also serving on the Editorial Boards of the Journal of Biomedical Optics (JBO) and Current Analytical Chemistry, on the Executive Board of Prevent Blindness Ohio, and on the Scientific Advisory Boards of few companies. He was an adjunct professor at the School of Biomedical Engineering, Science and Health Systems of the Drexel University in Philadelphia from 1998-2005. Currently he is holding two adjunct professorships in Italy and Switzerland. Dr. Ansari has over 85 published papers (basic, applied, and clinical research) in peer-reviewed journals and proceedings and 7 invited book chapters including Duane's Clinical Ophthalmology, Handbook of Coherent Domain Methods, and Tele-ophthalmology. He is also an inventor (three issued patents), an FAA-licensed pilot, a motorcyclist, and a boating enthusiast.

Among many honors, Dr. Ansari is a recipient of the prestigious Public Service Medal, two NASA's Space Act Award, the Abe Silverstein Medal, the Wings of Excellence Award, STAIF Best Paper Award, and the STARS Award from the State of Texas (when he served as a Professor in the School of Health Information Sciences with a joint appointment as a Professor in the department of ophthalmology and visual science in the school of Medicine, University of Texas at Houston).

Lecture Delivered at the

Josh Literary Society Symposium

August 15, 2009

University of Calgary, Alberta, Canada

"Josh's Vision: In Search of Truth and Change; A journey through his time and beyond"

Dr. Rafat Ansari

Ladies, Gentlemen, and Distinguished Guests:

Disclaimer: First, I wish to make this important disclaimer. "I am here in a personal capacity. I am not representing anyone or any organization but myself. The views and opinions expressed in this lecture are strictly those of mine and NOT those of my employer (NASA) or the Government of the United States of America".

Introduction:

This symposium pleasantly coincides with an important date in the lives of the citizens of the Indian subcontinent. Today is August 15th; India's Independence Day. And yesterday (August 14th) was Pakistan's Independence Day. It's very comforting to see that members of both communities are gathered here today to honor Josh Malihabadi and to remember his many contributions. This gathering shows the common culture between the two countries which binds them together. Let me wish you all a very happy and peaceful 62nd Independence Day.

I would like to thank the organizers of this meeting for inviting me to speak today. I am especially honored to share this podium with some of the great scholars of our time. Professor Pervaiz Hoodbhoy is doing an outstanding job in promoting the vision for a peaceful and just society, Dr. Abdul Hameed Nayyar, the nuclear peace activist, has the vision of protecting the world from self annihilation, and professor Anis Alam is striving for a educational system which promotes free thinking and debating controversial ideas which are absolutely necessary in creating independent institutions and productive societies.

Few Words about Calgary Days:

It's truly a great honor for me and my wife to be here in Calgary. We have many fond memories. The University of Calgary is my alma mater. I was a graduate student here exactly 30 years ago. On this campus, my advisor Professor George Fritz taught me the theory of chaos and how to find order from the disordered systems known as Brownian motion or stochastic phenomena.

Here in Calgary, in 1979, I met Mr. Iqbal Haider in a mushaira, listened to his poetry, learned about his dedication and passion to poet Josh Malihabadi, and met his charming wife Niggi and the rest of his family. They have been extremely kind and generous to me and my wife. We became best of friends. At that time we both had full hairs on our heads. Now the aging process has taken a toll and now we both have become follically-challenged.

I moved on with my professional career and Iqbal Sahib continued to do great work in advancing the Urdu language in North America as well as in the Indian sub-continent. He truly has a "fire in his belly" for Josh, his poetry, and his vision for a just society. Thank you Iqbal sahib!

Confession:

Let me be very frank and honest in the beginning of this lecture. As a scientist, involved in space medicine research, I am not an expert in Josh and neither in Urdu poetry. However, I do enjoy listening to Urdu poetry. And if I do not, my physicist wife Surryia of 35 years makes me listen to it as she writes Urdu poetry in her spare time. But this does not make me an expert commentator in this subject matter since Urdu language has a marvelous history of several hundred years in the Indian subcontinent.

Josh in My Life:

I heard about Josh in my early years as a child growing up in Karachi. My father and uncle in Bombay (now Mumbai) and Poona (now Pune) knew Josh personally in the 1940's when he used to write songs for the Indian black & white movies. My uncle did few small roles in these movies at that time and my father used to join him during the shootings. They had high regard for Josh which remained with them until they passed away. In 1954, my father was very happy that the Indian Government awarded Josh one of the highest national civilian honor award Padma Bhushan for his contributions in literature and education.

I consider myself to be very lucky and privileged to have Faiz Ahmed Faiz as my Urdu professor when I was a student at the H.A.H College in Karachi (1968-1970). Like Josh, Faiz Ahmed Faiz was a famous poet and one of Josh's contemporaries. During our classes, Faiz often praised Josh. Upon Josh's passing in 1982, Faiz Ahmed Faiz said "--the best craftsman of Urdu poetry had passed away, as Josh chiselled his verses to perfection because of his profound knowledge of Eastern literature and grammar--".

I am awestruck and inspired by Josh's power of imagination, a passion to search for and tell the truth, a vision for universal brotherhood and tolerance. And to laugh often, live fully, love everyone, question own-self, and learn from others throughout life. This is indeed a recipe for eternal peace and happiness. He had a vision; a grand vision. This is the basis of my talk.

Josh's Vision:

To me, vision simply means eye-sight or an ability to see. Light makes possible to see, in vivid colors, what is around us. In the absence of light we are practically blind. Therefore, astronomers look at the heavens using radio waves, infra-red, microwaves, and other forms of radiation that our eyes cannot see. But Josh Malihabadi's meaning of vision is immense. It covers a variety of things beyond the physical spectrum of light and radiation. To him, vision means to dream, hallucinate, imagine, visualize, reveal, predict, foresight and picture beyond the physical universe, and to present new and innovative ideas to challenge all of us. This is why to this day he is remembered as Poet of Revolution, Poet of Youth, Poet of Wine, Poet of Music, and Poet of Nature.

Unfortunately, a man of this caliber and intellect; a man who gave everything for freedom, free speech, and free thinking, Josh lived a very sad life in Pakistan.

A Walk through His Times:

Let's take a brief walk through the period he lived in. Josh was born in the town of Malihabad famous for mango groves and only 13 miles from Lucknow, India. In his home, the Hindu festivals of Holi and Dewali were celebrated with as much fan fare as the Muslim festivals of Shab-e-Barat, Ramadan, Eid, and Muharram.

Josh did not go to college because of his father's death in 1916. He did not have fancy college degrees but he was taught Urdu, Persian, Arabic, and English by some of the best teachers of his times. They include Farsi: Maulvi Niaz Ali Khan, Urdu: Maulana Tahir, Arabic: Qudrat-ullah-Baig, and English: Master Gomti Parshad.

Upon his birth in the year 1896, India suffered a major famine. It affected about 70 million people and killed about 1 million. Just three years before his birth, a young Indian-born British-educated lawyer Mohindas Karamchand Gandhi with a valid first class ticket was thrown out of a train in South Africa because he was a colored man. Later, this extraordinary man, through non-violence, brought freedom to India. And Josh fought shoulder-to-shoulder with Gandhi, Nehru, Maulana Azad, Sarojini Naido, and others for the independence of India. Late Indian Prime Minister Indira Gandhi once said "---Josh Sahib was great friend of her father's and perhaps one of the few who could take the liberty of upbraiding Nehru if he thought Jawaharlal had stepped down even for a moment from his lofty pedestal".

The period Josh lived in was full of human tragedies, pain and sufferings. He saw two world wars, holocaust in Germany, use of atomic weapons affecting thousands of people in Japan, several conflicts of the cold war era, and mass migration during the partition of India. But this was also a period of superb human triumphs. He saw the development of motorcars, airplanes, telephones, man landing on the moon, eradication of many diseases such as small pox and TB. 24 years before Josh's birth, a great philosopher and free thinker, Bertrand Russell was born in UK. This Nobel laureate stood up for social justice, change, and tolerance around the world. Josh was inspired by this man which is reflected in his poetry and prose. For example, in (Har Fard hay khair say malul….) Josh writes:

ہر فرد ہے خیر سے ملول و غم گیں
آزردہ و افسردہ و بیمار دِ جنوں
دانا کی نبا لیں کہ خدا ہے موجود
ناداں اس نگریں خدا ہے کہ نہیں

"Everyone in whirlpool of agony caught

Anguished, sick and suffering lot

The wise emphasizing that God exists

Foolish confused, God is there or not"

Around this time, another Nobel laureate Albert Einstein (1879-1955) was busy inventing photo electric effect and the theory of relativity which changed the world.

In Search of Truth:

Josh has written eloquently on almost every subject matter that touches every aspect of human life. In the interest of time, I'll not discuss his enormous body of work. For English readers, I recommend Mohammad Yamin's translation of Rubai'yat of Josh Malihabadi -A Drop and the Ocean.

Good scientists are always in constant search for truth and objectivity. And many times, they pay a very heavy price for it. Galileo lost his life because he said the earth revolved around the sun. This was a revolutionary idea at the time because the Roman church believed that the earth was at the center of the universe and sun revolved around the earth. Today we all know the truth. I am sure you know that brain studies were ceased during the Middle Ages (1100-1500 AD) due to a church ban on human dissection and the study of anatomy. Today, it's one of the basic requirements for medical education.

I am especially impressed with Josh approach and a good grasp of scientific knowledge. For example, in Reflections (Paida hua Aasaab mein Ek turfa khinchao…), he connects the infinitely small to infinitely large like an expert physicist:

The moment I placed an atom on my palm

The weight of entire solar system descent

پیدا ہوا اعصاب میں ایک طرف کھنچا ؤ
معلوم ہوا مستانہِ افکار کا سہا ؤ
درتے کو تیلی پہ جَو، پل کہر رکھا
محسوس ہوا نظام شمسی کا وبائؤ

On another occasion in (Ek zarra-e-mubham hay…..), he observes like an expert astronomer:

When I looked through the granary of stars I found

Our world is less than even a grain

اک ذرّہ مبہم ہے ہماری دنیا
اک قطرہ شبنم ہے ہماری دنیا
تاروں کے جو کھلیاں کھنگالے تو کھلا
اک جو سے بھی کچھ کم ہے ہماری دنیا

This observation has been confirmed by almost every astronaut who has flown in space and by magnificent photographs of the cosmos obtained recently by the Hubble space telescope. Remember, Earth is the only blue planet in our solar system that has life. Let me remind you our home planet is located in the Milky Way Galaxy which spans a distance of 100,000 light years with 100 billion stars (and yes that is B as in billion). Our neighborhood i.e., the interplanetary space around Earth is filled with plasma, gas, dust, rock, and radiation.

On the vastness of space and our existence, Josh remarks in one of his Rubai:

جب غرفہ علم دلکر کھولا میں نے
اپنے کو تنے بانٹ سے تولا میں نے
میں ہوں کہ نہیں یہ جانچنے کی خاطر
اپنے کوکئی بار ٹٹولا میں نے

"My vision blew open the eternal designs

II was released from my thoughts confines

To examine whether I exist or not

I touched myself a number of times"

In another example (Yeh dhun hay kay jaib mein hon maah....), he desires to explore and conquer the universe:

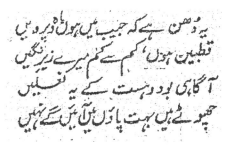

"I'm obsessed to pocket the moon and galaxy, complete

North to South Pole under my command treat

The shoes of knowledge of what is and was

Are too undersized to fit my feet"

Josh in the Era of Increased In-tolerance and Bigotry:

The wikipedia on the internet describes later years of Josh's life as follows: "It is reported that he was not entirely well-received in Pakistan where his iconoclastic ideas and socialistic leanings and views were not in tandem with the political and the social set up of the country. In fact, he deeply regretted his decision (as he would tell his close friends and acquaintances) and felt slighted that he was not accorded the respect and importance he had expected on becoming a Pakistani citizen. He died a sad, broken man".

No wonder! Upon migrating to Pakistan in 1958 until his death in 1982, he found his adopted "Land of the Pure" slowly drifting to extremism and religious intolerance. In the early-mid 1970's, under pressure from ignorant and hateful political and religious leaders during the regime of the democratically elected Prime minister Zulfiqar Ali Bhutto, Pakistan's national assembly declared Ahmadi's as non-Muslims or infidels (kafirs). According to Kunwar Idris, 105 Ahmadis have been killed since the community was declared non-Muslims in 1974. The situation became worst when General Zia-ul-Haque ruled the country with an iron fist by the so called Islamisation of Pakistan. During his dark period (1977-1989), many draconian measures were passed such as Hudood ordinances and blasphemy laws which resulted in gross violations of human rights and open season of discrimination was unleashed against minorities (Hindus, Christians etc). Even Shia Muslims were not spared. To this day, Zia's legacy and his vision of intolerance, is thriving; all in the name of Allah. Pakistan's anti-blasphemy law, enacted by President General Zia-ul-Haq in1986 and later amended by the parliament in 2004, is one of the most stringent laws. The penalty includes a mandatory death sentence for defaming Prophet Mohammad and life imprisonment for desecrating the Holy Quran. According to official reports, to date, over 500 people have been charged for breaching the Blasphemy Law. I strongly recommend everyone to look at Dawn.com which traces the history of some of these cases that have been highlighted in the media since 1990. Few months ago, The whole world has seen 17 year old girl brutally flogged in Swat and just two weeks ago, a church, over 100 Christian homes and 7 people including women and children of their community were burnt alive in the province of Punjab. And honor killing of women is a frequent occurance. Josh would have been outraged.

Probably Josh never thought of Pakistan becoming such an intolerant nation. Perhaps he believed in the 1948 statement by the founder of Pakistan (Muhammad Ali Jinnah): "In any case Pakistan is not going to be a theocratic State to be ruled by priests with a divine mission. We have many non-Muslims --Hindus, Christians, and Parsis --but they are all Pakistanis. They will enjoy the same rights and privileges as any other citizens and will play their rightful part in the affairs of Pakistan".

Josh's Love for Urdu and Migration to Pakistan:

Josh struggled to free India from the British rule but he did not opt for Pakistan at the time of partition in 1947. It's reported that he migrated to Pakistan in 1958 to the chagrin of his best friend Indian Prime Minister Nehru. At that time, Josh thought that urdu is "dying" in India and he can work with Maulvi Abdul Haque in Pakistan to promote this language. Perhaps he thought that he is well suited for Pakistan since Urdu was the official language of Pakistan which at that time included East Pakistan (now Bangladesh).

Let's look at some statistics and let me be little critical of Josh's vision of working in Pakistan to promote Urdu. Urdu is mainly spoken in south Asia (mostly India and Pakistan) by about 65 million people compared with Hindi (490 million) and Bengali (230 million). 52 million people in India are native Urdu speakers compared to about 13 million people in Pakistan (mainly in the city of Karachi). Although, Urdu is an official language of Pakistan but it's only spoken by only 8% of the population as a native language. Pakistan is home to diverse group of languages which include Punjabi, Pashto, Sindhi, Saraiki, Urdu, and Balochi. Up until 1971 before the break up of Pakistan into Bangladesh, it also included Bengali. Maulvi Abdul Haque's constant push in the 1950's and in the 1960's to make Urdu as the language of ALL backfired badly especially in East Pakistan which pitted Bengali speakers against Urdu speakers resulting in mass murders, rapes, and finally breakup of the country in 1971.

So Josh's reason for migrating to Pakistan came in full circle. In 1968 upon his visit to old Delhi, Josh was asked by a journalist: "what he thought about present-day Urdu poetry. He

shook his head and said Urdu was "dying" in Pakistan, but it was heartening to note that India "still paid lip service to it". In the following Rubai Josh seems cautiously optimistic:

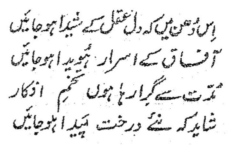

"For long I am sowing the seed of thoughts

Wait until the new trees of knowledge spring"

"For long I am sowing the seed of Thoughts

Wait till the new trees of Knowledge spring"

The languages flourish and progress as their speakers make progress in art, science, literature, and technology.

Vision of Tolerance:

Let's talk about tolerance. Josh was born in a Sunni Muslim family. His Grand Mother introduced him to Shia Islam. Josh married his cousin Ashraf Jehan –a Sunni Muslim. Upon his embracing of Shia Islam, Josh's father-in-law got very upset and filed a law suit asking for annulment of marriage (nikah). It took six years for the Indian-British court system to render a verdict after many religious scholars testified. The decision upheld that a marriage between a Shia boy and a Sunni girl is legal. At that time, Josh's father spent 40,000-50,000 Rupees on this law suit. At the end, everyone thought that Josh will convert his wife to Shia Islam. But he proved them wrong. Josh said "religion is voluntary and there is no compulsion in it. Ashraf Jehan bore many children with him and remained his loyal wife as a Sunni Muslim. He writes "my wife remained a Sunni Muslim until her death and I (Josh) am neither a Shia nor a Sunni; and now I can't decide even if I am a Muslim?" He asked: "Who will make that decision!!" A journalist once asked Josh his view on religion. He said "he was not a religious man and had his own religion -- the religion of man -- ". For example, in (Tachand koi dair-o-haram…..) he says:

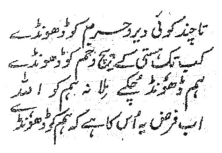

"I'ave searched mosques and temples but could not see

Existence how long to explore your obscurity

I looked through each nook and corner but couldn't find God

Now it's His turn to look for me"

Vision of Compassion and Firmness:

Josh was a man of great compassion. He felt the pain of others and wrote about it. He considered the entire world to be his family. He writes "when cooking fire is not lit in the kitchen of a poor, smoke billow from my chest. When I see a hungry orphan with bare bones and visible rib cage, I feel bones poking in my own body. When I hear the sound of crying, tears start flowing from my eyes. When I see a funeral procession coming from some one's house, I feel death in my own home.

Josh was inspired from the sacrifice of Imam Hussain in the battle of Karbala which shaped his personality. He always stood up for his principles with pride and firmness. The Governor of UP Sir Harcourt Butler and Josh's father were good friends. After the death of Josh's father, Sir Butler offered Josh a job of his choice of either a deputy collector or the special manager of the court. He even waived the requirement of the BA degree required for this job. But Josh politely refused by saying to Sir Butler that he considers British Government as an occupier of India and thus he cannot work for his government. In another example, in1925, while working at the Osmania University in the State of Hyderabad, Deccan supervising translation work, he was exiled from the state for writing poetry (nazm) against the ruler (Nizam of Hyderabad). Later, in Pakistan, he stood up against the tyrannical rules of army dictators for which both he and his family paid dearly.

Vision of Freethinking and Freespeech:

I was a student at Karachi University when Josh published his autobiography "Yaadon ki Baarat". Josh was invited to speak at a literary function at the university. Some faculty and students were offended by his book. They insulted him and did not let him talk. I always wondered why this happened in a university setting. Universities are supposed to be the cradle of free thinking, to discuss and debate controversial ideas. Dr. Rubina Saigol, a human rights activist and educationist, in her 2007 book "Social Science in Pakistan: A profile" explains the underlying reason for such behavior "overwhelming ideological orientation of teachers across the disciplinary spectrum revolves around religious and nationalist thinking.....so deeply rooted are the teachers and students in the hegemonic version of state and society that even the social sciences, which are tasked to produce alternative visions, fail to do so."

Josh strived and emphasized the importance of knowledge and wisdom. In (Hai kaon jo is dhouein ko gulshan.....) he says:

ہے کوئی ،جو اس دُھویں کو گلشن کر دے ؟

ٹکڑے اس تیرگی کا دامَن کر دے

دل پر بَے، گھٹا ٹوپ اَندھیرے کا دَباؤ

اللہ ،کوئی چَراغ رَوشن کر دے!

"This into a flame of furnace turn

To make hearts abode of vision, is there none?

The darkness of ignorance is so dense

Light the lamp of wisdom and knowledge, please someone"

Josh was ahead of his time. After the release of "Yadon ki Barat", he became a personal non-grata in the conservative circles of the Pakistani society especially upon his mentioning of extra marital affairs with other women and homosexual experiences with boys during his youth. It's interesting to note that Urdu Digest in the 1960's published an article "Mun Ke Aik Talib-e-Ilm" (I am a Student). This was written by a student who attended a madarasah (religious school). The article highlighted acts of homosexuality and child abuse by the mullahs of these institutions. But no one was outraged and no action was taken. Columnist Irfan Hussain recently wrote " Despite our prudish pretence, the fact is that we are relatively tolerant of homosexual behaviour. Our literature contains many references to romantic attachment between men. And for years, homosexuality in Pashtun society has been an open secret, although it might well be exaggerated. According to local tradition, many men live by the credo "Women for duty; boys for pleasure." When Josh shared his personal experiences with great honesty and candor, all hell broke loose. Mahatma Gandhi sums it up: "hypocrisy and distortion are passing currents under the name of religion".

Remember Singapore; the envy of the modern world and the smallest nation (merely 274 square miles) in Southeast Asia. From a small fishing village at the southern tip of the Malay Peninsula, after getting independence in 1965, it transformed into a strong economic power house and a model nation of prosperity and tolerance. It is home to many nationalities and religions: Chinese, Indians, Malays, Eurasians, and Arabs. In the late 1970's, Singaporian Prime Minister Lee Kuan Yew visited Pakistan. When asked how he saw the economic prospects of Pakistan, he replied "he wasn't all that optimistic because Pakistanis seem to spend more time thinking about the hereafter than what is to be done here and now." No wonder! Josh was not happy in Pakistan. This is what he had to say in (Jodat ka gohar mahr-e-mobin…..):

جودَت کا گوہر ، مہرِ مُبیں سے بہت سے بہتر

حکمت کی حَلاوَت ، اَنگبیں سے بہتر

عالِم کا دیا ہُوا گُمان بَد کبھی

جاہِل کے عَطا کردَہ یَقیں سے بہتر

"The pearls of intelligence are rare and few

Wisdom is delicate like a drop of dew

Even the vile suspicions given by the learned is better

Than the gift of faith that ignorant give"

A great American President Abraham Lincoln (1809-1865) said "with Malice toward none, with charity for all, with firmness in the right, as

God gives us to see the right, let us strive on to finish the work we are in, to bind up the nation's wounds". He ended slavery and preserved the union from the American civil war. Can the politicians and religious leaders of today stop malice toward each other and show charity for ALL? This is a requirement for building a tolerant society. Josh talks about this vision in his Rubai:

بے چارہ، عداوت میں گھلا جاتا ہے
وہ آگ لگی ہے کہ بجھنا جاتا ہے
جب تک میں زندہ ہوں، اُسے چین نہیں
یہ سوچ کے، دشمن پہ ترس آتا ہے

"The heart which loaded with malice be

Burns in its own flame unfortunately

Each soul despises his enemies, but

I am the one who pities his enemy"

And in (Insaan ki tauheed ka mushtaq hoon mein...) he says:

اِنسان کی توحید کا مُشتاق ہوں میں
شمعِ حُبّ عمیم کا طاق ہوں میں
مشرق کا نہ پابند، نہ مغرب کا اسیر
اِنسان ہوں، باشندۂ آفاق ہوں میں

I await the oneness among men to arise

I, the mantel where the candle of existence lies

Am restricted to the east nor prisoner to the west

Know me! I'm inhabitant of endless skies"

Our Future; A Global Vision:

Today, the world is more connected than ever before; we are a global family and therefore whatever we do anywhere on this planet, it affects the rest of us. And let's not forget, a big segment of world population is still living in dire poverty on less than $1.00 a day. Unfortunately, some among us have perpetrated the Holocaust in Germany, genocide in Rawanda and Darfur, ethnic cleansing in Bosnia, and other awful things in the Middle East, Mynamar, Tibet, Kashmir, Pakistan and Afghanistan. But still there is a lot of goodness among people. Just look at the volunteer work of Abdul Sattar Edhi and late Mother Teresa.

"The time to live is acutely short my friend!

Milk every moment, each possibility squeeze"

تاروں میں ثمگانت ڈال ذرّات کوگرو

پیمانہ روز شب میں اِک بوند نہ چھوڑ

ہاں مہلت زندگی کی نہایت کم ہے

ہرآن کو دے دے ، ہر دقیقے کو نچوڑ

One of the greatest astrophysicists of our times, Stephen Hawking says: "Life on Earth is at the ever-increasing risk of being wiped out by a disaster, such as sudden global warming, nuclear war, a genetically engineered virus or other dangers we have not yet thought of".

Not too far from Calgary, the southern Alberta town of Drumheller is the dinosaur capital of Canada. This place is the living proof that once gigantic animals roamed freely in this valley. About 65 million years ago dinosaurs suddenly vanished; perhaps due to a collision between the Earth and an asteroid. And this can happen again since we live in a "shooting gallery" surrounded by near-earth asteroid belt.
Hawking's vision: "It is important for the human race to spread out into space for the survival of the species. If humans can avoid killing themselves in the next 100 years, they should have space settlements that can continue without support from Earth". So the key word here is to avoid wars and live in peace; a vision shared by many scientists, poets, writers, and philosophers since the time of Aristotle. Such an

undertaking will require research collaborations among the nations, generating new knowledge, and developing advanced technology for all humankind to travel freely throughout the cosmos. I am amazed when Josh in (Tahqiq kay sholon ko hawa deta....) comments:

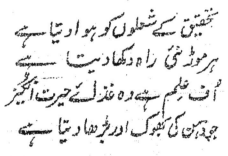

"Research surpasses destinations designed

Pursuits of vision new horizons find

Knowledge is that miraculous food

That whets infinitely the hunger of mind"

As I said earlier, research generates new knowledge but every researcher in the world will admit that how little he/she knows because an answer he/she finds for a question raise many more questions which is a very humbling experience. Josh recognizes this in (Phoolon say jo gulzar mahak....) and beautifully presents it:

پھولوں سے جو گلزار دہیک اٹھتا ہے

کانٹا سا معاً دل میں کھٹک اٹھتا ہے

جس وقت کہ علم کا جلاتا ہوں چراغ

تو چہرہ جہل اندھیرک اٹھتا ہے

"When I light the candle of knowledge

The dark face of ignorance glows"

Once Josh complained: "I find the young people these days are devoid of both good reading and good writing." So the young folks in the audience, who are pursuing advanced degrees, please pay special attention and always remember above rubai from Josh.

Conclusion:

Ladies and Gentleman: In conclusion, make no mistake; Pakistan is not a country in the Middle East. 62 years ago, It's carved out from mother India. Dr. Anis Alam has written: It has been the birth place of Hinduism, Buddhism, Jainism, Sikhism and it has welcomed Muslims, Christians, Jews, and Zoroastrians." He correctly points out: "Pakistani social scientists should study and explore their society so that they can identify the problems and suggest their solutions to help the people to transform themselves into a prosperous, peaceful and humane nation". This is exactly the Josh's vision. His vision will not be achieved until we clear our minds from obscurantism, gender biases, and religious intolerance.

Stephen Bauhart

Stephen Bauhart was born in February of 1982, in Vancouver, Canada. He was an inquisitive child who was interested in the workings of the world from a very young age. At the age of six, he began writing poetry, which has become a lifelong pursuit, with its first major milestone being a collection of poems entitled "Holy Jokes." Not long after his first foray into poetry, he discovered Kahlil Gibran which kindled an interest in philosophy, literature, history, and culture which has become central to his character.

He completed a double major in philosophy and literature from the University of British Columbia, which lead to a Masters in continental European philosophy from the University of Warwick, and is leading to the pursuit of a Ph.D in literature. His first major academic interest was Friedrich Nietzsche, with his Masters thesis being an examination of presentations of weight in Nietzschean philosophy, but he has always had a strong cross cultural interest. As an undergrad he developed an interest in the Taoist text the Chuang Tzu, which inspired him to take many courses on Eastern religion. Kierkegaard, Rousseau, Chuang Tzu, and Nietzche are the figures which have most shaped his academic interests and life philosophy.

Religious, moral, and existential philosophy is his primary interests, and he is fascinated by the interaction of Western and Eastern cultures in the intellectual realms. Josh Malihabadi is a notable new academic interest, and has opened a world of largely unexplored cultural crossover between Germanic philosophers and Pakistani and Indian thought.

Josh Malihabadi: A Poet in and against Nietzsche's World

By Stephen Bauhart

It is often easy for western poetry enthusiasts to forget that there are thriving poetic traditions beyond the western world and English language. Surely we are all familiar with the odd passage from the Tao Te Ching, know a few monolithic lines from the Bhagavad Gita, or can name some popular styles of Japanese poetry, but what of poets active in the past centuries from Africa, Asia, or the Middle East? This paper will focus on a particular tradition, and in that tradition, a particular poet - Josh Malihabadi, a twentieth century poet writing in the Urdu language and in a distinctively Urdu tradition. Josh, apart from being a very skilled poet, is a figure particularly well suited as a bridging point between Urdu and several facets of the western intellectual tradition. Josh's major intellectual influences range from figures in the Urdu tradition to giants of western thought from Shakespeare to Tolstoy to Nietzsche. Reflected in his work are themes, images, and existential concerns that represent a variety of sources one might not expect from a poet seemingly foreign to the western intellectual world. This paper will take a very brief look at the tradition and history that Josh is engaged in, followed by an intensive interpretation of his rubai'yat in A Drop and the Ocean. This interpretation will look at the work in itself, focusing mainly on how the image of the tavern is central to his work being viewed as a journey of intellectual and spiritual development. Following this, evidence from the work will be given that shows, at the very least, Josh was aware and indirectly dealing with major issues in the western academic world of his time or, at the very most, that his rubai'yat could well be a direct response to existentially oriented concerns and thoughts of Nietzschean philosophy.

For those of us unfamiliar with it, Urdu poetry is heavily influenced by Arabic and Persian traditions. The early period of Urdu poetry spans from roughly 1200 to 1700, during which Urdu began to flourish as a literary language in the south of India before and during the period of Mughal rule. This period is marked by an influx of Persian and Arabic influences and an establishment of Urdu as a literary language, but mainly in the south of India. (Habib XV)

Following this, roughly coinciding with an increase of British influence in India culminating in British rule, what is known as a classical period of Urdu poetry arose. The language became a literary force further north in India in places like Delhi and Lucknow, though it still followed classical Persian forms to a great extent. This period lasted roughly from 1700 to 1850 (Habib XVI). Next we enter what's called a modern period of Urdu poetry. Under British rule for this period, Persian was replaced by English as the state language and an influx of new ideas sparked tension and innovation in the classic Persian forms that dominated Urdu poetry at the time. Following this, we enter the 20th century modern period during which new forms began to gain popularity. (Habib XXI-XXV)

This is the period in which Josh finds his home. In a time of popular new forms, ideas, and notable political change, Josh is a figure who is both historically grounding and transitional, showing a love of classic forms of Urdu poetry and engaging modern ideas with those classical forms. The work that is the focus of this paper today, A Drop and the Ocean, is otherwise called The Rubai'yat of Josh Malihabidi. Rubai refers to a type of quatrain with a rhyme scheme of AABA. Rubai'yat is a sequence or collection of rubai, not unlike a sonnet sequence in the way they function together. Rubai'yat joins a indeterminate number of rubai together in order to form a cohesive unit. Though it would be possible for there to be one, in A Drop and the ocean, no obvious linear story is told, but the poems are meant to operate together to convey ideas and messages, a sense of progression and change, that couldn't be accomplished by a single poem. The introduction to A Drop and the Ocean translator Mohammed Yamin describes Josh as having "skilfully created turbulent seas out of the still and tiny lakes of rubai'yat" (6) – and now it would be appropriate to examine some ways in which Josh has turned these small fragments into a leviathan of purpose and meaning.

Tavern Poetry

The very title of Josh's work implies a greater organization and purpose than a mere haphazard collection of poems. Each one taken in itself is an interesting aphorism of sorts. Together, as a progressive whole – and I will stress, progressive, as I will show that there is progress and development from start to finish in the work – they paint a picture of a journey, using a series of locations which can be taken both literally and metaphorically. The significance of the journey can be in part gleaned from an examination of these locations.

A Drop and the Ocean is replete with repeat imagery, much of which is common in Urdu poetry. Much like in western poetry one might see repeated references to a grim reaper as a symbol of death or a rose as a symbol of love, in Urdu poetry one very often sees images of mad lovers, wine and wine givers, oppressor's swords (XVIII Habib) among others. Like the rose in western poetry, these images are as much a part of the tradition as they are something distinctive in the individual author's work – the images are used widely, but many authors impart new meaning, or make those images their own. Josh makes extensive use of several of these classic images, in particular wine and the wine giver. M.A.R. Habib says "Urdu poets have long had a tendency towards abstractness" (XVIII), and Josh lives up to the claim in his use of these images. Wine for Josh represents intoxication, intellectual bounty, sometimes both together, and possibly a host of other themes which I believe would warrant extensive exploration. While I will reference the image of wine with some frequency, it is an image not common to Urdu poetry which is central to this paper's project – the image of the tavern.

The actual word tavern appears in only five poems in the work, though arguably it is the locale or subject of more, but several of the appearances are very conspicuous and have structurally significant positions. The collection has several major headings in it. The first two poems go with no heading, the third under the heading of Reflections, poems four to one hundred and forty five going under the heading of In the Name of Power and Existence, one hundred and forty six to two hundred and forty two under the heading of Anguish, and the remaining two hundred and forty three to three hundred and three under the title Beauty and Glamour. So there is one short unnamed section, one short section, and three major sections which divide the vast bulk of the collections' poems between them. The image of the tavern makes its first appearance in the final poem of the first major section, several times in the second major section, and then again in the second to last poem of the second major section. The final poem of the second section is almost a continuation of the idea presented by the second last poem involving the tavern. The tavern is then explicitly mentioned only once in the third major section of the poem. So we can see, the image occupies prominent positions in the last poems of the first two major sections.

It could just be mere coincidence that the image of the tavern appears in these prominent section ending locations, but an examination of the content of several rubai strongly suggests the tavern is actually a very significant image in the collection. The fifth poem in the collection, and the second poem in the first major section, is this:

I've searched mosques and temples, but could not see
Existence! How long to explore your obscurity

I looked through each nook and corner but couldn't find God
Now it's His turn to look for me.
10

Coming so early in the collection, my immediate thought was that this is a starting point of a new type of journey. This idea was reinforced by the general content of the In the Name of Power and Existence. The first major section is very focused on a tension and conflict with the divine, asking whether man is the only son who would become an orphan in the father's lifetime with God filling the father role (28) claiming "Religion perishes while the city of heretic thrives," (24), even claiming at one point that his confidence has "Separated from me even God's nothing." (17). The complexity of the relationship with God in the first book alone would require a dissertation in itself to unpack, but it is clear there is a tension with a God who is absent. This tension and absence still references God, at times questioning God, at times requesting things, at times hostile and believing or simply not believing. What is clear is a departure from a previous state – perhaps one of faith, though there is no evidence that God was ever present. With this in mind, the fifth poem about searching the mosques and temples is a launching point that fits the themes of the first major section of A Drop and the Ocean, those of religious crisis and an absent God, very well. The narrator in his crisis of faith considers his time spent searching mosques and temples, religious places of gathering, and finds them, and his relationship with the divine, wanting. It seems implicit, and supported by the latter content of the first major section, that this is a launching point for a journey to a different type of locale, not unlike the prologue of the Canterbury Tales or Zarathustra's reasoning for his descent from his mountain to the marketplace – Josh is dissatisfied with the temple and mosque, and he is leaving them. This is the stage setting for a journey to a new type of locale.

The first section then is rife with the tension of leaving, both literally and metaphorically, the place of the gathering of people for divine purposes. After much consideration of this tension, it seems no mere coincidence that the section that began with leaving a religious place of gathering ends with the arriving at a secular place of gathering – the tavern.

> *O venerable sky! The tavern is still young in age*
> *Men pour in and in drinking spree engage.*
>
> *The arch is piled with heaps of burnt nights*
> *And the story is still in the first stage.*
> 45

Prior to this, it should be noted that the image of wine and drinking has been intimately tied to knowledge and learning. At one point grapes are described as being "the bunch of knowledge" to which people say "the grapes are sour," (26), and wine as coming from the cup of curiosity (15) with quite destructive ends, and also described as "the wine of thoughts" which "doesn't quench my thirst." (33) A reference to the poisoned cup of Socrates further implies the peril of drinking. (29)   These images make it clear that drinking, intoxication, and eating are all tied in to the act of acquiring, consuming, and being overcome by knowledge. In the Name of Power and Existence can be looked at as the telling of an intellectual journey from a place of religious worship and consideration to a place of secular pursuits.

The journey starts with a temple, motivated by an absence of and dissatisfaction with God, and ends with a tavern, with knowledge being the object required to sustain the human being along the journey. Knowledge proves to be a destructive pursuit, since knowledge seems to not quench the thirst or hunger the narrator supposes it might. The arrival at the tavern, a place where food and drink are freely distributed, is one that that this implies to be unfulfilling. The tavern might be assumed to represent any number of things associated with the acquisition of secular knowledge – a school or university, or perhaps even the entire philosophy behind the secular-rationalist pursuit of knowledge.

Of course, the unfulfilling nature of this hall of drink and food, the tavern, this place where the representation of knowledge, wine, flows free, is almost immediately suggested to be problematic. The dark tone of the poem to finish off section one is suggestive, but upon the narrator reaching the tavern, the next major section entitled Anguish begins. Whereas the previous section was rife with religious tension and an exploration of the thirst for knowledge, the second major section is, as its name suggests, very melancholy.

In this section we see a notable change in the image of wine and a further exploration of Josh's time in the tavern. The tavern had been revealed as a place of "burnt nights" and associated with the "first stage" of a story, but also as a place where people came to engage in a drinking spree. The tavern was, ultimately, social at the end of the first major section. By the time we see the tavern in the second major section, the drinking spree is over and the tavern is revealed to be a transitory place in itself.

Neither that pouring of wine nor joy's cry!
How travellers come, stay and fly

Some left at night, some at dawn,
The only one left in the tavern is I.
53

The tavern is now empty, and evidently some left at night, some during the morning, but in what we can presume is the day, Josh is alone in the tavern. The tavern is revealed to be transitory for others, but Josh remains. One should wonder, where are these others going, and why is it that Josh has nowhere to go? Immediately following this poem though is another with a tavern reference:

When starving solitude makes existence a crime
The journey's length seems affliction prime

At night the empty tavern makes me recall
The travellers lost in the whirlwind of time
54

If there is a recurring theme in these poems, it is of loneliness, and specifically, that Josh is now in a state of anguish, we can presume in part, because he is alone and has nothing to satisfy his grief in this lonely state. The hallmark of the tavern, the "drinking spree," has also left him wanting as we see a stark change in the image of wine.

> *A source of continuous fright, nothing else*
> *A leisure for soul to ignite and nothing else*
>
> *The wine contained the soul of the skies at one time*
> *Now it has the sediments of night and nothing else.*
> 52

The tavern is empty and he is alone, the wine, the sign of knowledge and intoxication from the first major section, is now a "source of continuous fright" and contains nothing but "sediments of night" where previously it seemed to contain promise and progress towards something better. Upon reaching the tavern and spending some time there, he finds its joys fleeting, and one might read the anguish that is the namesake of the second major poem as very existential in nature at this point. In the absence of God, the narrator is reliant on the presence of men to bring him contentment. One might even consider Pascal's assertion that "all the unhappiness of men arises from... that they cannot stay quietly in their own chamber" (Pascal) or Rousseau's assertion that "social man lives always outside himself; he knows how to live only in the opinion of others, it is, so to speak, from their judgement alone that he derives the sense of his own existence." (136) and see that Josh is tapping into an anxiety about being alone, of not having oneself reflected in other humans, in Western thought. This is partly the grounding of a type of existential crisis of existence, and for some of faith, that truly began to bloom in Western thought in the works of Kierkegaard and Nietzsche, the latter of whom he was heavily influenced by. Josh is alone, devoid of God, and without wine and humanity for him to turn to, he is in anguish.

God is...? Josh writing in and against Nietzsche's World

At this point it seems appropriate to take a break from the interpretation of Josh's journey and discuss how this journey reflects at the very least an awareness of the increased understanding of existential crisis in Western thought, and at the very most a direct awareness of Nietzsche's treatment of that subject. This will lead to a continued interpretation of the third major section of Josh's collection, Beauty and Glamour, and seeing how it culminates in a solution for his anguish.

Without a doubt, Josh was aware of Nietzsche's famous proclamation "God is dead!" (125) and the thought that accompanied this idea. The statement is dramatic, attention grabbing, and polarizing – but actually, as I'm sure Josh was also aware, reflects a very complex idea rather than what it seems to superficially. There is little evidence suggesting that Nietzsche meant by this simply that there was once a divine being and He literally died, but rather that the "death of God" was an event – the single greatest event - in the maturation of human thought. Specifically, he says "God is dead. God remains dead. And we have killed him." (125). This statement is importantly distinct from the atheist claims that there is no God, that there never was a God – Nietzsche's claim reflects that there was at the least a very real idea which had tremendous power in the scheme of the human understanding of the universe and ourselves, and intentionally or unintentionally, human understanding evolved in a way that stripped this idea of its central role in the human conception of the universe and ourselves. Whereas secular rationalist traditions almost rejoiced in doing away with what they perceived as a mere delusion or fable, and these traditions were quite prevalent in western thought prior to this, Nietzsche broached the issue in a way not widely considered before by secular thinkers. His concern was, what do we do now that we have undermined this idea that was of such important for determining humankind's place and what it all meant in the world? If this had been a political coup, God would have been a leader figure absolutely central to making a government run, and He has been deposed – but no-one has been put in His place upon the throne. Thus we are not usurpers, as there was no positive plan upon the death of God, but we are underminers and murderers (in Nietzsche's eyes) who did away with the deity figure as a central explanatory idea of human thought without anything to put in its place. Nietzsche importantly posed the question, how do we deal with the loss of this central explanatory power, and thus raised the existential concern of the passing of this idea.

It should also be noted that Nietzsche was not convinced that purely rational, secular knowledge was a viable substitute for the God idea. Speaking of the sciences, Nietzsche actually is concerned that they have the power to analyse and weigh, but in themselves and with rational methodology in general, the power to create values, goals, and meaning is conspicuously absent. He says "if all the jobs (of analysis) were done, the most insidious question of all would emerge into the foreground: whether science can furnish goals of action after it has proved that it can take such goals away and annihilate them." (7) His view on value creation is a complex one where only as beings with the ability to create our own values can we effectively navigate the value void left by the death of God, and that creative ability falls into an abstracted realm of an art form. But importantly here, pure knowledge, the type represented by secular rationalism, is not an answer to existential issues for Nietzsche, and he is unsure at best whether pure rationalism can lead to value creation.

The saga of Josh's narrator is one that fits comfortably into this world of Nietzsche's at this point – in fact, it is almost tailored to it, and in some ways is a narrative of someone undergoing the types of concerns that Nietzsche raises in the absence of God. Josh begins searching for God and, If we can recall, he says "I've searched mosques and temples, but could not see/Existence! How long to explore your obscurity" (10) – so his God is absent and ineffective. Left wanting by religious pursuits and declaring "it's His turn to look for me" (10) he engages in secular pursuits trying to find the answers he seeks. Pursuing wine, a representative of knowledge, he is left wanting, and eventually finds the tavern, an alternative to the mosque. The tavern representing a gathering place of humankind and, with wine being an icon of knowledge, he is ultimately left alone and in a state of existential anguish, bereft of God, finding the wine – secular knowledge – is not satisfying in the existential sense that he is wanting for. Essentially, unable to find God, a pursuit of knowledge without God fails Josh as a way to alleviate existential anguish. Much like Nietzsche, Josh sees rationalist pursuits of knowledge as valuable, but as not the answer to the absolute questions which trouble us on an existential level - it does not solve anguish. At the very least, Josh's attention to the existential conundrum of a person without God trying to find answers in a world through a secular pursuit of knowledge shows that he is aware of some of the intellectual issues of Western thought in the time he was writing. Though, I believe that the closeness of the structure of his thought on this issue to Nietzsche's is a nod towards Nietzsche's particular concerns – how does one deal with the absence of God? Can secular knowledge provide an answer? Josh at this point has given no clear answer to the first question, but to the second, it seems as if the second major section Anguish suggests that secular knowledge and the pursuit of the company of tavern dwellers will sooner or later leave him dealing with Pascal's old problem - that all of humankind's miseries come from not being able to sit in that quiet room, alone. For Josh, when the tavern is quiet, and without a deity figure, he is left in anguish.

Even if Josh is manifestly aware of Nietzsche's project and actively engaging with it, it is not the case that he doesn't diverge from Nietzsche's appraisal of the situation later. The narrator is no Zarathustra, and Josh's God, while absent, has a different relationship with the narrator than that of any figure in Nietzschean philosophy. This is an excellent point to continue with the analysis of A Drop and the Ocean, focusing on the latter part of the Anguish section and what could be called Josh's positive program in the final section Beauty and Glamour.

The latter part of Anguish starts to take on a more positive note than the previous part, though it offers no clear solution. The tavern does become a place of mixed good and bad.

> *This evening the joy of friends' company maintain*
> *Tomorrow only a prick of its memory will remain*
>
> *Sing a delightful song again tonight*
> *Lay the foundation of a new cry of pain.*
> 64

We see in this a contrast to the anguish of loneliness of Josh's previous descriptions of the tavern, and now it is a source of joy as well as sorrow – the happiness that is had there being the grounds for future pain. He further expresses some contentment in the tavern in the final section of Anguish:

> *These heavy eyelids and the aching member*
> *The dizzy moons and the night-bird's taper*
>
> *How exhilarating is this night at the tavern!*
> *This intense intoxication, this deep slumber.*
> 70

And Josh finishes the section of Anguish in a sort of intoxicated stupor. No solution has been found since the experience is "exhilarating" but not satisfying or lasting. Pure intoxication has brought him to a positive experience, at least.

This leads into the final major section of the book, Beauty and Glamour. This section is rife with images stressing the danger in beauty, expresses disdain for public readings of poetry, introduces the potentially very significant new figure of Gabriel in many poems, but these are not the issues which immediately concern me in this paper. This section introduces a notable change in Josh's relationship with God which both shows Josh's most significant departure from a Nietzschean perspective. That being said, that God of Josh, a figure that did not feature prominently in the section of Anguish, and featured only as an absence in In the Name of Power and Existence, is not dead. Rather, in Beauty and Glamour, God actually assumes an active and arguably positive role.

> *It drops healing balm when a lethal sword I bend*
> *A spring jets out, when I press a rock's end*
>
> *God has bestowed in me such profound miracles*
> *Dews drop from flames when a command I send*
> 80

God here is described as being the agent that has given Josh the ability to create "profound miracles," but it should be noted that Josh is the one creating the miracles. Josh has an active creative power that he previously showed no sign of. The only reference to the tavern in Beauty and Glamour is also a notable departure from its previous presentations:

> *Does someone in the tavern have qualities like mine?*
> *Endowed with thunder and melodies fine*
>
> *I am gifted with such modulation that is*
> *Wallowing in blood and the colour of wine.*
> 76

Josh is noticing himself now. He is not analysing the world, he is not attempting to intoxicate himself – he recognizes himself as a creature with powerful creative potential that is wallowing in wine. Josh started his journey leaving the temple, moved on to find the tavern, and now it seems that Josh has stopped searching for new locales to find what he's looking for and is turning to a recognition of his own splendour, his own ability to create thunder, melodies, and even miracles. And where his journey started with him searching for God, a final turn marks the change in Josh:

> *Eyes chasing and straining to see*
> *Distressed sun and the moon weary*
>
> *A light is traversing to and fro*
> *Perhaps God is looking for* me.
> 81

The God that Josh originally engaged on his journey to find is now looking for Josh. In the light of Josh's recognition of his own powers, his own splendour now, this is a change of the utmost significance. Josh has found a way to become significant to God and, it would seem he has done so by recognizing his own power to create.

Josh's God is not dead as it is for Nietzsche, but Josh's problem, until now, has been how does one establish a relationship with God? He originally could not find Him, he then thought to abandon him in the tavern, the hall of man, and it was only through reaching a bottom point of sorts, wallowing in the tavern, that he then came to recognize his own powers which extend so far as to perform "miracles." In a discovery and recognition of his own agency, his own power to be in some small way godlike, he turned the tables and made himself an object of interest to God. I cannot help but recall Nietzsche's comment on humanity's murder of God – "Must we ourselves not become gods simply to appear worthy of it?" (125) It seems that Josh's solution to an absence of God was to in some small way realize his own godlike power to create, and in doing so, he found a solution to the problem posed by his absence of God.

The relationship with God is still a tense one, but it is a relationship. One of the last poems rages at God "You expelled me down to earth to tatter into age/Tell me God! Are you fully content?" (86) and he further states "I am not the son of that disgraced Adam" (86) distancing himself from God's creation, but also disgrace in the eyes of the Divine. The tone is much more one of a relationship that is closer in rank – while he may be at odds with God, he is not as far from God as he was before. God is a figure he can speak with, that he can disagree with – and when God fails him, he is an agent with creative powers of his own. And that is the note on which Josh's journey ends.

We switch the dark night into moonlit
With straws fabric of a garden knit.

Each particle of the path with gift of imagination
We turn into the market of Egypt.
87

In the final drop in the ocean, Josh brings moonlight to the night, knits the fabric of a garden, and turns a particle into a market of Egypt. Josh finally moves forward on his journey, finally comes to terms with God, in virtue of his power to create. Be it Nietzsche's constant reference to creators as higher men or the assertion of Josh's contemporary, Jean Paul Sartre, that human beings are created and not found, Josh is examining the solution to our existential problems and coming to similar conclusions of some of the giants of Western thought - that we move past our crisis through an active recognition of our creative powers.

   To conclude, in A Drop and the Ocean Josh has taken us for a journey from a crisis of faith to an attempt at finding salvation in the workings of humankind, only to return to a more mature relationship with God as a final solution. His musings suggest an inadequacy of the pursuit of secular knowledge for solving existential anguish and that a relationship with the divine should focus on our creative powers to be successful, and need not necessarily be one of pure reverence for the God figure rather than a relationship of one creator to another. Unlike Nietzsche's though, Josh's God is alive, and a relationship with that God is important. Josh is a figure who is rooted in the rich Urdu tradition of poetry, but incorporates important elements of Western thought into his work. A scholar wishing to examine Josh's work should use resources from both Western thought and Josh's native Urdu to try and best understand what Josh contributes to an understanding of a post-modern existential crisis.

- Stephen Bauhart, January 30th, 2011

Works Cited:

Habib, M.A.R. "Introduction." An Anthology of Modern Urdu Poetry.
Ed and Trans. Habib, M.A.R. New York: Modern Language Association, 2003. XIV-XXXII.

Malihabidi, Josh. Rubai'yat of Josh Malihabadi, A Drop and the Ocean, Second Edition. Trans:
Mohammad Yamin. Collierville: Published by author, 2009.

Nietzsche, Friedrich. The Gay Science. Trans: Walter Kaufmann. New York: Vintage Books, 1974.

Pascal, Blaise. Pensees. New York: Dutton, 1958.
27 April. 2001 < http://www.gutenberg.org/files/18269/18269-h/18269-h.htm>

Rousseau, Jean-Jacques. A Discourse on Inequality. Trans. Maurice Cranston. London: Penguin Group, 1984.

Dr. Gauhar Raza

Josh Malihabadi

An active participant in building Indian Identity

By **Dr. Gauhar Raza**

It was the best of times, it was the worst of times, it was the age of wisdom, it was the age of foolishness, it was the epoch of belief, it was the epoch of incredulity, it was the season of Light, it was the season of Darkness, it was the spring of hope, it was the winter of despair, we had everything before us, we had nothing before us, we were all going direct to heaven, we were all going direct the other way – in short, the period was so far like the present period.

Charles Dickens

Let me begin by reiterating the most common statement often repeated by nearly every scholar that Josh, 'the Shayer-e-Inqalab' was a product of his time. But let us also not forget that Josh consciously participated in this production process. With all the literary skills at his command he chiselled out his personality and carved his position among the leading poets of his time. He received inspiration from varied sources and in turn inspired hearts and minds of his fellow beings.

Shabbir Ahmad Khan[13], was born at a time that is best described by the opening paragraph of Charles Dickens' most celebrated book 'A Tale of Two cities'. "It was the best of times….". The memories of brutalities that followed the first war of independence, 1857, were fading away and the masses were about to rise against the imperial powers once again. It was the worst of times. The basis for a united struggle was yet to emerge. There was confusion all around. The old-outmoded social structures were crumbling and new ones had not yet emerged. It was the age of wisdom, the novel ideas of democracy, fraternity, equality clashed with unjust social orders and were about to shape the future struggles against imperialism. It was the age of foolishness, many thought that the wheels of time could be turned backwards and the golden age of the past could be brought back. Those who firmly believed in shaping individual and collective destiny through struggle were ready to lay down their lives. The sceptics propounded that trying to struggle against the most powerful nation was a futile exercise. There were a handful who dreamt of a bright future and there were many who drew solace in the darkness of the past nostalgically seeing it as something that was better than their present.

In short the time when Josh was born, in a feudal family in a small place near Malihabad, around 25 to 30 kilometers from Lucknow, the capital of Awadh[14], was a period of intense churning and hectic political activity.[15]. During the first war of independence, it was this region that had resisted the British forces for the longest period and had sacrificed the largest number of people between 1857-59. The victory of the British Empire ensured unprecedented and uncontrolled imperial-loot which in turn led to successive famines. Millions perished. The epicentres of epidemics and famine shifted from one region to other. Bengal, Orissa, Maharashtra, North-western area were intensely effected by these cycles, millions died of hunger and plague in the next 40 years. The common people explained these away as divine retributions, but those who could see a pattern in the repetitive cycles, tired to establish a causal relationship. The press and folk art forms started articulation of the idea that the visitations were not sent by the gods but were man-made-disasters and were a result of the

British policies. The understanding that the drain of Indian wealth and the rampant British loot were the root cause of the misery of the people began to gain ground.

The political/religious leadership that emerged after the defeat of first war of independence can largely be grouped in three broad categories. Firstly, there were those who believed that society should be reformed by embracing new ideas percolating from the west and by being loyal to the British Empire. They also believed that participation and cooperation in governance and proliferation of modern education would emancipate people from drudgery. They saw modern knowledge and technology as the most potent source of power and lack of the same as the prime cause of subjugation. Secondly, there were those who thought that salvation lies in the great and golden past. The Hindu religious leadership searched for this golden past in the age old scriptures, (for example they drew spiritual, moral and ideological inspiration from the Vedas and the Puranas) and Vedic or Gupta periods (for demonstrating to themselves and others that the spiritual, moral and ideological tenets worked at some point of time and if practiced properly will bring the golden age back once again). The Muslim leadership located this glorious past in the Quran, hadith and Caliphate or selective parts of the sultanate or the Mughal period. Revisiting Islamic scriptures was necessary for developing a model code of conduct and the periods had to be specified to show that the code had worked in the past and shall work in future if applied properly. For them the reason for the Muslims falling upon bad days was the in contamination of the revealed truth and corruption of eternal moral values. Reforming society was one of the most important objectives of the thinkers of this period belonging to the first two categories.

The third category of political leadership that emerged during this period consisted of those who firmly believed that exploitation of man by man was the root cause of all the social, political and economic evils that dogged Indian society at the time . They dreamt of a society free from economic and social subjugation and proposed that imperialists will not leave a colony like India without armed struggle against British Rule. At the level of ideas the three streams were quite distinct but in reality the boundaries were quite hazy. In the arena of struggle the actors often switched roles. Before the turn of nineteenth century, it can be observed that the 'moderates', time and again, behaved like extremists, revolutionaries at times made use of a deeply religious discourse to arouse sections of society against the British and several religious leaders were inspired by 'modern ideas' of the west and in order to justify their fascination for these Ideas they tried to locate them in religious scriptures.

It was an era of profound confusion and society was in a state of perpetual agitation. The confusion was quite natural. The landmass that is known as India today did not exist as a nation state. It was an utterly fragmented society. The deep fault lines of social and economic division crisscrossed and ran through the social structures in every direction. It was a country divided in hundreds of princely states, these were almost independent nations unto themselves. How strong the loyalty to the king, nawab or raja would have been during those days can be gauged by the residual present day allegiance of a common man to the descendents of erstwhile Rajas, Maharajas and Nawabs etc in Hyderabad, Rajasthan, Madhya Pradash and in many other parts of the country. The highly complex caste system, the linguistic differences, food habits, diverse belief systems and religious distinctions divided people into small fragments.

The first two decades of the 20th century witnessed major upheavals, congress had split, religio-political groups had emerged and the revolutionaries had organised themselves in small yet quite potent groups and were gaining popularity among the people. With colonial oppression continuing its relentless march through these decades, the distinction between the three streams became more and more pronounced. This was the period when Josh was born and brought up.

During his formative years Josh, who was trained in feudal ways of life, received traditional primary education, first at home and then in Lucknow. Z Ansari in his article on Josh asserts that Indian social structure has, quite inflexibly, preserved the pride of racial qualities and wrote '......In his childhood Josh must have heard lullabies that sang of the valour of the Afridi Pathans, tales that carried the message that the (Afridi) Pathans were special people, stubborn, obstinate and yet kind-hearted. Warriors, ready to die for their honour, in short the same qualities that were also passed on to a Rajpoot child as a legacy of previous generations.'[16]

Josh often reminded his audience, through prose, poetry and during formal and informal conversations that he was an Afghani Pathan. The other part of his legacy that he constantly harped upon, was the great scholarship of his ancestors. In almost every articleor book that he wrote(including Yadon Ki Baaraat) this claim is repeated [17]. Ehtesham Hussain writes 'Josh often recalls his Afghani lineage. He frequently recounts that his ancestors were proficient with (both) the sword and the pen'[18].

It was probably, this cultural indoctrination that moulded Josh into a rebel at a very early stage[19]. He was born into a Sunni family and initially tried to locate his identity and thoughts in 'Hanafi ' belief system. He practiced the tenets so seriously that 'he grew a beard and prayed, cried and asked for forgiveness' for hours at night in solitude. Soon he got disillusioned and became a Shia changed his name from Sabbir Ahmad Khan to Shabbir Hasan Khan[20]. Against the wishes of his father (Bashir Ahmad Khan) Josh started writing and reciting poetry when he was nine years old. Khan Saheb tried to dissuade him, warned him and also appointed an informer who regularly reported on Josh's poetic activities. When, despite his best efforts, Josh did not change his ways the father relented he not only allowed him to write poetry but also sent him to learn Urdu poetry from a famous poet of Lucknow. Mirza Mohommad Hadi Lukhnawi[21].

In Rooh-e-Adab Josh admits that even when he was very seriously practicing the 'hanafi religious path' there was an element of doubt residing (deep down) within him, like a spring, in some unknown corner of consciousness. 'The spring (gradually) unwound, and after some time a kind of revulsion grew. Eventually I (Josh) reached a stage when I (Josh) gave up Namaz, shaved off my beard and gave up crying in the middle of night'. [22] The news of these changes reached his father who thought that his son will stray from the straight and narrow he patiently discussed the matter with his son over and over again. Progressively the dialogue got converted into admonishment and when even his scoldings did not cut much ice, the father threatened to disinherit Josh . A will that debarred Josh from inheriting family property was later written and sent to a judge.

The 'legal document' was changed during an emotionally charged meeting between father and son. Recalling the meeting Josh wrote '--- my father's voice echoed. Shabbir for the sake of wealth people kill their mothers, fathers, brothers and sisters, they even give up their faith (for acquiring property). But you held on to your convictions and cared not for wealth and property. Even if a person like you converts to the faith of a fire worshiper he should be respected.' Josh perfected his rebellious actions at home. Later, the rebel was to grow into the poet of the revolution (Shair-e- Inqlab)..

Josh received his early education in Arabic, Persian, Urdu and English at home. His Arabic teacher was Mirza Hadi Mohommad Ruswa of Umrao Ada fame. Persian was taught to him by Maulana Qudrat Ullah Beg who is famous for writing a Mathnavi of 5000 couplets without using words without dots (nuqta). Niyaz Ali Khan and Maulana Tahir also taught him Persian and he learnt English from Master Gomti Parshad.

His formal education was repeatedly disrupted and he changed his schools frequently. The list of schools which he was admitted to, is long. Sitapur School, Husainabadi School, Jubilee High School and Church Mission High School. In 1913 he went to MAO College Aligarh and left it soon and joined St. Peters College, Agra where he completed his Senior Cambridge course. In 1918 he went to Shanti Niketan where he spent about six months. While this frequent shifting of schools disrupted his formal schooling it increased his exposure to the great ferment that was to reshape India in the coming decades.. Lucknow, Aligarh and Agra were not only centres of higher learning but were also focal points of intense literary and political activities and Josh benifited greatly from his experiences in these centres of learning and enquiry .

The Rebel Josh had mastered languages for which he had a natural talent and flare. Even at the age of nine years, writing poetry was a serious affair for him. His interest was focussed on very few things ' reading books, observing nature, human behaviour, meetings with friends, poets and writers' were his favourite engagements[23]. In Rooh-e-Adab Josh wrote 'whenever I took time off from composing poetry my favourite pass time was to collect children of my age and gave them lectures on whatever, wrong or right, passed through my mind'. He goes on to narrate how he tormented his so called students during these sessions. Josh never changed; he often whipped his audience like a traditional teacher and dared them to disobey

Mujh ko eeza de, Kisi Hasti mein yeh quwwat nahin Doost ya dushman, koi ho, is qadar taaqat nahin
Juz Khuda, ab aadmi ki josh par qudrat nahin
Kiyon ki mujh ko ahle dunyan se koee haajat nahin
Or
Kya yehi rasm hai ke baad-e- wuzoo
Barf ho jaye aabidon ka lahoo
Zauq-o-taqwa zauq-e-taqwa ??? mein dil ka naam na aaye
Aadmi aadmi ke kaam na aaye

Or adab kar is kharaabaati ka jis ko josh kahte hain
Ke yeh apni sadi ka haafiz-o- Khaiyaam hai saaqi

His rebellion was not restricted to revolting against family traditions or religious beliefs alone he changed his official name from Ahmad to Hasan and his pen name (takhalloos) from Shabbir to Josh. It was this rebellious streak that also made him move away from ghazal as a form of creative expressions. By the age of sixteen Josh had read almost all important poets Persian and Urdu poets. Haafiz, Khaiyaam , Urfi, Nazeeri, Nazeer, Saadi, Daagh, Mir Anees, Sarshaar and Sharrar had impressed him most. Among all these poets his favourite was Nazeer Akbarabadi[24].

Though Josh had taken to Ghazal writing under the prevailing literary atmosphere of Lucknow and Under the influence of teachers like

Mriza Mohommad Haadi he found the form restricting his restless expression . An encounter with Salim Paanipati , an ardent follower of Haali, opened for Josh the flood gates of Nazm. Josh acknowledged 'Salim Saheb, with his loud laughter on ghazal goee (ghazal writing) turned me towards nazam goee, around 1914 or a little earlier ' . The restless rebel poet was now free to conduct experiments and explore new vistas.

Writings of Anis, Dabeer, Shibli, Haali and finally Iqbal's Shikwa and Jawab-e-Shikwas [25], had challenged the enviable position of ' the Ghazal' as the only legitimate form of poetry in Urdu language. In the 19th century you were not considered a poet if you did not write 'Ghazals' this was despite the fact that when he said "Kuchh aur chahiye wusat mere bayaan ke liye" Ghalib, had already realised that some thing other than the Ghazal was required to meet the needs of expressing the changes that had begun to influence life and society in his times.

Once in a while a poet was permitted to dabble in other forms. These writings were to gradually prepare the ground for a shift in content. Poetry was trying to break the shackles of 'Husn-o-ishq' (beauty and love) and come out of the prison of 'expression through indirect and unrealistic imageries'. Portrayal of reality as it was, opened up the possibilities of initiating the use of a conversational and didactic mode. The ground had been prepared for writing about real daily life issues, mundane topics, ordinary people, deteriorating economic conditions, notions of democracy, imperialist oppression, etc. and Urdu poetry gradually began to move towards hard core political questions.

Josh entered this emergent arena at the best and worst of times He was already equipped with a highly developed sense of poetic expression he had access to a large cache of vocabulary and tools of moulding words into various lyrical forms. His mastery over urooz , his sharp memory and deep study of great Persian and Urdu poets gave him an edge over many of his contemporaries. He wrote

ahiJabke Mudat se yehi pesha-e-aabaa hai to hum
Saheb-e- Saif-o- Qalam hon to koee door nn

Or
Shayeri kyon na raas aaye hamen
Yeh mera fann-e-Khaandaani hai

He wrote more than 100,000 couplets, a substantial part of it is lost
(this is true of many highly prolific poets for example scholars claim
that only one fourth of what Nazeer Akbarabadi wrote has survived).
A number of scholars have criticised him of being reckless in
selecting what he wrote. They argue that as Ghalib did he should
have weeded out all that which did not pass the litmus test of 'the best
of Urdu literature'. I am of the opinion that the wealth of poetry that
Josh has left, on the one hand gives us an opportunity to make a
correct assessment of his contribution and on the other it let us peep
into the long period of upheaval that India and later Pakistan was
passing through. The benchmarks and parameters of judging what is
'good quality literature and what is not keep changing with time. For
example Ghalib excluded

Hai Kahan Tammanna Ka Doosra Qadam Yaarab
Ham ne Dasht-e-Imkan Ko ek Eik Naqsh-e- Pa Paya

Ghalib excluded the couplet because of the alliteration in the latter
half of the couplet "Pa Paya". At the level of thought the couplet is
one of the finest among the great wealth of ideas that Ghalib's poetry
represents.

The point that I am trying to make here is that the enormous treasure
that Josh Malihabadi has left, not only gives us an opportunity to
examine the turbulences that marked the times that shaped the first
half of 20th century-India, it also gives us a chance to understand his
level of participation in building the socio-political consciousness that
was a hallmark of the times.

There is no evidence that Josh received training in any of science
disciplines or ever studies Marxism seriously (in a letter quoted by
Ehtisham Husain Josh includes Karl Marx in the list of writers,

philosophers and poets who impressed him)[26]. Therefore, it could be safely assumed that his 'materialist' and 'secular' understanding of nature and society is rooted in his keen observation, ability to question and fearlessly challenge and reject irrational beliefs. Probably he is the first poet who introduces theory of evolution and historical materialism into Urdu literature[27]. For example his poem 'Naya Milad' describes how out of the womb of the old social structure new society is about to take birth. The notion of evolution and historical materialism recurs in many poems however, in 'Naya Milad' in the first segment he wrote

Khasta jan tehzib utari ja chuki thi qabr mein
Aur nayi tehzib muzmar thi hijab-e-abr mein

In the second part of the poem he asserts that the old stagnant social order was bound to crumble and concludes

Jang ki bhatti se aane hi pea hi baad-e-murad
Irtaqa payindabaad-o-nau-e-insaan zindabaad
His journey to fame and title Shayer-e-Inqalab, began much before he came in direct touch with revolutionaries of the Progressive writers association.

The literary atmosphere of Malihabad, visits toDhaulpur, Lucknow, Aligarh, Agra, constant influx of famous lawyers from Allahabad to his house and the six month stay at Shanti Niketan (1920) where he also met Tagore, influenced his thought process and broadened his knowledge base. It is possible that it was during this time that he encountered and engaged with the revolutionary ideas that were increasingly influencing the literati and the youth. The young and perpetually restless Josh constantly to raise questions and looked for answers.
Kisi muqam pe haasil naheen qaraar hamen
Misal-e-Joo-e-rawaan beqaraar hain hum log

The restless Josh could not stay too long at one place and it was this need to be constantly on the move that took him in 1920 to

Ahmedaabaad to a meeting of the Khilaafat committee. , It was here that he recited a poem in a public meeting organised by the f Khilafat committee. According to Josh 'this was the beginning of his hate towards the British (rule)'[28]. Though during this period (1920 to 1924) he had fallen in love and was busy writing love poetry, the hatred towards oppression grew and matured his strong dislike for institutionalised religion and accepted notions of god continued to haunt him and found expression in his poetry of this period.

In 1922 the Governor of UP called him and offered to include his name in the list of those who were likely to be appointed as Magistrates in the near future. Josh not only declined the offer he also bluntly and fearlessly confronted the Governor and told him 'you are a ghasib (forcible Occupier). You have snatched our freedom. I will not join your service'[29]. As he matured his attacks against the fundamentalist became increasingly vigorous. In fact these attacks were to continue throughout his life. Even during his stay in Hyderabad, despite evident dangers his tirade against institutionalised religion[30] continued relentlessly.

Bijliyan jis Nakhl par   raqsaan hon phal Sakta nahin naheen
Teri is duniya ka mujhse kaam chal saktaa nahin
Main paron ko tolta hoon aashiyaane ko sanbhaal
Yeh hai duniya, aur apne kaarkhaane ko sanbhaal

In many poems he challenged the authority of those who portrayed themselves as sole repositories of religious knowledge and wisdom. 'Maulvi', 'Fitnay-e-khanqaah' and 'Sheikh ki Maanajat' are some examples. Much later when he started writing Rubaa'is (quatrains) the intensity of his attacks on irrational beliefs increased many folds. For him every prayer of 'the Sheikh saheb' amounted to unconditional support to the ruling classes and their unbridled oppression of the pauperised masses. In his opinion, organised religion, always played second fiddle to Capital.

Aql ki jin pe band hain raahen
woh bashar hain meri charaagaahen

Sun meri baat mera kehnaa maan
ya Ghafoor-ur-raheem, ya Rehmaan

Ahle zar ko kisi bahaane bhej
Saans lete hue khazaane bhej

Or he challenges the prevalent notion of god

Kahte hein mazahib jise Dara-e-do aalam
Woh hai to ta'ajub, jo nahin hai to ta'ajub

Hum aise ahl-e-nazar ko suboot-e-haq ke liye
Agar rasool na hote to subha kaafi thi.
(Shola-o-Shabnam p105)

Or for example see this rubaa'i of a later period where he says
'O God, those who learn only through wrote are nothing but idiots'
Gard hai, sab atey hue hain Ma'abood
Sab ek sabaq ratey hue hain ma'abood

Haan dekh, ke is khema-e- zarnigaari mein
kitne ahmaq datey hue hain maa'bood
The flowing couplet is no less potent in its attack on those who blindly
follow traditional religion tenets
> *Haqqa ke saaheban-e-riwayat ke deen se*
> *Pakiza tar hain ahl-e-daraayet ke kufriyat*

In the above couplet, word "darAyet' has been used by him for 'men of scientific knowledge or scientific temper'.

In 1961, he wrote an article for Josh Number, in which while trying to dissuade the editor of Afkaar from bringing out a volume on him, he wrote '-----in the eyes of people (qaum) my worst fault is that I do not accept axioms (aqwaal) and declarations, traditions and annals, all encompassing claims and absolute dictates and conventions, without testing them on the touchstone of firm logical arguments. Doubt, for me, is the key to wisdom (scientific)[31] and truth. I prefer revolt over imitation (taaqleed), I favour kufr-without-understanding to faith-without-understanding and I have proved to be so courageous in announcing the truth as I know (Kalma-e-haq) that I cannot even think of shying away in front of the biggest powers of the world[32].

Despite the fact that Josh had never formally studied science as a subject nor was he exposed to a materialist approach in his education, accept for reading some rationalist literature during his stay at Hyderabad, his personal experiences, his travels and his questioning mind, had combined together to reinforce his commitment to scientific temper and rationality[33]. It should be pointed out here, that even rationality and scientific thinking did not succeed in convincing him fully.. Ali Sardar Jafri argues that Josh was not a non-believer, but he was committed to separation of politics and religion[34]. A number of incidents narrated in his autobiography stand witness to his transitory slip into the frame of a believer [35]. And Yet the loudest messages he gave through his poetry and prose were rooted in rationalist thinking. He at times out rightly denies the existence of God or tries to subvert irrational thought processes from within,even while using traditional and religious imagery to subvert outmoded ideas.

Mabood naheen hai koyi quwwat ke siwa Insaan yaqin hai aur allah gumaan
Mabood nahin, nahin koi cheez nahin Illa agaahi-e- rumooz-o-israar

Kar Sakte naheen gunaah jo ahmaq, unko
Be rooh namazoon mein laga deta hai

Rabab farsh pe rakh de, ke josh se is waqt
Zameer-e-arsh-e-bareen ham kalam hai saqi

Yeh kaun hai, jibreel hun, kyon aaye ho
Sarkar, falak ke naam koyee paigham ?

When Ghalib first saw electric power in use, he was able to visualise the changes that this new invention will bring about. And Josh, similarly saw the steam Engine as the prime mover of change. He considered it to be a symbol of cultural advancement, industrialization, world of wisdom and victory of knowledge over ignorance:

Jangalon ke sard goshe, rail bal khati hui
Jehel ke seeney pay zulf-e-ilm bikhraati hu i

Bazm-e-wahshat mein tamaddun naaz farmata hua
tund injan ka dhuan,maidaan pe bal khata hua

Fitrat-e- khaamosh mein bhartaa huaa soz-o-gudaaz
San'at-e-purkaar ke chaltey hue jaadoo ka naaz

Al- amaan duniya-e-danaayi mein danaayi ka zore
bhaap ki phunkaar, lohe ki garaj, paani ka shore

(Banbasi Baboo, Shola-o-shabnam 149)
The same train for him becomes the symbol of inequality and socio-economic disparity, and he observed:

Allah Allah is qadar adl-o-tanaasub ki kami
is taraf bhi aadmi thay us taraf bhi aadmi
Ah is manzil se be-maatam guzar saktaa hai kaun
Juz khuda is zulm ko bardaasht kar sakta hai kaun

Rail ki patriyan is a poem though which Josh describes entire social structure of that period.

The train also enters his love poetry:
Gaadi guzar chuki thi patri chamak rahi thi

The years when Josh was maturing as a poet were also the years of heightened political activity in India, this ferment suited Josh's personality ideally and he was pulled in by the rising crescendo of the anticolonial struggle. . It is during this period that from a simple rationalist Josh graduated into a serious social and political commentator. His Collection Shola-o-Shabnam containing his writings of this period includes more than 50 political nazms like 'Paiman-e-Mauhkam', 'Ghulaamon se Khitaab, 'Tarke Jumood', Nara-e-Shabab, 'Husn Aur Mazdoori', 'Aasar-e-Inqilab', 'Mulkon ka Rajz' and others that are informed by the political discourse referred to above..

Despite the fact that in many of his nazms, Josh repeatedly invokes the imagery of 'a golden past' and advises   his reader or listener to seek inspiration from the 'valour' 'bravery , 'courage', 'fearlessness' and 'commitment' of ' our' ancestors, spiritual and secular, he does not want to go back into that golden past, nor does he ever seek to turn back the wheel of history, his call to the youth was to always march on ahead and to fashion a new world, a new society.

After 1920s, competing notions of 'Indianness' and 'identity of India' vigorously struggled for space on the political arena. Both the People and the leadership were in search of symbols and motifs denoting a common identity, motifs around which all the British subjects who lived in the Indian subcontinent could be rallied. Religious, linguistic, regional and caste identities were invoked by various leaders at different times, to channelize the anger of the people against imperialists,

Most of these identities were (are) dwarf identities, they included comparatively small sections and excluded the majority. However, in order to reckon with the immensely powerful British Raj which constituted the 'other', a decidedly inclusive identity was required. At many levels Indian freedom movement was a project to search for a shared identity that could produce the greatest possible opposing force against the British domination.
The History of the formation of Nation states tells us that all nations were born first in the minds of the people who lived within a linguistic or geographical boundary. It is only after a prolonged struggle, through mass actions, that they become a reality on the ground.

Forming the Indian 'nation state' was still a distant reality but it had taken birth in the minds of the people who inhibited this landmass. Three distinct streams of political consciousness were trying to give it a shape. The leftists (revolutionaries or progressives), the centrists and the communalists were trying to define 'Indian identity' in their own idiom. For the leftist the basis was class struggle, abolition of feudal structures and elimination of capitalist mode of production etc. For the centrists it was removing the alien British while the communalists located their Idea of India in religious constructs.

I, like many others, put all the communalists in one category for the simple reason that there was no substantial difference in their consciousness. The only difference between them was that as you moved from one set of communalist to another the religion changed and thus changed the number of citizens included in the respective sets of ' the self' and the 'the other'. Take for example Hindu and Muslim communalists, both believed in the two nation theory, both argued that the basis for citizenship and nation state should be religion, both believed that those who did not subscribe to the state religion should be reduced to second class citizens and both made out a case for the exclusion of the 'other' from governance. In short the communalist were experimenting with dwarf exclusivist identities while the other two streams searched for a universal inclusive Indian identity.

Where did Josh Malihabadi place himself? While this 'Maha Manthan' (the great churning) was going on Was he a mere onlooker, at the periphery. No. Josh's voice was loud and clear. He synchronised his consciousness very closely to the progressive positions[36]. With all the creativity at his command, he, as a poet, as a writer and as an extremely forceful and effective communicator participated in the construction of an inclusive Indian Identity[37]. The India that he voted for was fearless (paimaan-e-Mohkam), egalitarian (bhooka Hindustan), just (zaeefa), self reliant and confident (Kahaan Tak), free of exploitation of man by man (Zawaal-e-jahaanbaani), rationalist and scientifically tempered (Mard-e-Inqilaab and Tark-e-Jumood), anti war (Kisaan), free of tyranny of feudal lords, nawabs and kings(Zawaal-e-Jahaani or zamaanaa badalne waalaa hai), liberated from religious bigotry (Sharik-e-zindigi se Khitaab) and communal hatred (sada-e-bedaari i and many other nazms and rubbaiyat).

He was not a supporter of women's liberation, and did not subscribe to 'tu is anchal se ek parcham bana leti to achchha tha' but he aspired for an India where women would not be subjected to extreme poverty, deprivation and hard labour (husn aur mazdoori). There are a whole host of poems which can be used to create an India of his dream but in 'Mulkon ka Rajz, Josh compares ten countries and this collection of ten short poems clearly portrays his desire to learn from the experience of other nations and create an India that is not inflicted with a sense of inferiority.

Let me quote just two couplets to illustrate his opposition to feudal structures and consciousness, his firm belief in the evolution of ideas through experimentations and the efforts he was trying to make in creating a scientifically tempered society.

Hazaron tajrubon ke baad ab insan   yeh samjhaa hai
ke shaahi se nahin   hotaa shraafat ka chalan paida s-o-s 34

Musallat hain azal ke roz se jo ibn-e-aadam par
Main un auham ko sardar garebaan kar ke chhodungaa s-so-s p 98

Josh who relied on a direct and open method of addressing and arousing his audience/readers was confident that social change would be brought about by the most oppressed sections of society (see Baghaawat) audience

Aye hind ke zalil Ghulamaane-e-ru-siah
shayer se to milao khudaa ke liye nigaah

Or this couplet in the same nazm
Tujh par mere kalaam ka hota naheen asar
Chaunkaa rahaa hoon kab se main shaane jhinjhod kar   (ghulamon se khitab p 13)

Josh was a hard core secularist, he understood that communalism is a potent tool being used to prolong imperialist rule in India and he hated the British for dividing the Indian people on the basis of religion. He detested those who had imbibed the communal consciousness. Since 1930s till the assassination of Gandhi, communalism was on the rise and accounted for the largest number of deaths after Second World War. He wrote extensively on the subject a few couplets are cited below to illustrate this point further:

Lekin aye aaqil musalmanon, mudabbir hinduo
Hind ke sailab mein eik shaakh par tum bhi to ho   *shola-*
o-shabnam p 101

Ho jo ghairat doob mar, yeh umr, yeh dars-e-junoon
dushmanon ki kwahish-e-taqseem ki saide-e-zuboon
sos p16

Yeh sitam kya 'aye kaneez-e-kufr-o-imaan kar diya
bhaaiyon ko gaai aur baaje pe qurbaan kar diya

In 1931, communal riots broke out in Kanpur, almost 2000 people were killed, Josh's anger and frustration could not be restrained and he wrote 'Maqtal-e-Kaanpur'.

The anger with which he wrote this poem is evident from his choice of very strong words that he chooses to describe the communalists and their acts of violence and destruction. The poems begins with a litany of abuses, words to be found in all good dictionaries but not normally part of a literary vocabulary, words that he deliberately chose to express the anger and revulsion of civil society.
I quote a couplet which is relatively mild in its choice of words yet razor-sharp in conveying the message

Is tarha shiddat kare insaan' aur insaan par
Tuf hai tere deen par, lanat tere imaan par   s-o-s p 66

He did not stop at admonishing the communalists, he went a step further and probed the ultimate objective of communal violence:

Rukne hi waalaa ha aazadi ka jaan parwar jehaad
Aye firangi ! shadmaan bash, O-ghulaami zindabad   *s-o-s p 16*

While assessing his contribution Hilal Naqvi writes 'Josh circumscribes such a vast span of our literature and history that he has become a part of our consciousness'[i]. Naqvi further asserts that his contribution can only be assessed properly when we shed our narrow thinking and give up our tribal loyalties to the various groups that exist in literary circles. Prof. Ihteshaam Husain also raises this issue in his writing on Josh. And that brings me to the last point that I wish to make about Josh, through out his life, Josh experimented with various thought structures and continually explored new vistas of viewpoints[ii]. He came under the influence of Spiritualism, rationalism, liberalism, materialism and many other isms in between but sooner or later he was confronted with the same inadequacy in each school of thought – the mismatch between what was professed and what was practiced by the followers of that school. The result was distancing and withdrawal from or a rejection of that school and the idea that the school propounded   He was born an Afridi Pathan but he could not become a Pathan in the traditional sense, he located himself in the ' Hanafi' belief system but soon came out of it and became Shia. Instead of becoming a committed Shia, he transformed Marsia writing and introduced the notion of revolution into it[iii].

He joined Aligarh but left his studies midway. The poetry he wrote during this period was strongly critical not only of the Aligarh School of thought but also of the entire value system that Aligarh sought to nurture, a crime for which Aligarh was never to forgive him. '.

 Rationality fascinated him but he did not completely break from traditional thought processes. Freedom movement attracted him but he was strongly critical of the congress leadership on several major issues. He was quite impressed with Marxism and came close to the progressive movement[iv]. He participated in shaping the progressive writers association but did not join the communist party. He was an Indian who wrote many poems in praise of the country, received many prestigious awards, but finally migrated to Pakistan. He was a Pakistani but never reconciled with that fact[38] neither was he ever accorded the status and respect in Pakistan, that he so richly deserved.

We notice the same restlessness, this unending search for 'better than the best' in his creative output as well. He would choose one genre of expression, stay with it for a while, get disillusioned with its limitations, leave it, at times go to the extent of condemning the form itself and move on to explore another form, so on and so foryh. Josh experimented with all forms of Urdu poetry. He began with Ghazal, got disillusioned and started a campaign against ghazal writing. Shifted to Nazam and Marsia and then for a long time he wrote rubais. he wrote a large number of qatas, the number of rubais he composed exceeds rubais written by any other poet[v].

The trajectory of his expression is marked with many discontinuities, what however remains as an abiding constant in his writing is his curiosity and his ability to question and seek answers. A transparent honesty of purpose and commitment to basic human values that were ingrained in his personality formed the connecting thread[vi] that ran through all his writings. The graph that he drew on the canvas of Indian literature was a result of his fearless commitment to his ideas that changed with time. He never hesitated to announce them loudly. The most shocking discontinuity was his migration from India to Pakistan. How was he received in Pakistan is described by Hyderi Kashmiri, he says 'writers poet, media persons and cartoonists unsheathed their pens and went at him hammer and tongs. Articles and poems were written against him, caricatures were drawn, the religious zealots of all shades Wahabees, Barailwees, Deobandees, Qadiyanees, Sunnis and Shias forgot their mutual differences and formed a united front and began sounding the drums of war against Josh'[39].

His messages were clearly spelt out and he left no room for ambiguity, this absence of ambiguity in his writings led to a strange situation, he was not Pathan enough to be owned by the community as their poet. He was not Sunni enough to be owned by the Hanafis. He was not Shia enough. He was not Aligarian enough. He was not Congressi enough. He was not Marxist enough,. He was not Indian enough and he was not Pakistani enough to be owned by any one of them as their own Shayer-e-inqalab.

 When looking back on his life and ruminating on his achievements and short comings Josh was to write 'It is a fact that my fame has a strong resonance and the vibrations are felt across India and

Pakistan............my acquaintances and contemporaries are divided into two categories. There is a small collective of friends and contemporaries who like me because of a shared background and temperament. And there is a big group that dislikes me because they do not have any thing that is common between them and the first group, they are our opposites and suffer from prejudices of various kinds'. Rasheed Hassan Khan's article is a good example of hateful criticism of Josh Malihabadi's poetry[vii].

Josh did not know that he had a large following among every cluster of Urdu reading population s precisely because he had been rejected by every fundamentalist and communalist set up and his poetry had established hiom as an iconoclast, something that has been the prime mover of Urdu poetry down the ages,. Even today Josh has many fans and they do not belong to 'a small group of friends and contemporaries'. Put together their number is quite large and they are spread all over the world.

After the fall of the Soviet Union, aided and abetted by imperialism, religious fundamentalist of all shades and colours have surfaced. On the one hand imperialist forces are usurping one nation after another and on the other religious bigots are holding the world to ransom. A situation not very different from the times in which the genius of Josh flourished, Let us, in this gathering of the fans of Josh recall his strident anti imperialist and progressive legacy and repeat his revulsion of the politics of hate

Is tarha shiddat kare insaan' aur insaan par
Tuf hai tere deen par lanat tere imaan par

When Shabbir Hasan Khan, Josh wrote these line the world was passing through the great depression, 'in short' in the words of dickens, "the period was so far like the present period".
Had Josh been alive today, his writings would have been in the forefront of the struggle against the subversive ideas spawned by the 'Clash of Civilisations Theory' and his onslaught against this anti people concept would have reverberated across the world of literature with the same energy and anger as did his writing in the dark days of enslavement and the after math of the division of the sub continent.
, vol 122-123, Karachi, p 17

[1] For details see http://www.indianetzone.com/12/malihabad_uttar_pradesh.htm and http://www.maplandia.com/india/uttar-pradesh/lucknow/malihabad/
~~dia/uttar-pradesh/lucknow/malihabad/~~

[1] Ansari, Z, Lakhloot Josh Malihabadi, [1] Josh was born on 5th December, 1898. His family name was Shabbir Ahmed Khan, which was changed to Shabbir Hasan Khan when he was nine years old (1907). Sehba Lakhnawi. Josh Malihabadi: Zindigi, Shakhsiyat aur Fun ka eik Jaiza. (Josh Malihabadi: An Overview of Life, Personality and Artistic Work), Josh Number, Afkaar, Oct.-Nov., 1961 Guftgoo, Bombay, 1968, p27

[1] For example see Sayyad Mehmudul Hassan, Josh ki Shayeri mein Fikri Pahloo, in Josh Shinasi, Ed. Kazim Ali Khan, Shia College Lcknow, Lucknow, 1986, p130

[1] Hussain, Ehtisham, Josh: Eik Taarufi Mutala,(Josh: An Introductory Review) Josh Number, Afkaar, Oct.-Nov., 1961, vol 122-123, Karachi, p 107.

[1] Waheed Akhtar, Urdu ka Akhri Classici Sayer, in Josh Shinasi, Ed. Kazim Ali Khan, Shia College Lcknow, Lucknow, 1986, 39-69

[1] For details of how he became Shia and changed his name read Mahir-ul-Qadri, Josh Number, Afkaar, Oct.-Nov., 1961, vol 122-123, Karachi, p 240-241

[1] ibid. p111

[1] Rooh-e-adab p11-12 as quoted in Hussain, Ehtesham, Josh Eik Taarufi Mutala, Josh Seminar Number, Josh Number, Afkaar, Oct.-Nov., 1961, vol 122-123, Karachi, p 114.

[1] Hussain, Ehtisham, Josh Eik Taarufi Mutala, Josh Number, Afkaar, Oct.-Nov., 1961, vol 122-123, Karachi, p 109

[1] Ayjaz-ul-Haq Quddoosi, Resh Aur Rindi Ka Rishta, Josh Number, Afkaar, Oct.-Nov., 1961, vol 122-123, Karachi, p 208.

[1] Both Hali's Mussadas and Iqbals two Shikwas illustrate the confusion that India was passing through. These writings could be read as good examples of clash of ideas and search for a future in the glorious past.

[1] Hussain, Ehtisham, Josh Eik Taarufi Mutala, Josh Number, Afkaar, Oct.-Nov., 1961, vol 122-123, Karachi, p131

[1] Qamar Rais, Josh ki Shayeri mein Ehtejaji Lehje ki Manwiyat in Ed. Ali Ahmad Fatimi, Josh Bani-2, July-Dec. 1980, Allahabad, p26 GAUHAR SAHEB AISE CHAND ASHAAR INAAYAT FARMA DEN

[1] Ansari, Z, Lakhloot Josh Malihabadi, Guftgoo, Bombay, p30

[1] Ansari, Z, Lakhloot Josh Malihabadi, Guftgoo, Bombay, p30

[1] For a fairly detailed account of his stay in Hyderabad read articles by Tamkeen Kazmi, Josh Meri Nazar Main, Josh Number, Afkaar, Oct.-Nov., 1961, vol 122-123, Karachi, p 169-176 and Md. Habib Ullah Rashdi, Josh: Huderabad Dakan Mein, Josh Number, Afkaar, Oct.-Nov., 1961, vol 122-123, Karachi, p 177-197.

[1] In 'A dictionary of Urdu, Classical Hind and English, John T Platts, Urdu Academy, Delhi' one of the meaning of Irfan is science, I presume that Josh has used Irfan in the sense of scientific knowledge, wisdom and temper

[1] Josh Mallihabadi, Khatarnak Iqdam, Josh Number, Afkaar, Oct.-Nov., 1961, vol 122-123, Karachi, p16

[1] Ali Sarada Jafri, Kalidi Khutba, Josh Seminar Number, Irtaqa, September, 1999, Karachi. P 22

[1] Josh had read 'The Riddle of the Universe' by Haeckel (1901), Articles of Voltaire, 'The Existence of God' by Josheph McCabe (1937) and 'The Evolution of the Idea of God' by Grant Allen (1897), Josh Number, Afkaar, Oct.-Nov., 1961, vol 122-123, Karachi, p133

[1] For example Josh, in 'yadoon ki barat', his autobiography recounts that once he had 'godly revelation' during the sleep and when he woke up his room was full of fragrance. The book was published in 1970 and soon became best seller, see Hilal Naqvi, Josh ki Shakhsiyat Ke chand Asaasi Phlu, Josh Sadi Number, Irtaqa, Karachi, September 1999. P41

[1] Ali Sarada Jafri, Kalidi Khutba, Josh Number, Irtaqa, September 1999, Karachi,. P 17

[1] Iqbal Hyder, Josh: Eik Mufkkir Shayar in Ed. Ali Ahmad Fatimi, Josh Bani-2, July-Dec. 1980, Allahabad, p59-77

[1] Hilal Naqvi, Josh ki Shakhsiyat Ke chand Asaasi Phlu, Josh Seminar Number, Irtaqa, Karachi, September 1999. P42

[1] Mohsin Ehsaan, Qalil-ul-Alfaz Kaseer-ul-Maani, Josh Number, Irtaqa, Karachi, September, 1999. P74

[1] Jadid Urdu Marsiye ke Khadokhal: Mirasi Josh Ke Aaine mein, in Josh Shinasi, Ed. Kazim Ali Khan, Shia College Lcknow, Lucknow, 1986,P187

[1] Sayyad Mohomad Aqeel, Josh ki Shayeri mein Inqlab, Baghawat aur Militancy, in Ed. Ali Ahmad Fatimi, Josh Bani-2, July-Dec. 1980, Allahabad, p26

p 26

[1] Saleem Akhtar, Kya Aaj Josh Mailihabadi ki Zaroorat Hai, Josh Seminar Number, Irtaqa, Karachi, September, 1999. P 220

[1] Farid Parbati, Josh Ki Rubaiyan, in Ed. Ali Ahmad Fatimi, Josh Bani-2, July-Dec. 1980, Allahabad, p104-118

[1] Khaliq Ibrahim Khaliq, Josh: shakhsiyat aur Shayeri, Lucknow ke Hawale se, Josh Seminar Number, Irtaqa, Karachi, September, 1999. P 315

[1] Akbar Hyderi Kashmiri, Josh Malihabadi Kuchh Ahem Malumat aur Gair Murattaba Kalam, in Josh Shinasi, Ed. Kazim Ali Khan, Shia College Lcknow, Lucknow, 1986, p 111

[1] Rasheed Ahmad Khan, Josh Ki Shayeri mein Lafz aur Maani Ka Tanasub, in Josh Shinasi, Ed. Kazim
Ali Khan, Shia College Lcknow, Lucknow, 1986, p70-87

Wasimul Haque PhD

Edmonton, Alberta, Canada

Josh: Through the Prism of Colonial and Post-Colonial Culture

If one believes in the famous Persian poetic line ' Shairi juzwest az paghambari', then it is logical to say that poets have been the torchbearers of truth in a fashion similar to the prophets who have changed history through the gospels of Vedas, Quran and Bible.

Josh's message was the message of truth, a message to denounce tyranny and condemn religious orthodoxy; He thus championed the cause of reason, respect for human dignity, freedom and democracy. His audiences were the inhabitants of this world living under shackles of Imperialism or Colonialism.

In theory, Imperialism is driven by ideology, whereas Colonialism is driven by commerce. In practice, it is often difficult to distinguish where one ends and the other begins. One of the greatest scholars of English Language, Edward Said in his books ' Orientalism' and 'Culture and Imperialism' elucidates the mind-set of colonial masters, their understanding of the "East and West' or 'Orient and the Occident'. According to Said, " Orientalism is fundamentally a political doctrine willed over the Orient because the Orient was weaker than the West, which elided the Orient's difference with its weakness-------- As, a cultural apparatus is all aggression

(Orientalism)

Said further elaborates, " Imperialism did not end, did not suddenly become 'past', once decolonization had set in motion the dismantling of the classical empires".

(Culture and Imperialism)

In the twentieth century, a large part of Asia, Africa and Latin America living under colonial rule were showing signs of resistance against their imperial masters. The common masses, intellectuals of various colors, labors and peasants rallied under the banner of freedom to oust their colonial masters.

Josh can be best understood if one can capture the essence of 'colonialism' and 'imperialism' and analyze the poetic messages of Josh and other revolutionary poets of his time. Josh was one of the early Urdu poets who challenged the British Colonial presence in India and thus impacted the Indian Freedom Movement.

Josh's message is clearly reflected in the following lines (written and recited at Bhagwat Singh's hanging):

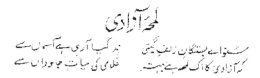

Listen

Oh, dwellers of the planet Earth,

The thundering sound, which is coming from the heavens

One solitary moment of life in freedom is better than eternal life of slavery

In another poem he declares his ideals in a language, which clearly reflects his revolutionary character

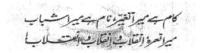

My mission is change,

My name is youth,

My slogan is revolution,

Revolution and Revolution.

The freedom struggle of India gave Urdu poetry a new temper, and a new ecstasy. He used the battle of Karbala as the symbol of resistance and the blood of Hussein as the glory of the struggle. The Battle of Karbala is simply the challenge to the establishment (Yazid) by upholder of justice (Hussein). Karbala, Yazid and Hussein have become the centre-piece of all political struggles in the Muslim world. The occupation of Iraq and Afghanistan by the American forces and the resistance is the new Karbala and Yazid is the new colonial power. Josh attempted to galvanize the youth of Indian sub-continent by illuminating their contemporary struggle of liberation from colonization with Hussein's Battle:

ہاں جوش اب پکار کہ اے میر کربلا   اس بیسویں صدی کی طرف بھی نظر اٹھا
اِس دیکھ یہ خروش یہ ہلچل یہ زلزلہ   اب سینکڑوں یزید ہیں کل اِک یزید تھا
طاقت ہی حق ہے،شور ہے یہ گاؤں گاؤں میں
زنجیر پڑ رہی ہے پھرانساں کے یاؤں میں

"O Josh, call out to the Prince of Karbala [Hussain],

cast a glance at this twentieth century, look at this tumult, chaos, and the earthquake.

At this moment there are numerous Yazids,

and yesterday there was only one.

From village to village might has assumed the role of truth,

Once again, Human feet are   in chains"

Josh expresses the agony of occupation through this beautiful quatrain. Here he addresses the state of his own existence, where an aggressor occupies his land. His mind is in restless state when he thinks about his future.

فردا کی زمین پر مکاں ہے میرا

امروز، اک عصر بے زباں ہے میرا

بویا ہی نہیں گیا ہے اب تک جو شجر

اس کی چوٹی پر آشیاں ہے میرا

(Roman urdu version)

Farda ke zameeen par makan hai mera

Imroz ik asr asr-e be zuban hai mera

Boya hi nahin gya hai ab tak jo shajr

Iski choti par aashiyan hai mera

My dwellings on the land of tomorrow rest

My today is a voiceless age at best

That tree is not even planted in the ground

On top of which is my humble nest

(Translated by Mohammed Yamin)

In the following quatrain (rubayii) Josh emphasizes the power of reason or logic as the template of intellectual development. Here, we see that Josh resonates at the same frequency as Al-Farabi and Ibn-Rushd (Aver roes). These philosophers contributed to the awakening of the Western world from the Age of Darkness. It is that darkness which prevailed in the colonized world that was shaping the destiny of the Indian citizens of that time.

کھولا ہے تو ہر ایک گرہ کو کھولو
منطق کی ترازو پہ ہر اک شے تولو
مانا کہ یہ عالم ہے کسی کی ایجاد
اور، علّتِ ایجاد ہے کیا؟ اب بولو

(Here is the Roman Urdu version)

Kholla hai to har aik girrah ko kholo

Mantiq ki tarazo pah har aik shai taulo

Mana ke ye alam hai kisi ki ejad

Aur ellat-e ejad hai kya? Ab bolo

Open each knot, if you must open

Weigh objects on scale of logic now and then

I admit, Some One has invented this world

And now tell me the idea behind the invention

(Translated by Mohammed Yamin)

In the next quatrain Josh highlights the state of abject poverty of his compatriots. It is hunger, which suppresses or eliminates the finer human instincts like creativity and aesthetics.

جس دیس میں آباد ہوں بھوکے انسان

احساس لطیف کا وہاں کیا امکان

اک فکرِ معاش پر نچھاور سو عشق

اک نانِ جویں پہ لاکھ مکھڑے قربان

(Here is the Roman Urdu version)

Jis des men abaad hoon bhoke insaan
Ehsas lateef ka wahan kya imkan

Eik fikr-e mayash par nichawar sao ishq

Eik nan-e jowen par lakh mukhre qurban

In a land where people do not have enough to eat

Aesthetic, creativity and refinement never meet

An empty stomach extinguishes flame of love

Pretty faces are all yours; this piece of bread is mine

(Translated by Azmat Qureshi)

The country with hungry people inhabited

Among men delicate feelings aren't created

Single worry for livelihood hundreds of loves surrenders

For one barley bread, millions of charming faces are   resisted

(Translated by Mohammed Yamin)

In the above two quatrains, his poetry is unique in style, is lucid, elegant and has a mastery of language which has the power to structure a text as a skilful architect. Josh is revolutionary and at times anarchic. One can easily capture his feelings of despair. It is imperative for a reader to understand his poetry in the light of history of colonial culture prevailing in India at that time.

The following English quatrain reflects an unconscious bond between these two great poets, Omar Khayyam and Josh, born and lived at different times. They have both challenged orthodoxy in Islam and championed the cause of learning for human progress.

Those who went in pursuit of knowledge

Soared up so high, stretched the edge

Were still encaged by the same dark hedge

Brought us some tales ere life to death pledge.

(Omar Khayyam)

In the next two quatrains, Josh again sheds light on the importance of knowledge and wisdom, which has been the focus of one of the greatest mathematician, philosopher and a poet, Omar Khayyam of Nishapur.

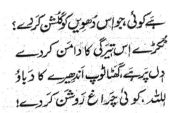

(Here is the Roman Urdu version)

Hai kyoi jo is dhoyen ko gulshan karde?

Tukre is Teergi ka daaman kar de

Dil par hai ghata top andhere ka dabao

Lilah kyoi chiragh roshan kar de

This ice into a flame of furnace turn

To make hearts abode of vision and foresight, is there none

Darkness of ignorance is so dense all around

For God's sake, light lamp of wisdom and knowledge, someone!

(Translated by Mohammed Yamin)

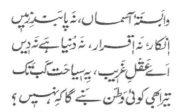

(Here is the Roman Urdu version)

Wabista asman nah paband-e zameen

Inkar nah iqrar nah dunya nah deen

Ai aql ghareeb yea seihat kab tak

Tera bhi kyoi watan banaye ga ke nahin

Bound to the earth nor to the sky's dome

Neither deny nor accept; between faith and disbelief roam

O poor wisdom! How long will you traverse thus

Will any where ever be your home?

(Translated by Mohammed Yamin)

The parallelism between Josh and Omar Khayyam has been well documented by other expert scholars on Josh. Some of the poetic parallelism can be seen in other poets who were also under the colonial domination in their native counties. When Josh was actively involved in the liberation movement in India, several poets of his time were involved in liberation movements in the Turkish and Arab world.

NAZIM HIKMET was a Turkish poet, and known around the world as one of the greatest international poets of the twentieth century, and his poetry has been translated into more than fifty languages. Between the ages of 27 and 34, he published nine books - five collections and four long poems- that revolutionized Turkish poetry. Hikmet's imprisonment in the 1940s created uproar among intellectuals worldwide. In 1949, a committee of intellectuals Pablo Picasso, Paul Robeson and Jean Paul Sartre campaigned for Hikmet's release.

It is through these lines of his famous poem 'A Sad state of Freedom', one understand the parallelism of thoughts in Josh and Nazin Hikmet's poetry.

You waste the attention of your eyes,
the glittering labor of your hands,
and knead the dough enough for dozens of loaves
of which you'll taste not a morsel;
you are free to slave for others--
you are free to make the rich richer.

The moment you're born
they plant around you
mills that grind lies
lies to last you a lifetime.
You keep thinking in your great freedom
a finger on your temple
free to have a free conscience.

You love your country
as the nearest, most precious thing to you.
But one day, for example,
they may endorse it over to America,
and you, too, with your great freedom--
you have the freedom to become an air base.

You may proclaim that one must live
not as a tool, a number or a link

but as a human being--
then at once they handcuff your wrists.
You are free to be arrested, imprisoned
and even hanged.

Nazim Hikmet

Another poet of eminence against the imperial attitudes was a Syrian known as Ali Ahmed Said (pseudonym, Adonis). As a poet and a theorist on poetry, and as a thinker with a radical vision of Arab culture, Adonis has exercised a powerful influence both on their contemporaries and on younger generations of Arab poets.

These few lines from his poem echo the same agony which Josh had experienced during his life:

Mask of Songs

In the name of his own history,
in a country mired in mud,
when hunger overtakes him
he eats his own forehead.
He dies.
The seasons never find out how.
He dies behind the interminable mask of songs.

The only loyal seed,
he dwells alone buried deep in life itself.

(Adonis)

The legacy of colonialism has been the instrument of power in Pakistan. Urdu poetry has become the vehicle of defiance against the troika of feudalism, militarism and religious fanaticism. There were, or, are several voices from the Progressive Writers of India and Pakistan which have battled newer waves of colonialism in the sub-continent. There are now resurgent voices in the literary arena that may be following the footsteps of Josh, Faiz, Ali Sardar Jafri and Kaifi Azmi to keep the flame of resistance against Imperialism burning.

Bashinda-E- Afaq

(Citizen of the Universe)

By Shaista Rizvi

Josh Maliahabadi and his uncompromising passion for expressing absolute truth had always been a remarkable and esteemed objective through out his creative life. To him serving the oppressed and disparaging the oppressor is merely pivotal to human values. He was a non- conformist in the very core of his thoughts. He envisioned the concepts of anaesthetizing religion, concocted boundaries of country and obsessive love of our language as prisons which divide confine and segregate mankind. He had the squall to scrutinize and disregard any dogma that impedes unity in mankind. This is more vital now that it was ever before. Who could not agree with me more today after helplessly watching our world racing back in time to a degree that it seems to be on the verge of disintegration. In spite of intellectuals foreseeing those dangers nothing was done to prevent the chaos we are in today.

Our era has witnessed immense landmark being embarked in the realms of science and technology, on the contrary humanity suffered most heinous crime against it in recent times which surpasses the brutality of dark ages. One seem to wonder that why such a paradox exists in our thoughts and actions. This discussion could be endless, without any conclusion but looking at our world closely unfolds the painless disparity in material, social and intellectuals realms which divides mankind in such a way that any common denominator is hard to find. Josh like many enlightened minds of twentieth century pre - empted us about this and resolved to encouraging knowledge and awareness and rationalism to combat those divisive forces. Our mutual and most vicious enemy is intolerance stemming from ignorance without any doubt.

His relentless pursuit of rationalism propelled him to attack mindless dogma and implored his fellow human being embracing centuries old beliefs he deemed obsolete. By referring to a few of his verses will make his vision more candid to comprehend.

تفریق جو سکھائے، وہ تاریخ پھاڑ دے
جغرافیہ کا محبسِ دیریں اجاڑ دے
نقشوں کی، نیش دار لکیریں بگاڑ دے
ایمان اور کفر کو، دامن سے جھاڑ دے
للّٰہ، افتراق کا دروازہ بند کر
اٹھ، اور لوائے وحدتِ انساں بلند کر

THAFRIQ JO SIKHAAY WOH TARIKH PHAR DAY.

JUGHRAFIA KA MAHBAS-E-DEREEN UJAR DAY

LAFZON KI NEESHDAR LAKEERAIN BIGAR DAY

IMAN AUR KUFR KO DAMAN SAY JHAR DAY

LILLAH IFTERAQ KA DARWAZA BAND KAR

UTH AUR LEEWAY WAHDAT-E- INSANE BALAND KAR

He advocates and impresses upon us to have a fresh start shedding all the animosities stemming from manipulated pages of history, divisive geographic borders drawn by hatred and oppression. His message is robust and zealous particularly in the region that he was emerging from. The orient in general and the sub – continent in particular had ingrained the teachings of Buddha, Nanak and countless Sufis who spread message of love and peace to their fellow human beings. In particular he shared the intellectual dais with literary giants like Iqbal and Tagore. Josh was an extension of those great souls with increased vigour and dynamism. He made his mark with his consummate eloquence supreme   mastery with diction.

The following splendid quatrain exemplifies his point of view   in his favourite terminology.

"اقوامؔ" کے لفظ میں کوئی جان نہیں

اِک نوع میں ہو دوئی، یہ امکان نہیں

جو مشرکِ یزداں ہے، وہ ناداں ہے فقط

جو مشرکِ انساں ہے، وہ انسان نہیں

AQWAM KAY LAFZ MAIN KOI JAN NAHIN

IK NAU MAIN HO DOI YEH IMKAN NAHEEN

JO MUSHRIK-E- YAZDAN HAY WOH NADAN HAIY FAQAT

JO MUSHRIK-E-INSAN HAY WOH INSAN NAHEEN

We can connect with his vision more in Canada since we experiment a cohesive and multi-cultural society around us. As Canadian legacy in seeing beauty in diversity and celebrating differences to enrich the very mosaic of our society, it is imperative to keep strengthening the fibre that unites the mankind. This seems to be an insurmountable task today. To achieve this seemingly impossible goal we have to extract relentless strength from a great humanist like Josh. He envisioned a society that we are fortunate enough to cherish. Which he used to refer as " ganga- Jamani " denoting an all-inclusive and all embracing culture of the sub-continent since his early years and once put in global perspective claimed to be "the citizen of the universe " denouncing all divisive forces impeding harmonious co-existence of mankind.

This will be a point of great interst to my readers that the term 'Bashinda-e-e Afaq 'was coined by Hazrat-e- Josh. The concept and reference behind the term was absolutely unheard of in 1960s when published. It was a good six or seven years earlier when his potent mind composed it. He pioneered the term and preceded the concepts of 'global village 'and 'one world 'which we undoubtedly resonate today but seven decades ago it was very alien even to the west .

We must take a notice of his prophetic tone as well.

انسان کی توحید کا مشتاق ہوں میں

شمع حبِ عمیم کا طاق ہوں میں

مشرق کا نہ پابند، نہ مغرب کا اسیر

انسان ہوں، باشندۂ آفاق ہوں میں

INSAN KI TAUHEED KA MUSHTAQ HOON MAIN

SHAMM-E- HUB-E-AMEEM KA TAQ HOON MAIN

MAGHRIB KA NA PABAND NA MASHRIQ KA ASEER

INSAN HOON BASHINDA-E- AFAQ HOON MAIN

(Translation)

I yearn for the dawn of the oneness of mankind

Like a niche on which the candle of humanity glows!

Neither bound to the East nor tied to the West

Being a man, Citizen of the Universe I am

His legacy is the ultimate pursuit of truth. To him it is immaterial to contemplate about the outcome of his quest a. It is of no consequence to him whether it is a mosque or a temple at the end of his pursuit. He is stead fast in the pursuit of truth like a prophet. And I quote:

نہیں مجھ کو پروا، حرم ہو کہ دیر

رسولوں کے مانند نیّت بخیر

NAHIN MUJH KO PARVA HARAM HO KAY DAIR

RASOOLON KI MANIND NIYYAT BAKHAIR

To culminate to the highest level of gen it is vital to shed all divisive and debilitating beliefs that we have been plagued for centuries. It is an enlightened path and the entire divisive forces will only hamper the journey to discover our utmost potentials that mankind is endowed with. It was a dream for him to witness those potentials released and to see mankind cultivating upon them to reach a new horizon of justice, compassion and intellect.

His remarkable poem " Zindan-e- Musallas " denounces language , country and religion as three prisons and his signatory eloquence builds an eye opening discourse of the three pronged attack on unity in mankind as following couplets entail.

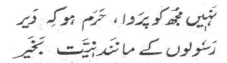

حبِ وطن کے شرریبا، اے اوجِ آدمیّت

کب تک نہیں پڑے گی حبِ جہاں کی ٹھوکر

یہ "غیر" کا تصور، افلاس آگہی ہے

رہتے نہیں میں پیارے، "اغیار" اس زمین پر

ہاں وحدتِ خدا کا اعلان ہو چکا ہے

اب، وحدتِ بشر کا، دنیا، کوئی پیمبر؟

Hubb-e watan kay sar par ay auj-e-admiyyat

Kab tak nahin paray gi hub-e jahan ki thokar

Yeh ghair ka tasawor iflas-e-agahi haiy

Rahtay nahin hain yaro aghyar is zameen par

Han wahdat-e-khuda ka ailan ho chuka haiy

Ab wahdat-e-bashar ka dunia koi payambar

His creative genius was always combating with the cosmic realities. He can not bear the thought of being the master creation as humans are believed to be and being ignorant of the very purpose of their creation. The traditional religious beliefs could not quench his intellectual curiosity. His intellect brings him to an interesting twist demanding the ultimate to search for the mankind because mankind has exhausted for centuries to find him.

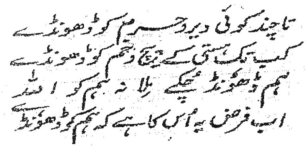

I HAVE SEARCHED THE MOSQUES AND TEMPLES BUT COULD NOT SEE

EXISTENCE HOW LONG TO EXPLORE YOUR OBSCURITY

I LOOKED THROUGH EACH NOOK AND CORNER BUT COULDN'T FIND GOD

NOW IT'S YOUR TURN TO LOOK FOR ME

(Translation of "Qatra –o- Qulzum
by Mohammad Yameen)

To him salvation does not come from the heaven we have to extract it from earth. Organized religion claim to offer salvation yet it has failed miserably to deal with its own paradoxes. He has faith in human mental faculties to resolve all the enigmas and mysteries haunting the very core of our existence. He thinks that one day we will even conquer death. This is where he shares his vision with men of science.

We draw passion and energy from his electrifying vision to propel us forward. We need to revive his message that he has amazingly delivered in colonial India to awaken the masses against their greatest enemies---ignorance, intolerance hypocrisy and mediocrity. He fought these negative forces all his life as his highly charged poem narrates:

MY FINGERS ARE BUSY WRITING OVER AND OVER

BLOODY STORIES OF DEATH AND NARRATIVE OF TEARS ALIKE . . . . .

(Lafani Huroof Elham o – Afkar)

لکھ رہی ہیں ، لکھ رہی ہیں، لکھ رہی ہیں اُنگلیاں

موت کی خونیں حکایت ، زندگی کی داستاں

جوت ہیرے کی جگائے، کولیلے کے آنگ میں

دامنِ طرزِ بیاں کو، ڈوب دیتی رنگ میں

روشنائی سے،ہزاروں خال و خد کو جھالتی

شعلۂ رخسار میں، نوکِ قلم کو ڈھالتی

He places great responsibility on men of letters. In his realm of thoughts 'pen is more influential than throne and cavalry. In another quatrain he emphasizes the power of pen in a robust fashion which is a signatory attribute of his poetics.

تَسبیح و عَمامہ و عَبا و خِنا ختم
تاج و اورنگ و قَلعہ و طَبل و عَلم
سَب کا اثر مُتَّفِقَہ ایک طرف
اور ایک طرف طاقتِ سرکارِ قلم

STRINGS OF BEADS, PROFOUND PRAYERS AND DEVOTEE'S TURBAN

THRONE, CROWN, DRUMS AND FORTIFICATION

THEIR COLLECTIVE POWER ARRAY ON ONE SIDE

AND ON THE OTHER THE MIGHT OF HIS MAJESTY THE PEN

A well crafted couplet is by far more effective than pages after pages of eloquent speeches. Especially a master craftsman like Josh Malihabadi knew the power of words and sounds. It is no exaggeration when he says and I quote:

یہ تابزباں، سُخن کے لانے والے
یہ، اپنے ہی خون میں نہانے والے
واللہ کے ہیں چشم و چراغِ آفاق
یہ ''فکر'' کو ''آواز'' بنانے والے!

MEN WHO RECITE THEIR VERSES PROFOUND

AND IN THEIR HEARTS CONCEAL A BLEEDING WOUND

ARE INSIGHT AND VISION OF WORLD BEYOND?

THOSE WHO TRANSLATE THEIR THOUGHT IN SOUND

His skilful subtlety baffles me when I see his treatment of grave realities in tender and delicate poetic terms. His beautiful imagery sets the stage for these two ruybaiyat in such a way that it has a mesmerizing affect.

اس بارگہِ کہن میں، ہم کیوں بولیں

اس کعبۂ حسنِ ظن میں ہم کیوں بولیں

اللہ ہے، "رحمٰن" و "روف" و "رزاق"!

سچوں کی اس انجمن میں ہم کیوں بولیں

LET THE ANTIQUATED SONG AGAIN BE SUNG

IN THE FLAME OF TESTS COMMON NOTIONS WEREN'T FLUNG

GOD IS BENIGN, MERCIFUL AND BENEVOLENT

IN THE SOCIETY OF TRUTHFUL WHY OPEN YOUR TONGUE

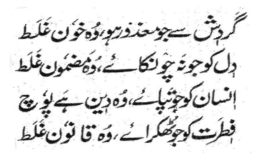

In Conclusion we must keep reminding ourselves that optimism, determination and an insatiable love for our fellow human beings are the ammunition we need to combat the challenges facing us today. As Dr Luther King JR once said and I quote "we must learn to live with each other or perish like fools.

We can and shall achieve that lofty goal if we commence our journey as "citizen of the universe "today as this great visionary envisioned.

He following quatrain expresses it in a splendid fashion

میں اور کائنات، اے محرمِ راز

مدت سے اب ایک ہیں، یہ فیضانِ گداز

لے کر جو مرا نام، پکارا کوئی

آفاق سے لبیک کی آئی آواز

MAIN AUR KAINATH AY MAHRAM-E-RAZ

MUDDATH SAY AB AIK HAIN, BAFAIZAN-E- GADAZ

LAY KAR JO MERA NAM PUKARA KOI

AFAQ SAY LABBAIK KI AYE AWAZ

Dr. Javed Qureshi

M.Sc.: University of Karachi, 1976
Ph.D.: University of Liverpool, UK, 1982
Field: Plant Biotechnology and genetic engineering
Post Doctorate: University of St. Andrews, Scotland and University of Toronto, Canada
Scientist: Monsanto Canada
Research Fellow: University of Adelaide, Australia
Senior Scientist: Novartis, North Carolina, USA
Current engagement: Professor of Plant Biotechnology, Foreign Faculty
University of Karachi

and

National Institute for Biotech & Genetic Engineering, Fasialabad
Publications: Over 50 papers in international journals
Poets I love: Ghalib, Josh, Faiz and Faraz

Josh: His love for humanity and passion for the pursuit of knowledge

Dr. Javed A. Qureshi

We are talking about a man who clearly was ahead of his time. This is particularly true in the context of the sub-continent, where time does move slowly than other places around the globe. There are numerous facets to the personality of Josh and his works. I am certain my fellow speaker will cover many of those. What I would like to do briefly is to focus on his work or message related to his love for humanity and for his quest for knowledge. He truly believed these two factors to be the essence of human dignity and its survival on this planet. Among his contemporaries and beyond, I have not witnessed any one so focused on the need for love for the mankind. Additionally, he constantly pounds away at the utter necessity of concentration, thinking and acquisition of knowledge regarding our being here on earth and exploring the universe. To him searching for and deciphering the intricacies of life is the essence of life. Ignorance to him is the cardinal sin. Therefore, the subject of thinking and opening the doors of knowledge and awareness is replete in his works. To propel his message, he has employed both poetry and prose. For poetry, he opted for (1) Nazm, where a particular subject is dealt at length (2) Rubaee,(Quatrain) where the message is sharp, swift and complete in four lines. As far as prose is concerned, his talent turns it into a missile that is guided as well as enormously explosive. It leaves you with no place to hide but to receive it.

Once during a speech, I was asked "what is the purpose of poetry". I was actually agitated by that question. I did answer that question and later wrote an article on that too. To me, poetry is an expression of inner feelings and lighter side of things. It does not have to have an obvious purpose. To put it crudely, food that we eat is a necessity, but putting a twist on it by adding flavors makes it more attractive and palatable. There are some things that you can only feel and extract pleasure or sorrow from them. What I am trying to say is that poetry is a medium for expression to those who have the inclination and the channel to deliver. There is no restriction on the kind of message it brings. Most of the time it depends on our own antennae as the audience to receive and decipher it. Having said that, it is a great advantage if the poet is resourceful and powerful enough to make his message heard loud and clear. Josh certainly is one of those voices. His message of rejecting hatred and adopting an illuminated path of brotherhood for humanity is ever so relevant today.

Before I move further quoting examples from his poetry and prose, let me share a thought with you since these proceedings are taking place in English. K.C. Kanda, in his book on Mir Taqi Mir, states: Translating the poetry of one language into another is a difficult task, more especially so when the two languages are as far removed from each other, geographically and culturally, as are Urdu and English. Josh himself once said " It is an impossible task, for poetry is a dainty porcelain vase, translation is sledge-hammer, poetry is crystal, translation is stone, poetry is a bubble, translation, the fierce gale". So you must forgive me for the crudity of some of the translations that I will be sharing with you today.

As I mentioned earlier, Josh was ahead of his time. He was very aware of that fact himself. He says:

My dwelling is built on the land of future

Current time is just a silent phase

I dwell at the peak of the tree

The seed of which is yet to be sown

To me the gist of Josh's message is in the following verses.

The dust of malice in your heart, need not be there

Hatred for the good or the bad, need not be there

Who says, your love of the flowers need not be there?

But yes, your hatred of the thorns need not be there

The same blood of the green flows in their veins too

The same spring breezes have nurtured them too

These verses clearly show how he saw the humans living with no malice and with the realization that our differences should not be a prelude to enmity and hatred. We must learn to co-exist caring and sharing.

Josh considers hatred and enmity to be the biggest weakness of human kind. To him, such negativity pushes us into a deep and dark cave where all pores of doing good are clogged. This leads to that path of destruction and violence which is so evident in today's world.

Josh says:

If you open your heart to enmity

You invite death riding on your shoulders

If you let the hatred of the enemy enter your veins

It is like dissolving poison in your blood

Coming to the subject of the necessity of modern thinking and acquisition of knowledge, Josh in utter frustration at the people of the sub-continent once wrote: A thousand pities that we have summarily dismissed our "heads" and have appointed our "ears" to be our guides. Having elbowed out intellect from its rightful place, we have embraced sentimentality and the abandon of religious mindlessness instead. We have desecrated our "brains" and have given place of pride to our "bosoms". As a result, in front of those nations, for whom the conquest over the forces of the universe is the crowning glory of life, we stand embarrassed as a bunch of poor, ignorant thugs – naked, hungry, and sick! It seems as though the spirit of the universe has lost all hope in us and has decided to write us off. Its is indeed because of this withdrawal and hopelessness that we are trying to open the mighty locks in the mansions of life and the universe not with incandescent flame of the intellect that will melt them open, but with silken braids and Turkish tassels! Therefore, those of you who have not listened to me so far, please heed to my words: We have to adopt true scientific attitude and forsake our enmity towards insightful wisdom. Until such time as we continue to romp in the fields of devotional music and kick back like a mule at the very mention of the word "intellect", life will continue to have no truck with us whatsoever!

The message of Josh continues with this Rubaee:

> *I started to hear, after my ears went numb*
>
> *I started to see, only after losing my eyes*
>
> *Only after having churned all the oceans of knowledge*
>
> *Did I find the priceless realization of my own ignorance*

How beautifully Josh has pointed out the importance of searching and acquiring knowledge. One can only start to understand the depth of the ocean of knowledge only after taking a dive in it.

It is not only knowledge that Josh is after. He also wants to question, criticize, dare and think.

Look at his expression:

> *Without questions, empty is the city of meaning*
>
> *Without a skeptic concern, desolate is the mind of man*
>
> *Without daring, intellect is but a bone-dry desert*
>
> *Without thinking, knowledge is nothing but a huge junkyard*

I would like to thank my dear friend Mr. Jafar Abbas for helping with the delicate task of English translations presented in this article.

Yaadon ki Baraat (The Procession of Memories) by Josh

Dr. Khalid Alvi

Josh Malihabadi's autobiography, Yaadon ki Baraat, is perhaps the most interesting biography to have been written in the sub-continent. No other work in Hindi, Urdu, Punjabi or Bengali compares. Its publication in _1972___ changed the face of autobiographies in Urdu! Many other writers of Urdu have tried time and again to imitate the style of Yaadon ki Baraat but these experiments have been mostly unsuccessful. The most notable among such efforts are the works of Qudratullah Shahab and Kishwar Nahid. Yet others have tried evidently and deliberately to escape the style of this phenomenal work. One way or the other, it has not been possible for any writer of merit to ignore the work and its impact.

If we try to measure the truthfulness of the work to estimate its worth as a biography, it would indeed make for a very sorry exercise. But if we consider the elegance of composition and language that Josh pours forth his memoirs in, the book is a delectably unmatched. Amongst Indian autobiographies, the work of writer Kamala Das, My Story, has enjoyed much popularity and attention but its fame stemmed out of non-literary reasons.

I talk about My Story because I want to highlight some of the similarities between this and the work under discussion. Kamala Das has dealt with the amorous affairs of her younger days with bold confidence and Josh also ponders over the various episodes of love in indulgent and excessive details. In this context, his preoccupation with 'truthfulness' can be gauged by the decision to include his first two affairs in the autobiography both affairs were with men and while the first one was unsuccessful, the second reached its 'logical end.'

To include such incidents in the written testament of one's life is the kind of courage which is peculiar and particular to Josh. These are issues which even with passing generations, do not cease to be potential sources of trouble and scandal. Josh is very vocal in his disagreement with his co-religionists because of their tendency to remain silent about their sex/intimate stories. It is because of this weakness that Josh unhesitatingly addresses all of them as namards (impotents)! A number of critics proclaim him to be a 'progressive' writer only because of such uninhibited gestures and remarks.

Because of these and other reasons, Yaadon ki Baraat is perhaps the most commented upon biography in Urdu. There were cases filed and fought in Pakistan. The Indian press in Hindi, Urdu and English was full of articles written either in support of the work or condemning it. Due to so many views and sentiments afloat about the work, it has become almost impossible to maintain an independent perspective about it. Some unbiased critics of the Urdu language have proclaimed that this book represents the best of Urdu prose literature but it is at best a work of fiction and should only be treated as such. I am personally of the opinion that such a great book of Urdu prose has not yet been and would be hard to match even in future. When compared to other great works of literature like the Bagh-o-Bahaar, Fasaanaa-e-Ajaayab, Aab-e-Hayaat or Ghubaar-e-Khaatir, in terms of the elegance of composition, even these so not shine as brightly. Though, in terms of the appeal of the content, Aab-e-Hayaat can be placed second. Abul Kalam Azad, who is a highly popular and appreciated prose writer, also seems bland in comparison. Both the 'great' Azads of Urdu literature have their unique shortcomings.

As far as Muhammad Hussein Azad is concerned, if he ever thinks of a story to be told, he moulds it into a sher to authenticate the story and if he is struck by a sher, then he transliterates it into a story which turns out to be much more interesting as compared to the real story. The other Azad, Maulana Abul Kalam, seems to write only so that he can use labyrinthine shers from both Urdu and Persian. The result is that his prose ends up becoming a collection scary and sublime words rather than being enjoyable and captivating.

Some people are of the opinion that in the name of blunt and honest truthfulness, all Josh attempts and achieves is to publicly publish indecency. Some critics also believe that under the guise of reality, a number of historical personalities and events have been misrepresented and what is attained at the end is rather a falsification of the actuality. It has likewise also been claimed that Josh has attempted to attack the established moral and religious sentiments through his biography as he had done previously with his shayari. The publication of Yaadon ki Baraat in all major Indian languages, including English, brought with it an onslaught of accusations which made the book out to be a Pakistani writer's attempt to soil the reputation of the late Nehru and Maulana Azad. In Pakistan on the other hand, it was always believed and expressed that Josh lived and behaved like an Indian, a foreigner in that country.

Interestingly, Yaadon ki Baraat provides validation for such claims as were made by Pakistan and these were proved right to a great extent. I believe that Josh was aiming for such justifications and validations at all through this work. He was only trying to serve 'history' rather than any faction or opinion. But even more than this, by presenting his version of history, he was also indulging in a pro-active and decisive act of self-fashioning and imaging. And to this end, he used 'untruth' just as freely. But these 'untruths' do not have any deeper and more vile/evil reason other than grasping the unwavering attention of the readers. Moreover, all these statements have been made with absolute simplicity and innocence. In the very beginning of the work, Josh attempts unsuccessfully to justify these 'deviations':

I have never been a master of good memory. Now the situation is such that I cannot even remember in the morning what I had eaten for dinner the night before. A couple of months back, I had left home to take a stroll under the stars but on my way back forgot the way to my own home.

One day, after I finishing a letter when it was time to put my signature, I could not remember my own pen-name and for some seconds, it was a very troublesome feeling. My heart began beating faster. If in the next second or two also I would not have been able to remember my pen-name, it would have been the end of me...

I have written these things because if any of the incidents of my life seem lesser or greater than reality or if there seems to be difference in the timeline, do not consider it to be deliberate and forgive me (13)

Utterances like these in the text prepare us for some of these 'untruths' and exaggerations and also make it evident that the writer is also conscious of the differences in timeline and versions of truth.

The appearance of truth in the text is also warranted by the fact that Josh has tried to bring to light each and every nook and corner of his eight decade long life in the course of this book. His childhood has been discussed in leisurely detail. The Bismillah ceremony of the young Josh and the rituals and the functions are also described. He remembers the rituals and the functions and also that there were plates of silver and pens of gold. He also remembers that his grandmother said to him, "Qalam goyad ke man shah-e – zamanam.(the pen says I am the king)

Intricate details like these which have been furnished by Josh do not testify to his fading memory. It might be another argument to claim that Josh remembered only those details which he wanted to remember. But wouldn't one's address be just the kind of detail that one wouldn't want to let go of? Wherever there seems to be an error in honest reporting, Josh appears to be very innocent. One can only call it innocence the way Josh blames the fault of his deviations on his poor memory even before he embarks on the journey of his memories.

To me, his attempts to portray his personal life in a particularly crafty and clever manner, highlight his innocent more sharply than his overt exultations otherwise would have.

To cite another example in support of my argument and as my final statement:

The Nawab of Tonk needed a favour from the Ministry of Finance. Bismil Sayeedi suggested that he should seek help from Malihabadi as he could get the work done through Nehru. The Nawab invited Josh to his house. Josh went with his wife and stayed at the Nawab's residence as his guest. The Nawab presented Josh a new car for his use while there. He also presented Josh's wife with jewels worth forty thousand rupees.

While on his way back from Tonk, Josh said to the Nawab that since the people of Tonk are accustomed to seeing me ride around in a Buick, if they see me leaving on board a bus, I would feel belittled. He asked the Nawab if he could take the car till Jaipur with his permission. The Nawab was more than happy to oblige. On reaching Jaipur, Josh called up the Nawab and informed him that they had missed the train to Delhi and consequently wished to embark on that journey further by car if he didn't mind.

On reaching Delhi, he again called up the Nawab and told him that he had been using the car ever since he had come to Delhi and even used it while he went to meet Nehru for the Nawab's work. He also told the Nawab that it was famous now in the city that Josh had been gifted the car by the Nawab. He asked if he should send the car back. The Nawab replied, "You can gladly keep the car as a gift." Thus Josh was able to exchange his old and battered car for a new Buick. There is even a couplet about this incident which has become very famous:

Aisi bigdi hai aql yaaron ki , josh sahib ki jaisey motor car .,

The minds of friends is so useless

As was the car of Josh

Though, this incident has often been cited as an example of the worldly cleverness and wisdom of Josh, I would like to believe that this is another example of his innocence. This is because the Nawab who had gifted Josh's wife jewels worth over forty thousand rupees could not have begrudged the gift of a car worth half that value to Josh (The incident is reported to have taken place in the mid fifties when a car would have cost about fifteen thousand rupees.) this especially when he was the one asking for Josh's help.

Wherever Josh wants to prove a point, he brings in a story to his defence. Ghalib very famously commented once — what I want is that in the world, if not in the world then in Hindustan, if not in Hindustan then in Delhi, there would be no hungry poor. The same emotion was expressed through the pen of Josh as well, "whenever it happens that there is no fire in the hearth of a poor man, my heart burns instead; whenever I see the ribs of an orphaned child, my body starts burning to the bones; when I hear sobs in any corner, my own eyes start flowing; if I see a funeral in a house, I feel the gloom of the funeral even in my house." (Yaadon Ki Baraat; 23)

Ghalib could only empathise with the hungry orphans but Josh goes a step ahead and declares that he cannot even handle the sight of a funeral. Ghalib wrote once, "us mughal borns are very unique, we almost annihilate those whom we love". Ahmad Faraaz has expressed a similar opinion in a sher.(Hum mohabbat mein bhi Ghalib ke muqallid hain Faraz-jis pe martey hain usey mar ke rakh detey hain.

Even in love we follow Ghalib, O Faraaz,

We use our charms to kill those whom we love the most.

With this one line of Ghalib in mind, Josh recounted eighteen of his love affairs in Yaadon Ki Baraat, the central idea however, remained the same. Before the publication of this work, these affairs might have been born out of the influence of his shayari, but after the publication, some of them might have their origin even in the success of this book.

An eighteen year old once came to meet Josh after hearing him at a mushaira, "instead of sitting on the sofa, she came and sat on the lower side of my bed where I was. I thought I would stretch my legs back towards me but before I could do more than think about it, she put her soft hands on my knees and said, 'please be at ease!' her touch penetrated till my blood and unsettled it!"

"...Allah! Don't lose yourself so in your philosophy. I came with such hopes and excitement to meet you but didn't so much as look at me one glance. Today I feel very... towards you I feel very ..."

"I have read all your poetry and Yaadon Ki Baraat, reading such tumultuous emotions, the philosopher in me died and the poet came back to life. I held on to her tightly and my tears started rolling down." (ibid 781)

These references are important for a lot of reasons. The girl in the conversation above has been identified as a student of philosophy and interestingly, Josh also considers himself to be a philosopher. Till now, women fell only for Josh's poetry but here is the first instance, of a girl falling in love with him because of his philosophy and his biography. There seem to be a number of shortcomings apparent even in these stories. I have also noticed poets like Anand Bakshi, Hasrat Jaipuri and Javed Akhtar surrounded by girls after concerts but these girls do not approach the poet because of physical attraction.

The writer of Yaadon ki Baraat is narcissistic to the extent that he is unable to transcend the boundary of his own personality. He is sure that the reader will agree with and believe whatever he writes about himself. He speaks about Nehru also in a similar vein, "I have seen him as a child at Anand Bhawan; then he was a wonder and so was I" (ibid 194) further talking about Mirza Qadr he says, "among the historians of my childhood, he is the only one alive and he reminds me of how delicate and comely I was." He also did not hesitate from expressing his opinion about his eligibility for the Nobel, "I wish someone would go and tell the blind and orthodox people associated with eth Nobel Prize that they are unaware of true poetry and if they want to really appreciate real poetry then they should read it in its original language ... what blindness is this that you refuse to look at the living form of poetry, it is only when translation kills the spirit of the text and turns it into a cold corpse that you embrace it!" ()

One of the characteristics of Josh's writing and his temperament is that every character and every man who he describes turns into a wonder. He proclaims himself to be the most handsome man and he does not let slip any opportunity to emphasise on this point whether it be in his own words or through words spoken by some beautiful woman. the whole world acknowledged his poetic merit but he also considered himself to be a philosopher and to prove this he sometimes uses the statements of philosophy students and sometimes uses his own very primeval articulations about the body and the soul.

Josh was convinced that Yaadon Ki Baraat would prove to be an irrefutable justification of the accusations made against him by his critics in Pakistan. The two very serious accusations against him were – firstly that he was an atheist and the second that though he lived in Pakistan, he was not a patriot.

But Yaadon ki Baraat as a text is full of evidence in favour of his innocence. Despite this, if one decides to overlook the beauty of expression in the book, there are many shortcomings that can be highlighted. Josh has not cared to include any dates of relevance in his life like his trips to Hyderabad and to Delhi; one has to sit and calculate all these dates, josh does not help at all. Similarly, he gives no details about when he started publishing the magazine 'Kaleem.' His exploits in the movie world are also not listed with dates. Important events of his life like his going and coming back from Pune are other such examples. If one tries to figure out the dates and arrange the events chronologically, it becomes very difficult because of the peculiar structuring of the book. The events have been narrate in a random fashion in an order which seems to be based on the temporal order of memory of the poet rather than in order of actual occurrence.

Though Josh was witness to many events of historical importance like the Jalianwala Bagh massacre, the Swaraj Andolan, the salt march, Simon commission, on-cooperation movement , WWII, Indian Independence and then partition, the annexation of Hyderabad and the martial law in Pakistan. But surprisingly, he does not mention any of these important events.

Josh was a great fan and a great friend of Nehru, but it wasn't because of his political genius or because Nehru led such a large nation but because, "when I saw Nehru for the first time, he was a wonder and so was I"(194) such was his political imbecility that he considered Gandhiji to be the foremost enemy of human pleasure only because he called for a total ban on the wine shops and the whore houses in every city. (93)

Josh was forced to take a lot of flak due to his being an atheist and his oppositions to certain fundamental Pakistani ideologies. He has tried to answer a lot of these allegations in the book. He says, "during the last phase of the publication of Kaleem, I became a very ardent supporter of Pakistan and even crafted a poem specially for the nation which I read very passionately."(249) moreover, Josh has tried his best to portray himself as somewhat of a religious saint so that the religious factions of Pakistan could re-conceptualise him in a spiritual and religious way.

According to an incident stated by him, during the Khilafat committee meeting going on in Ahmadabad, there was a very beautiful girl standing behind the tent. In the heat of the moment and noticing that the light was dim at that time, Josh kissed the girl and after that, relieving himself of any moral scruples decided to go on a trip to Ajmer with his grandfather. While on the train about four stations before Ajmer, Josh spotted another beautiful girl standing on platform and disembarked from the train. As a consequence, he missed his train and reached Ajmer by a later train. On seeing him, his chhotey dada said, "let's go and visit the khwaja's dargah." To this Josh replied, "I am the guest of the khwaja. I will not go to his dargah till he comes himself to invite me." After this incident, when Josh went to sleep, he dreamt about a very impressive old man standing near his bedstead and smiling at him. "when I asked who he was, he said that his name was Muinnuddin Ajmeri and that he had come to invite me." (197)

Adding to this, he recalls another dream as a result of which every religious muslim could be forced to kiss his hand in reverence.

"last night I saw a very strange dream about a wise old man who was standing in front of me. The moon was revolving around him and when I looked at him, my vision suddenly became blurred. I rubbed my eyes and looked keenly at him again ... when I recognised him, I fell at his feet and began rubbing my face on them ...   I broke down into tears and asked him – are you the same prophet of mine who visited me once when I was but a child? Hearing this, he smiled gently and said, yes I am that same Mohammed who visited you in the earlier dream ... he motioned towards the man standing near my feet and asked me to go to him."

After this Josh clarifies that the man mentioned above was the Nizam of Hyderabad. Whenever Josh fabricates a tale, he does not spend much time in the details. He just wants the reader to believe in his tales without any questions. The real incident behind this story/dream is that Josh had written a letter to the Nizam of Hyderabad that he (Josh) wanted to write a history of the dynasty of the Nizams in the style of the great poet Firdausi. In response to this letter, Josh was invited to come to Hyderabad. Josh's application and the specimen of poetry he sent to the Nizam can still be viewed.(Ref Josh Malihabadi – EDT,Qamar Raees P 290)

Another reason that can be given for this vivid and artistic imagination is to justify fully a Marxist poet seeking employment in the court of a feudal Nizam. At another place, he also claims that he could summon spirits as well. This claim he substantiates not just through his own statements but claims that even people like Raja Kishan Prashad Kaul, Faani Badayuni and Azaad Ansari also believed that Josh could summon spirits and get answers to any questions asked.

After recounting many unbelievable stories, he writes, "Faani called the spirit of Meer Taqi Meer and asked him, how good a poet is Iqbal? The spirit replied that according to him, Iqbaal was but half a poet."

This sort of strategy using the spirit to critique Iqbal is something that only Josh could do. This is particularly interesting considering Josh considered Iqbal to be his rival.

According to one incident, when Raja Kishen Prashad urged Faani to call a spirit, Faani quipped that it was a difficult task and he should ask Josh as his business was prospering then. Josh promptly summoned the spirit of the Raja's father. (493) Interestingly, Qudratullah shahab also mentions summoning spirits to obtain written answers, in his biography. Like Josh's spirit, Qudratullah's spirit also answered every question correctly and was called ninety.

There are some other people also who were among Josh's friends and who prophesied. Mehboob Shah Majzoob was another who could fathom what a person was thinking. (583) Alvero could also answer any question put to him and could know any question which barely thought and not spoken.

Every friend to be featured in Josh's album is extraordinary. He showcases each personality in the way he sees fit and oversells but in no instance does he let anyone be judged better than him. He writes this about Tagore, "There is one thing which I do not like about Tagore and that is his ostentation. If a foreigner would come to interview him, he would get dressed and sit in an important place which was ritualistically diffused with scent and beautiful girls were made to stand beside him." He had already declared Iqbal to be only half a poet. It is his habit to first praise a person and then in a single sentence to demolish their credentials. He declares Faani to be great poet in his opinion but in the end writes, "Faani spent almost all his time in the house of his beloved and the rest of the time, he went on talking about his lover."

Suha Bhopali was a learned man but he was addicted to both liquor and women. Wherever he would see a beautiful girl, he would ask for a kiss. "Please one kiss, one kiss."

Dr. Saxena was the professor of Philosophy at Hindu College but he was mortally afraid of his wife. One day he was sitting inside a car with Josh and drinking when they were spotted by a constable. Dr. Saxena got so scared that the glass fell from his hand and he ran straight to the house of the police commissioner Shankar Prasad who was his old friend. For eight days he kept hiding in the house of Shankar Prasad.

Josh does not stop at these incidents. He says that Wasl Bilgrami was a person who would go and kiss girls he met while travelling.(505) About Agha Shayar Qazal Bash he says that he was so scared of loud noises that he would hide in his house because of the scare. Colonel Ashraf Haq, according to Josh, wrote bad poetry and spoke of indecent and sensual things in front of his daughter. He was moreover a famed doctor but for every patient he asked his assistant to prescribe 'ADT' (any damn thing). (509) Maani Jaysi, says Josh, was ruining himself in the love of a Eurasian boy. Majaaz, according to Josh, destroyed himself due to alcohol. There is no man in his descriptions who does not have a comic shortcoming and Josh appars to be a better man than all of them as a result.

Josh himself is a bundle of contradictions. He prided himself on his Marxist and Socialist beliefs but also recounts proudly how he fired the barber's boy only because he did not salute Josh. He was also a short tempered man who did not hesitate in resorting to the cane if the need arose. Once, to prove his love to a boy, he picked up a knife and put it to his chest, which was dripping in blood within seconds.

Once when he was going with his Anglo-Indian girlfriend in a tonga, a British man objected. Josh snatched the horse whip from the driver and beat up the British man. This very girlfriend was once lying down in Josh's lap and drinking when her uncle spotted her and fired a gun!

There are many incidents like these which have been recounted which seem to be untrue but so not serve the purpose of enhancing Josh's image. The decision to include these is very unclear. I think that these varied incidents are a result of the different emotions that Josh went through at different times to create a certain image for himself. Sometimes he wanted to portray himself as a young lover, sometime as a socialist revolutionary and at other times as a feudal lord. All these images have got so mixed up in the book that now no single image has remained complete and independent.

As I have already suggested, if one reads this text as a biography, a lot of questions arise. If however, one reads this text only as an interesting treatise, it adds to one's repertoire, especially when Josh describes the seasons, youth or even nature. One might have read about the monsoons a lot of times but monsoons through Josh's eyes and pen have a different kind of magic.

--jhoomti,jhumakti jhoolti,jharjharati,jham jhamati,jhaum jhum barasti,joban wali jonti barsat,ghup andheron aur ghanghor ghataaon ki chhaon mein,ghirti ghoomto ghumarti,gungunatimgumakti ,gaati,garajti goonjti ghad ghadati,ghoongro wali barjkha.

The words are chosen with such expertise that one can almost feel the rain falling. Monsoon was exciting for Josh not just because of the rains but also because of all the girls who used to play in the rain with him, "the girls were so full of passionate and blossoming youth that if they so much as stretched themselves fully, their bodices would come undone." (69)

When he describes the beauty of a woman, he tries to capture the full delicacy of her charms. When he talks about the time when he started drinking, he mentions a woman thus, "with in the brimming cups of her bra, were the humming of the yet unbuilt Taj Mahal."

When he talks about summer, he gives it myriad names like Dhupya, Dundkya, Dehkarya, Paseenya, Nichodya, Bhadya, Bhanbhodya, Tanoorya, Changezya, Akal Khara, Ghunna, Roodha, Baddatta and Habda. Josh derived all of these words from the different dialects around India, these cannot be found in any dictionary. Not only this when he mentions the beginning of his philosophical observations,he mentions that " my observation started with stars.I used to think what are these bright objets?what is the secrets of their brightness?when I got slightly matured I started to think over entire solar system and I was determined to understand everything" Now Josh starts his untranslateable urdu-I thought –zato sifat ke tamam masaail ko

ulyon,palton,pighlaaaon,khurchoon,kuredon,naapoon,tolon,janchoon,
parkhoon,thonkon,bajaon,kootoon,chhanon,phatkoooon,usaaoon,chhuo
on,chakhhoon,soonghoon,bulwaaoon,sunoon aur dekhoon. Can
anybody translate this and even one can not find all these words in
any dictionary.

If you want to read the descriptions of the feudal life, of the
pain, of festivals like holi and Diwali, Ramzan, of ceremonies like
weddings and circumcision, of women's jewellery, their palatial
homes, children's education or the lives of the prostitutes from the
mouth of a magician, then you should read Yaadon ki Baraat. As far
as the verse is concerned, this is one of the most beautiful books
written in Urdu and its charm cannot be translated. The book is a
testament to the literary and verbal cornucopia of the Urdu language.

JOSH MALIHABADI & SHALIMAR PICTURES

by

Dr Kusum Pant Joshi & Lalit Mohan Joshi

South Asian Cinema Foundation, London

Josh Malihabadi (1894 –1982) hailed as *Shair i Inqalab* or Poet of Revolution for his passion for freedom and his fiery anti-colonial poetry[40], was a distinguished

---

[40] Writing about the powerful impact of Josh Malihabadi in the 1930s and 40s, Yavar Abbas, then a young undergraduate at the University of Allahabad, writes: "Josh was the darling of the young and the dread of the old Raj. His inspiring and aesthetically beautiful poetry sent the young blood coursing through our veins:
Suno ai saakinon kitaai-e-khaak
Nidaa kyaa as rahi hai asmaan se
Ke aazaadi ka ek lamhaa hai behtar
Ghulaami ki hayaat-e-jaavedaan se

literary figure from a landed family of Afridi Pathans based in Malihabad in northern India. He was one of those literary figures who, like Munshi Premchand (1880-1936), Sumitra Nandan Pant (1900 –1977), Govind Ballabh Pant (1898–?) and Amritlal Nagar (1916 –1990) in the 1930s and 1940s, and Ismat Chughtai (1915 –1991) in the 1950s, had strayed into the *filmi duniya* (or world of cinema). Having already won laurels for eloquence as a poet, it was not surprising that he was offered the position of film lyricist in a new film studio, Shalimar Pictures in the early 1940s.

Josh's Malihabadi's employer and colleagues in Shalimar Pictures

The owner of Shalimar Pictures was Wahid-ud-din Zia-ud-din Ahmed or W.Z Ahmad for

short. An ambitious man with fluency in many Indian languages and an interest in dialogue writing, Ahmad had worked as an Urdu translator and writer for some significant films directed by Modhu Bose[41] starring his talented wife, dancer and actress, Sadhona Bose[42]. For instance, in 1940 he had written for Bose's Kumkum and a year later for his Raj Nartaki / Court dancer. Then, eager to make his own films, he had established his film studio, Shalimar Pictures, around 1941. Like V. Shantaram before him, the studio was set up about 75 miles away from Bombay (now Mumbai) in the historic city of Poona (now Pune).

(Listen, you people of the Earth below
To the voice coming from up above
That a life span of a moment of freedom
Is better than eternal life without it)
And we took out "Freedom Processions" reciting in chorus his clarion call:
Kaam hai mera taghayyur, naam hai mera shabaab
Mera naara: Inquilaab-o-Inquilaab- o-Inquillaab
(My name is Youth, my work is change
My slogan: Revolution, again and again!)"
[41] Son of eminent geologist Pramathanath Bose, Modhu Bose had acted in the silent film The Light of Asia (1925) written and directed by Franz Osten with pioneering London-based English playwright, film script writer Niranjan Pal, as co-director. He had also spent time learning filmmaking in Germany and in British film studios and filmmakers including Alfred Hitchcock, before he returned to India in 1928. (For more, see: Directory of Indian Film-Makers and Films, compiled and edited by Sanjit Narwekar, Wiltshire, 1994, p.61.)
[42] Sadhona Bose was a granddaughter of the famous Brahmo Samaj social and religious reformer, Keshub Chandra Sen. She was a trained dancer associated with international figures such as Rabindranath Tagore, Inayat Khan and Anna Pavlova. Her sister was Nilina Sen who, after the sudden death of her husband, a prince from the royal family of Kapurthala, developed her old interest in classical music and became a famous musician under the name of Naina Devi.

Luckily for us, we have a collection of vivid essays on some prominent filmwalas (those connected with films) from the pen of one of the most gifted, controversial and witty Urdu writers of his times, Saadat Hasan Manto (1912–1955). From the dramatic vignettes conjured up by these writings, we can form a fair idea of Shalimar Pictures, its founder W.Z. Ahmad, Josh Sahib and other key members of his company's staff. Manto writes that he had first come across W.Z. Ahmad when V. Shantaram, the highly successful director and actor of Prabhat Studios, invited him to meet some writers and journalists in Poona in the 1940s. According to Manto, Ahmad was a sagacious and cool player with a politician's guile to set long-term goals and slowly work towards realising them. This was evident from the way he functioned. For instance, to turn Shalimar Pictures into a successful venture, he had assembled "a whole stable of writers and poets working for him, among them Saghar Nizami, Josh Malihabadi, Jan Nisar Akhtar, Krishen Chander and Bharat Vyas, apart from Dr Abdulla Chughtai and ... Masood Parvez."[43]

Besides adding lustre to the reputation of his film company, Ahmed's selection of these

men of letters enabled him to bask in their reflected glory as he sat in their midst. He also received special treatment from them. Again, we find this satirically described by Manto when he writes: "They would sit in Ahmed's room and hold heated discussions on the story being shot, sometimes for the whole night but without arriving at any useful conclusions, which was not surprising as the atmosphere was that of a court, full of sycophants. Josh would be kept happy with a pint of rum every evening. He would come up with a verse appropriate to the subject under discussion and receive effusive praise. Masood Pervez ...would add a few verses on the spot, which would inspire Saghar Nizami, who would recite an entire poem in his sweet voice. Krishen Chander, being a story writer, would just sit there like an owl, unable to join in the spontaneous versification. Very

---

[43] Bitter Fruit, edited and translated by Khalid Hasan, Penguin India, 2008, p. 548. The calibre of the people he assembled is evident from the lasting impact of their work. For example, Saghar Nizami's lyrics: Yoon na reh reh kar hamen tarsaaiye and Hairat se tak raha hai jahan e wafa mujhe, set to music by Pandit Amarnath and masterfully sung by Master Madan are an indelible part of the history of the ghazal in India. Similarly, Jan Nisar Akhtar is remembered for his Urdu poetry and lyrics and was part of the Progressive Writers movement; Urdu and Hindi writer Krishan Chander had left behind about a vast body of literary works including novels, short stories and plays; and Hindi poet and lyricist Bharat Vyas has a permanent place in the history of Indian cinema for lyrics such as: Ai malik tere bande ham and many others that he wrote for V. Shantaram's Prabhat Studio.

little work would be done during such meetings. Bharat Vyas would feel out of it because of his poor knowledge of Urdu. To make up, he would try to impress the company with his Sanskritized Hindi. And every time Ahmed sahib said something witty, Josh would shower him with praise, 'Ahmed sahib, you are a poet'.' When the meeting came to an end, Ahmed would shut himself in his room and try to write a ghazal, but as far as I know, he had not been able to compose one even once. All these people were Ahmed's groupies."[44]

In addition to the impressive array of literary figures in his payroll, Ahmad had also lured educated people with other skills from Mumbai into his organisation. One such individual was Mohsin Abdulla, scion of a well-known family[45] the likes of whom Himansu Rai had made special efforts to employ in his famous Bombay Talkies in a bid to win respectability for filmwalas.[46]

From Manto's writings, it is evident that W.Z. Ahmed knew how to cleverly run his ambitious film studio with limited financial resources. Thus, to play the female lead in his company's very first film, Ek Raat (1941)[47] that was inspired by Thomas Hardy's Tess of the D'urbervilles, he decided to use an unknown

---

[44] Bitter Fruit, op.cit.

[45] Mohsin's father was Sheikh Abdullah, a lawyer and philanthropist and his mother Waheed Jahan Begum was an enlightened woman. They founded a girls' school in 1905 that grew into the Aligarh Women's College. They believed in the emancipation of women and gave their daughters a liberal education. One of Mohsin's sisters was Rashid Jahan, who after studying in Isabella Thoburn College, Lucknow, studied at Lady Hardinge Medical College, Delhi and qualified as a doctor. In 1932, she gained notoriety for contributing a play and a story in an Urdu publication titled: Angarey that was condemned by conservative critics as a "filthy pamphlet ... which has wounded the feelings of the entire Muslim community." Due to her progressive views, Dr Rashid Jahan was attracted towards communism and joined the Communist Party in 1933. Another sister of Mohsin, Khurshid Jahan, was no less progressive than her sister, Rasheed Jahan. After completing her studies, she moved out of Aligarh and took the revolutionary step of joining the film industry where she starred in many prominent Bombay Talkies films such as Jeevan Prabhat (1937), Bhabhi (1939) and Naya Sansar (1941) under the pseudonym of Renuka Devi.

[46] Bitter Fruit, edited and translated by Khalid Hasan, Penguin India, 2008, p. 542.

[47] Ibid., p.544. Many people writing about Shalimar Pictures or Josh Malihabadi, have said that Man ki Jeet was based on Hardy's Tess. This includes Mushtaq Gazdar in Pakistani Cinema 1947-1997, Karachi, 1997, p.25. Manto, on the other hand, is the only person who has written that it was Ek Raat that was based on Hardy's novel. Since Manto was a contemporary of Josh Sahib and also knew many of those working in Shalimar Pictures, we feel we have good reason to accept Manto's account in preference to all the others.

female and for months on end, persisted in creating a hype about her. Summarising this publicity stunt, Manto writes: "The first production [Ek Raat] was already being aggressively advertised. I noticed that every ad was centred on a new actress described as 'the inscrutable Neena[48]'. I could not understand what mystery could be attached to an actress … For nearly two years, he kept selling Neena as 'the mystery lady'. I asked many people who this Neena was but no one knew."[49] After being thoroughly intrigued about the identity of the elusive Neena, Manto adds that he had eventually found out from Baburao Patel, editor of one of India's earliest film magazines, FilmIndia, that Ahmed's "mystery lady" was just a simple housewife. Baburao also revealed that Neena's real name was Shahida who was married to Mohsin Abdulla whom she had met, fallen in love with and married in Aligarh. He was the same Mohsin Abdulla who had abandoned Himansu Rai's Bombay Talkies to join W.Z. Ahmed to take charge of his studio laboratory.[50] Though thoroughly disinterested in acting, she had been initially pushed into the field by her prodigal husband and was later manipulated to star in Ek Raat by W.Z. Ahmed. He not only groomed her into an actress on whose shoulders he ran his Shalimar Pictures, but also succeeded in first getting her estranged from her husband and later to agree to marry him and become his wife.

Josh Sahib's entry into Shalimar Pictures

In the absence of original research-based writings on Josh Malihabadi's stint in films, it is indeed fortunate that besides Manto's writings, we have a detailed account in Josh Sahib's own words. This appears in his autobiographical work: Yadon ki Baraat in a chapter titled: Kuchch din filmi duniya mein.[51] He begins with an interesting description of how he happened to enter films which translates as follows: "I, along with Ummed Sahib Amethvi and Saghar Nizami Sahib, had gone to Mumbai for a mushaira [poetry recital]. On the evening following our arrival, the owner of Poona's Shalimar Pictures [Ahmad Saheb] came to the residence of Banne Sahib (Saeed Sajjad Zaheer). We were putting up there and after hearing our poetry, he took Banne Mian to another room where he kept talking to him for a long time. After he had left, Banne Sahib told me that Ahmad

---

[48] In October 2013, I asked filmmaker and ex-BBC broadcast journalist, Yavar Abbas Sahib about Neena and was given the following information:" Neena was the eldest daughter of Ain- ud-din, an Aligarh-based bureaucrat. Neena's father replaced my uncle as Diwan of the princely state of Charkhari in Bundelkhand. Our families were acquainted to each other and Neena's younger sister (Rashida) and I were very close when we were teenagers."
[49] Bitter Fruit, edited and translated by Khalid Hasan, Penguin India, 2008, p. 544.
[50] Ibid., p.
[51] Yadon ki Baraat, Lahore, undated, pp.265-271.

Sahib wanted me and Saghar [Nizami] Sahib to join him. "There won't be any restrictions on either of you except that you'll have to write some songs. Your salary will be up to 1100 rupees and Saghar Sahib's up to 550 rupees." My reply was:'This is a happy time but inappropriate for such talk. I'll give my response tomorrow.'[52]

In the morning, Saghar [Nizami] said it would benefit him greatly if I were to make my acceptance of the job offer, conditional on both of us being paid the same salary. His rationale was that this would push Ahmad Sahib to give in as he was very keen to have me. I agreed to carry out Saghar's wish and told Banne Sahib that my precondition for joining was that Saghar should also be given the same salary as what he was ready to give me or else I would decline his offer.

Ahmad Sahib accepted my demand. So, after a few days, both of us moved to Poona and started living in Tahir Palace on Shankar Sheth Road."

Josh Sahib's work at Shalimar Pictures
Available written material on Josh Sahib's work at Shalimar Pictures appears to suggest that Josh Sahib and his Shalimar colleagues engaged themselves in seemingly endless rounds of talking and enjoyment. Josh Sahib himself, for instance, writes that after coming to Poona, he had managed to get two of his other friends employed at Shalimar Pictures. He says that together they all formed a full-fledged "Chandaal chaukdi" (or gang of friends) making each day at Shalimar Pictures as festive as the day of Id and each night as bright and colourful as Shab e raat. He also adds that after an interval of eight or ten days, he would pay a visit to Bombay to meet his other friends who lived there. Such statements, should, however, not lead us to conclude that Josh Sahib's time at Shalimar Pictures was replete with socialising and enjoyment, but was devoid of productivity.

Between 1942, when Shalimar Pictures launched its first film, and 1947, the year India was partitioned in 1947, W.Z. Ahmad produced at least 6 films: Ek Raat (1942), Prem Sangeet (1943), Man ki Jeet (1944), Ghulami alias Rape alias Rape of Burma (1945), Prithviraj Samyukta (1946) and Meera Bai (1947). This means that throughout its existence, Shalimar Pictures released at least one film every year. Josh Malihabadi wrote nothing for the first two films and all the bhajans (or devotional songs) for the last film, (Meera Bai), were adaptions of the original songs of the medieval saint poetess Meerabai, by Pandit Bharat Vyas. But, in all Josh wrote at least ten songs for the three remaining films made by Shalimar Pictures. Of these, five songs were for Man ki Jeet, one for Ghulami alias Rape of Burma and four for Prithviraj Samyukta.

---

[52] Ibid., p.265-266.

Not all film lyrics written by Josh Sahib between 1942 –1947 are easily available.
Moreover, from whatever that has been unearthed for us to read and/or hear, it
can be
safely concluded that his Urdu poetry was far, far superior to his film lyrics. This
was sadly the result of his taking on the mantel of a song writer for popular or
mainstream cinema. As a film lyricist he had to respond to certain fixed demands
and work under some constraints. He could not function as a free spirit who could
write whenever he

Year	Name of film	Song Total	Lyricists	Music	Singers
1942	Ek Raat	8	Ghalib (1) Indrajeet Sharma (7)	S.K.Pal	Neena/ Rajkumari
1943	Prem Sangeet	10	Bharat Vyas (10)	S.K. Pal	Bharat Vyas/ Shanta Thakkar/ Amirbai
1944	Man ki Jeet	7	Josh (5) Bharat Vyas (2)	S.K. Pal	Sitara Kanpuri/ Zohrabai/ Shanta Thakkar/ Bharat Vyas
1945	Ghulami alias Rape of Burma	9	Josh (1) Bharat Vyas (5) Akhtar ul Iman (2) Majaz(1)	S.K. Pal	Renuka Devi/ Masood Parvez/ Bharat Vyas
1946	Prithviraj Samyukta	9	Josh (4) Akhtar ul Iman (4) Unknown (1)	S.K. Pal	Neena/ Bharat Vyas (1)
1947	Meera Bai	13	Meerabai bhajans adapted by Bharat Vyas	S.K. Pal	Sitara Kanpuri

Table showing films made by Shalimar Pictures, Pune (1942-1947)

wanted on whatever inspired or interested him. For each film assigned to him, he had to do a command performance or write to order by confining himself to the demands of the film. This included being mindful of the popular demands or taste of the common man on the street. Caught in a world where commercial ends were of the highest importance, there was little space for Josh, the Poet of Revolution or Josh the Iconoclast out to demolish feudalism with its oppression and man's exploitation by man, through the power of his mighty pen.

Even so, Josh Sahib did get a few opportunities for creativity at Shalimar Pictures. This
is evident in some of the lyrics he wrote for Man ki Jeet that caught public attention when they were first heard in 1944 and have also stood the test of time. Regarding their impact, Raza Ali Abidi, well-known Producer in BBC Radio's Urdu Service in his book: Naghmagar writes: "The year 1944 arrived bringing with it a revolution in the life of the King of music directors, Naushad Ali Sahib and the great poet D N Madhok. That year, their film Ratan arrived with a bang. Zohrabai Ambalewali who had sailed into the film world singing saucy numbers, took filmdom by storm … The lyrics of the songs in Ratan were not extraordinary. They lacked the elegance of the ghazal … [But] that year [1944] Man ki Jeet came with music of the highest order. The poetic quality deficient in Ratan, shone through brilliantly in the lyrics of Man ki Jeet because one of its lyricists was Josh."[53]

To the hit songs of Man ki Jeet that have been listed by Raza Ali Abidi: Pardesi kyun yaad ata hai; Ay chaand naa itrana[54] and Nagri meri kab tak (all three sung by Sitara)[55], must be added another lilting number in Sitara's voice: Man kahey ghabraye. But undoubtedly, Josh Sahib's most outstanding contribution to the film were the lyrics for the Nagri meri kab tak yun hi barbaad rahegi song. It has two parts and the lyrics are these are as below:

Part 1
Nagri meri kab tak yun hi barbaad rahegi
Duniya! Duniya yahi duniya hai to kya yaad rahegi
Nagri meri kab tak yun hi barbaad rahegi

---

[53] Naghmagar, Lahore,2010, Raza Ali Abidi, pp.126-127.
[54] Praising this song Pankaj Raag in his Dhunon ki yatra, New Delhi, 2006, p.187 writes "SK Pal's beautiful use of the bansuri [flute] in the background of this song sung by Sitara, raised it to great heights."
[55] According to Pankaj Raag, "This song [Ay chaand naa itrana] and Nagri meri kab tak, Pankaj Raag which SK Pal embellished with the notes of the mandolin, became immensely popular."

Aakaash pe nikhraa hua hai chaand ka mukhda
Basti mein gharibon ke andhere ka hai dukhda
Duniya yahi duniya hai to kya yaad rahegi
Nagri meri kab tak yun hi barbaad rahegi

Kab hoga savera
Kab hoga savera koi ai kaash bata de
Kis vaqt tak ai ghoomte akaash bata de
Insanon par insaan ki bedaad rahegi

Kehkaaron se chidiyon ke chaman goonj rahaa hai
Jharnon ke madhur raag se ban goonj rahaa hai
Par mera to fariyad se man goonj rahaa hai
Kab tak mere honton pe ye fariyaad rahegi
Nagri meri kab tak yoon hi barbaad rahegi.

Part 2
Ai chaand ummeedon ko meri shamma dikhaa de
Doobey hue khoe hue Suraj kaa pataa de
Rotey hue jug beet gayaa ab to hansaa de
Ai mere Himaalaa mujhe ye baat bataa de
Hogi meri basti bhi kabhi khair se aabaad
Nagri meri barbaad hai barbaad hai barbaad
Nagri meri kab tak yoon hi barbaad rahegi

Jo aankh ka aansoon jo aahon kaa dhuaan hai
Vaari mera dil uspe nichhaavar meri jaan hai
Mujrim hoon gunahgaar hun usko ye gumaan hai
Aavaaz do Insaaf ko insaaf kahaan hai
Ik bekas-o-majboor pe ye zulm, ye bedaad
Nagri meri barbaad hai, barbaad hai, barbaad
Nagari meri kab tak yoon hi barbaad rahegi.

Replete with leftist thought, with compassion for the sufferings of oppressed
humanity and yet redolent with yearning and hope for a better tomorrow, it was
set to melodious music that has pathos but without a loss of buoyancy, by the
highly talented music director of Bengali origin, Surya Kant Pal[56], and was sung
soulfully by Sitara Kanpuri. These lyrics also provide an excellent example of the
ease with which Josh Sahib and many Urdu poets and lyricists before and after
him were wont to effortlessly select Hindi words and phrases and use them with
grace and efficacy in their poetic compositions. In this, he was like someone

---

[56] SK Pal was a nephew of Ram Chandra Pal whose success in providing music
for south Indian films had led to his being recommended for employment in
Himansu Rai and Devika Rani's Bombay Talkies. SK Pal was music director for
all the films that emerged from Shalimar Pictures.

crossing over from one flower bed to another in his effortless quest to pick the best blossoms for his garland of flowers.

Yet, the Man ke Jeet song that created the greatest stir was Josh Sahib's: "Jubna" lyrics sung by Zohrabai Ambalewali. This was because the public considered its words vulgar. Criticising the lyrics, Pankaj Raag in his chapter on music director S.K. Pal, writes: "Man ke Jeet will be counted among Pal's most discussed films the reason being that a storm of criticism had been raised over the obscenity of the words of one of the songs [of Josh] that he [Pal] had set to music in this film." Its words are reproduced below:

Morey jubna kaa dekho ubhaar
Paapi jubna kaa dekho ubhaar

Jaise naddi ki mauj
Jaise turkon ki fauj
Jaise sulge se bam
Jaise baalak udham
Jaise koyal pukaar
Dekho-dekho ubhaar ...

Jaise dhanni kulel
Jaise toofan mail
Jaise bhanvaron ki jhoom
Jaise saavan ki dhoom
Jaise gaatee phuhaar
Dekho-dekho ubhaar ...

Jaise saagar pe bhor
Jaise udtaa chakor
Jaise gendavaa khiley
Jaise lattoo hiley
Jaise gaddar anaar
Dekho-dekho ubhaar ...
Morey jubna ka dekho ubhaar

The impact of the above lyrics is also evident from Shamshad Begum's response to it that has been described by Raza Ali Abidi: "That saucy song of Man ki Jeet had been written by Josh Sahib in his distinctive style and it was said that [singer] Shamshad Begum had refused to render it, although Zohrabai[57] quickly stepped

[57] A professional singer, Zohrabai Ambalewali shot into fame with her songs in a landmark film produced by Kardar Studios and directed by M. Sadiq, Rattan (1944), for which the music had been given by Naushad Ali then at his creative best.

in and took up the assignment because "joban" had featured many times in the private songs she had sung before she had entered films."[58]

The prudery that marked the reception of Josh Sahib's More jubna ka dekho ubhaar lyrics in 1944, was also unleashed against him over 25 years later in Pakistan, when he began to share his life experiences with the public through his prose writings. Recalling this episode Raza Ali Abidi, then a journalist in Karachi, writes: "Around 1970, Josh Sahib was writing his reminiscences. I was the News Editor of a daily in which his Yadon ki Baraat was being serialised. When Josh Sahib's pen began to move in an unfettered fashion, the newspaper edited out those bits. Josh Sahib was displeased and refused to write any further for the paper. He also despatched a letter to the paper's management which began with the words: Oh my squeamish fellow countrymen" – boldly announcing that he considered the paper's action to be a highly conservative over-reaction to his frank outpourings.

In fairness to Josh Sahib, it also needs to be said that though his "jubna" lyrics received considerable flak, as a lyricist he was perhaps merely responding to the practical need or demand of a specific situation in the film. Moreover, when we hear the original recording of the song today, the way it has been set to music and sung, makes it come across not as vulgar, sexy or even suggestive, but as a playful song. Additionally, as the following trite but nevertheless true adage goes: Nothing is good or bad, but only thinking makes it so. In other words, while one can interpret Josh Sahib's "jubna" lyrics to be cheap and vulgar, someone else can see beauty in his similes and consider the lyrics to be an imaginative description of the fullness and blooming of youth. Finally, the words of Josh Sahib's "jubna" song seem to have made a positive impact for their format is strikingly similar to that of a popular song written by Javed Akhtar for a 1994 film. We were heartened to find our view corroborated by Raza Ali Abidi for he writes: "Let today's lyricist Javed Akhtar not get cross, but upon hearing Man ki Jeet's ['jobna"] song, one's attention is drawn for a while towards a song written by him. Ek ladki ko dekha to aisa lagaa (1942 A Love Story) …"

Impact of World and Indian Politics
In the 1940s, while Shalimar Pictures was still functioning, India was passing through one of the most turbulent periods of its history. Besides the turmoil and tensions of the national movement that had been gathering strength since the 19th century, India had also become embroiled in the Second World War (1939 – 1945). Shalimar Pictures was also affected by these momentous events. As already mentioned, in 1945, for instance, they had made a film that bore the intriguing title of: Ghulami alias Rape of Burma for which Josh Sahib had written

---

[58] Naghmagar, op.cit., p.129.

one song. Since the film's title refers to Burma and also because the song that Josh Sahib wrote for it was a patriotic number[59], it is
perhaps quite logical to conclude that in all probability the film was inspired by the Japanese attack on Burma in 1942 and the consequent suffering of Indian and other soldiers and civilians affected by the attack and the deadly retreat from Burma in the 1940s.[60]

Ultimately, Josh Sahib himself became a victim of another drastic political development, the Partition of India in 1947 and the creation of Pakistan. Partition dealt Josh Sahib and his colleagues at Shalimar Pictures a severe blow because it prompted W.Z. Ahmed, along with his wife Neena, to suddenly disappear from the scene and quietly slink off to Pakistan. Remembering this calamitous episode, Josh Sahib writes that it had come as a rude shock and left them all high and dry. Shalimar Pictures folded up and like its other employees, Josh Sahib too had no choice but to abandon it. From his Yadon ki Baraat, we also learn that from Poona, he moved to Bombay.

Josh Sahib after the closure of Shalimar Pictures[61]
In sharp contrast to Poona, life in Bombay proved far from comfortable for Josh Sahib
and his family. He was lucky to be able to start living in the vacant residence of a close friend and fellow Progressive, Sajjad Zaheer. But, because of constant minor causes of friction and a desire to live peacefully, pushed him to move to another friend's place in Bombay's Jacob's Circle. Though they had a roof over their heads, Josh Sahib had no income and due to the prevailing political turmoil of the times, there was little happening in Bombay's film world. Of course, he had some friends here who did not abandon him. Saghar Nizami, who owed his

---

[59] The first line of this patriotic song were: Ai watan, ai watan, Tujhpe meri jaan nisaar.
[60] Burma was an independent kingdom which the British in India gradually annexed in the course of 3 Anglo-Burmese wars. In 1886, they converted it into a province of India with Rangoon as the capital. It remained so until 1937. In 1942, during World War II, the Japanese army unexpectedly invaded Burma. What followed is described as follows on the website of the Imperial War Museum, London: "British and Empire forces ... began the long and tortuous withdrawal to India. In what was to become the longest fighting withdrawal in the history of the British Army, the retreating troops faced problems of sickness and disease, impenetrable jungle, poor roads and constant harassment from the Japanese Air Force. They shared the retreat with thousands of civilian refugees fleeing northwards to India to escape the threat of Japanese brutality. The last exhausted stragglers finally crossed the last mountain range into India at Imphal in May 1942."[60]

[61] Our source for Josh Sahib's post-Shalimar days in Bombay, is primarily drawn from his Yadon ki Baraat., op.cit, pp.267-269.

position in Shalimar Pictures to him, visited him regularly and others linked with films, such as Agha Jani Kashmiri and K. A. Abbas, even tried to persuade him to go and meet film producers in the city to ask them for work. However, since he preferred to be offered work rather than go seeking it, he says nothing significant was forthcoming. The result was that, (although our search of post-1947 films has revealed that he wrote one song for a film released in January 1949)[62], his financial situation kept deteriorating and his wife's savings also started dwindling.

The passage of time failed to improve the situation. The sudden assassination of Mahatma Gandhi on January 30, 1948, in fact, created a big crisis. Josh Sahib describes it thus:
"One evening it seemed that hell had broken loose in the neighbourhood when I suddenly heard loud shouts of: 'Maro, Maro, Maro!' (Kill, kill, kill) from the nearby bazaar. I rushed to our veranda to ascertain what was happening, when someone started knocking loudly on the door of our flat. I took a bottle full of soda and opened the door. A neighbour, who looked like a Hindu, appeared and said: 'Mr Josh! Please leave this place. Someone has shot Mahatma Gandhi. Hindus suspect it is the work of a Muslim. So, please go away to a Muslim locality.' I immediately took my bottle and children and went to the house of my daughter's friend ... in Bombay's Bhendi Bazaar. There I heard a radio broadcast of Nehru announcing that the man who had shot and killed the Mahatma was a Maratha named [Nathuram] Godse. This prevented the killing of Muslims. Had he delayed this announcement even by five minutes, lakhs of Muslims might have been slaughtered."

Though the threat from reactionary forces unleashed by Gandhi's assassination soon lifted and enabled Josh Sahib to return to his Jacob's Circle residence the very next day, his financial state remained bad and even worsened. Noticing his wife's distraught appearance, he one day asked her the cause of her worrying. She is reported to have said that she had run out of money and was afraid that soon starvation would stare them in the face unless some remedial measures were taken. Pushed by this, Josh Sahib says he felt like casting away his pride, placing a pen behind his ear and like a hawker start parading the streets around Bombay's film studios crying out: "Lyrics on sale!" so that hearing him, someone would offer him work as a lyricist. Just then, he writes, the pride of the poet within him asserted itself. Issuing a stern warning lest he succumbed to the mundane

---

[62] This Bombay film for which Josh Sahib wrote the lyrics in his post-Shalimar period in Bombay was titled: The Last Message or Akhri Paigham (1949). It was earlier being named: Message of Mahatma Gandhi or Mahatma Gandhi ka Paigham and the first line of the song was: Jagmag jagmag hai sansaar jyoti se tere jiwan ke. (From: Hindi Film Geet kosh, Part II, Kanpur, 1984, p.503.) The title indicates that it was inspired by Mahatma Gandhi's message of peace and von-violence and that Josh Sahib's song was also a tribute to him.

demands of daily life, it threatened to break his legs if he dared to venture towards film studios asking for any such work!

Regarding what happened next, we have an interesting account in Josh Sahib's own
words: "A solution occurred to me like a flash of lightning. I ran to my wife, Ashraf Jan, and told her to be patient for just another five days. I said that if by then, our position failed to improve, she should give me about 30 or 40 rupees and a black blanket. Puzzled by my statement, when she asked me what I needed the money and the blanket for, I replied that I would buy some vegetables, place them on the blanket that I would spread right next to the wall of our flat and sell potatoes, cauliflowers and banda [a root vegetable] to my acquaintances. I added that my father had been very fond of banda and by selling banda, I, his son would at the end and the beginning of my life, establish a relationship with him through this vegetable! Upon hearing my explanation, my wife jumped up saying: 'Please don't do this! If you do, we will have no face to show to the world!' There were big tears in her eyes. My reply was: 'Forget about our feudal talukdari background. What shame is there in earning a living in an honest way? If there is any cause for shame, it is in stealing or robbing and in walking up and down the streets of film studios begging for work as a lyricist. Moreover, even if I did start selling vegetables, it would not be a loss of face for me, but a cause for shame to India!' My wife, however, seemed shattered by my utterances. Exclaiming: 'O Allah! Why have you abandoned us and become impervious to our sorry state!" she lay down and simply closed her eyes. Sensing her grief, I did the same in another room and dosed off. Then, I had a dream where I saw myself selling vegetables on a blanket spread out next to the wall outside my flat. I also saw some dead bodies passing by. When I asked, I was told they were the dead bodies of my ancestors."

Josh Sahib's financial problems and morbid dreams, however, were to soon end with dramatic suddenness. While he was still in Bombay, he got news of a vacancy for the post of editor of a public sector magazine called Aaj Kal. He applied and easily got the job. Thus ended Josh Sahib's brief sojourn in the film world. Though the limitations and demands of filmdom did not have the potential to provide a fertile ground to inspire and nurture his outstanding poetic genius, the Indian film world itself had surely gained by his brief foray into it.

ENDS

KUSUM PANT JOSHI

Dr. Kusum Pant Joshi is a Social Historian, researcher and author. Her books include: The Kashmiri Pandit– Story of a Community in Exile (1988), Kaleidoscope– South Asian Women in UK (2003). Recently, she co-edited a book on a UK-based film pioneer titled: Niranjan Pal: A Forgotten Legend

(2010). She has contributed to India Perspectives, South Asian Cinema and Hinduism Today and is the Chief Researcher in the South Asian Cinema Foundation (SACF). Kusum was a Modern Indian History Lecturer in the University of Allahabad and worked in the Central Office of Information (COI), London.

LALIT MOHAN JOSHI

Lalit Mohan Joshi is a film historian and documentary filmmaker and edits the thematic journal South Asian Cinema. He has written and edited several books including Bollywood –Popular Indian Cinema, Niranjan Pal –A Forgotten Legend and A Door to Adoor. His documentaries include Beyond Partition and Niranjan Pal – A Forgotten Legend. He is the founder Director of South Asian Cinema Foundation (SACF).

Tarika Prabharkar

Educated in India, Tarika holds an M.Phil degree in English Literature from the EFLU (The English and Foreign Languages University) and Master's degree also in English Literature from Hindu College, DU (University of Delhi).

Her work includes serving as the Fulbright Language Teaching Assistant (FLTA) for Hindi-Urdu at the University of California, Davis (2012-13). Otherwise, she has been teaching English Literature in the capacity of an Assistant Professor at various DU colleges since 2011. She also has experience working as an assistant editor at the publishing house Rupa & Co. She has been involved in social service with NGOs like Udayan Care and Nature Foundation (India), since her student days.

She is interested in the literary and historical perspectives of the Indian freedom movement and also in popular and canonical culture, socio-political theories, visual arts and Indian literature from different languages. Her research at the EFLU has been centered on the indigenous folklore, myths and rituals of North India.

Her presentations have been highly appreciated at International conferences like the Fulbright Mid-Year Conference, Washington Dec 2012; AVSA (Australian Victorian Studies Association) in February 2011, at the Adelaide University; the SGTC (Singapore Games and Toys Convention) in December 2010.

Reflections on Josh - The Socialist

Tarika Prabharkar

The peasant figure of British India lay at the heart of colonialism. At the beginning of the century, the problem of the peasants was brought centre stage by such influential works as R. C. Dutt's The Economic History of India and iterated by all the major leaders of the Indian struggle. Gandhi and Nehru both declared that the fight could not be won without the full emotional and organisational support of the peasant population. Like the politicians, the poets and artists also understood and emphasised on the fundamental necessity of addressing this issue.

Nehru's close associate and friend Josh Malihabadi, aka Shabbir Hasan Khan, also agreed ideologically but being a poet, his perspective and emphasis were oriented differently. Whereas Nehru was the optimistic political strategist, Josh saw the rawness and futility which underlay the rural life of the peasant whom he adorns with titles like Ameer-e-bostaan and Maahir-e-aaine-kudrat nazim-e bazm-e jahaan ('Kisaan'). The brutality of Josh's depiction comes closest to the expression of the real tragedy as opposed to the theorised idealism of rural life. The romaticisation of his life resulted in the absurd and confused usage of the peasant figure in between discourses like economy, patriotism and socialism. What makes Josh's depiction even more important and poignant is the fact that Josh marks a crucial departure in the tradition of Urdu poetry. He was the first poet of major influence and calibre who dealt with these 'secular' ideas. Most Urdu poetry before him was 'Ishqiya.' The form and idiom of his poetry still follow the old conventions but the subject he chooses to weave these images around is of revolutionary import. His poetry is the repository of his slightly eccentric political and ideological maverick self.

This is not to say that Josh remained the only poet to be touched by the revolutionary fervour. There were other influential writers in other genres who were embracing like ideas in the light of the Marxist ideas brought to the sub-continent very recently. Many other members of the Progressive Writers Association (PWA) like Premchand depicted the touching desperation of rural life without any hope of redemption. However Josh, with his characteristic flair, does not present the reality in a straight-forward manner. He weaves the idealism inherent in the portrayal of the peasant in his poem Kisan published in 1929. At least that is how he begins.

He paints the picture of a landscape utterly lorded and controlled by the peasant where he is called the son of the clouds (tifl-e-baraan), the king of the earth (taajdaar-e-khaak), he can understand the nuances of the early morning wind (waakif-e-tabaye naseem) and is the prime witness and secret keeper to nature's most intimate and beautiful secrets (husn-e-fitrat ka gawaah). His blood and sweat give the various luxuries of nature, like the flowers and fruits, their true natures and qualities. He is the painter, the magic life giver and reads the pulse of the earth for crops (din ko jiski ungliyaan rehti hain nabze-e-khaak par) like a doctor takes care of his patients. The cleverness with which Josh builds up a hierarchy and establishes the supremacy of the farmer is an example of the artistic exuberance with which he pampers his subject, the farmer. The epithets which are detailed with care infuse the image of the peasant with an epic grandeur which transports one effortlessly into the second phase of Josh's skilfully structured poem.

As far as the progression of ideas in the poem is concerned, the second segment of the poem progresses only in terms of ideology but not yet images. The reflections and visions evoked by josh still highlight how the peasant forms the cultural and 'vital' backbone of the society which is ideologically at his mercy and in his debt. Ironically however, no one seems to understand this debt apart from the poet. One finds to one's horror that even the peasant does not. It would be helpful to cite some lines from the poem to clarify this point.

Saaz-edaulat ko ataa karti hai naghme jiski aah!

Maangta hai bheek taabaani ki jisse rooe shah

Khoon jiska daudta hai nabz-e-istaqlaal main

Loch bhar deta hai jo shehzaadiyon ki chaal main

Jiske maathe ke paseene se pae izzo waqaar

Karti hai daryuzae taabish kulaahe taajdaar

Sarnigun rehti hain jisse quvvatein takhreeb ki

Jiske boote par lachakti hai kamar tehzeeb ki

Jiski mehnat se fabakta hai tan-aasani ka baagh

Jiski zulmat ki hatheli par tamaddun ka chiraagh

The reason why I accentuate these lines is because Josh has now made the crucial transition into the human society and culture from the natural landscape. While one can attribute the descriptions of nature as the kingdom of the peasant to the eccentricity of a poet but how does one justify the attribution of all culture and finesse of a civilisation to a lowly rural worker? This seems to imply ignorance on the part of the poet. The contributions of the peasant in the ideological workings of an edenic world where the class and social distinctions give way to a frank and honest appraisal of hard work where it is due seem to be gross exaggerations. The blunder seems even more incongruous keeping in mind the economic conditions of the Indian subcontinent at the time. How could one even dream of ascribing the 'loch' in the back of a princess to a peasant! The parallels are too fantastic to hold true. Also, the simplicity of the assertion heightens the irony to an unimaginable degree. That the farmer is responsible for fulfilling the basic human need for food is easily forgotten. If the aristocracy had to worry about essentials like food, the intellectual, political or social aspects of the society would never have been developed. The peasant is indeed in his silent and sturdy way, the source of all human refinement and luxuries.

Josh was an active freedom fighter and as such wallowing in these flights of fancy stands at odds with his practical and hard hitting views in other works like the Shikast-e-Zindaan ka Khaab. But Josh has been known for his rhetorical extravagance. Even in these lines, Josh's rhythmically brilliant poetry manages to distract the reader into a tacit submission into the rhythm of the work just long enough for him to reach the penultimate stage of his argument.

In the next couple of lines Josh describes the retreat of the peasant from his kingdom of the land towards his home. This is where the focus shifts from the territory of the man to the man himself. The 'symbolic' peasant has till now been described and detailed not through his own physical self but through the effects of his work. For the first time, the focus shifts to his own life where he reaps the benefits of supplying a whole culture with delicacy, finesse and leisure; the polarity is made brutally evident. He might be the reason why the society can get food, but he certainly does not partake of the bounty which he produces from the land. The land is apparently at his command to furnish gold if he asks. He, however, comes home to hungry children and a pallid wife. His loyal companion is the desperation and helplessness which has overtaken his household.

Sochta jata hai kin aankhon se dekha jaaega

Berida biwi ka sar, bachchon ka munh utra hua

Seem-o-zar, naano namak, aab-o-ghiza, kuch bhi nahin

Ghar main ek khaamosh maatam ke siva kuch bhi nahin.

One can get a sense of the conflicting worlds that the peasant straddles through his social function and position. The image of the delicate princess with the graceful gait is in stark contrast with the distressing demeanour of the peasant's wife. Josh's poetic effusions only make the images clearer and more intricately drawn.

What is sad however is that Josh lets his political ideology give a perfect ending to the dirge above. What Josh does masterfully is to pin the blame of the condition which has befallen rural India on sarmayadaari, capitalism. The capitalism of Britain was the root cause of the state of Indian economy, which was more or less hinged on agriculture. But Josh's political agenda takes over the fate of the peasant in the ideological curveball that he has sketched so brilliantly in the course of the poem. While in the earlier parts of the poem the focus zoomed in slowly from the broader panorama to the details of the peasant, in a later knee-jerk moment, Josh zooms out and puts the focus back on the 'general' evil of capitalism rather than the 'specific' lament of the kisaan.

This latter moment is the result of the political consciousness fostered through the experience of being a colonial subject which was very soon going to find a voice and companionship in the PWA. This ideology carves the forceful statement which makes the poem more than just a cluster of beautiful images. If however, Josh would have ended the poem with the poignant description of the life of the kaastkaar, the poem would have had a greater and more specific tragic appeal to it, unhampered by any ideological underpinnings. It would then have been a stirring humanist story with the kind of heart wrenching pessimism which is characteristic of Premchand.

This strategy of juxtaposing forceful contrasts also does not let the reader linger on and get lost in the rich tapestry of images he weaves in the poem. He takes the idealism of the portrayal of the peasant to a crescendo and suddenly leaves it to depict the reality of his life. The reader is brought back to the actuality of the situation with a sudden realisation which imposes a force greater than a constant iteration of his misery would have done. It makes the reader sit up and acknowledge the irony of all the images he/she has read and indulged in so far. But these are just some of the poetic charms of Josh which inadvertently and subtly exert their influence over the Urdu reader.

This also reminds one of the theories of tragedy put forward by Aristotle. According to Aristotle, the best kind of tragic hero was one who belonged to a high social position and virtue. This was because in this case, when the hero encountered misfortune, the contrast between his happy and sad days was greater than it would have be in any other case. A poor or a villainous man falling on hard times was no tragedy. Josh also builds up a certain persona for the kisaan, as the emperor of his domain. The tragedy which the consequent reality evokes is of a higher degree than it would have been otherwise. I am not suggesting that such were the motives of Josh in presenting his ideas in this particular way but such a strategy also holds forth for the poet's political ideology. Josh catches the pulse of the tragedy of the Indian socio-economic system through works such as these. During the colonial rule, the real tragedy lay not in the houses of the rich-who most often collaborated with the government-but with the poor farmers who bore the brunt of the imperial exploitation the most. Josh manages to re-introduce the figure of the peasant in all his mysteriously pessimistic glory though not yet defeated.

Mr. Yavar Abbas

JOSH MALIHABADI

Shabbir Hasan Khan JOSH MALIHABADI, one of the towering poets of Urdu, was born in a feudal Pathan family whose forbears came from Central Asia, via The Khyber, and eventually settled in Malihabad near Lucknow, the capital city of the kings of Awadh. Lucknow was then the cultural Paris of the East with Urdu language the literary currency of the elite. The newly arrived warrior Pathans drank deep out of this culture and became noteworthy poets and writers.

Josh's great grandfather Hisamuddin Tahawwar Jung Faqir Mohammad Khan GOYA rose to the rank of a General in the army of Awadh kings Ghaziuddin Haider and Nasiruddin Haider, but is remembered more for his illustrious Dewan-Goya - collection of his published poems. Josh's grandfather and father were also notable poets, but it was JOSH who finally exchanged the family sword for the mighty pen that he wielded with such dexterity for over seventy years. The writer of these lines, who had the great good fortune of knowing the poet at close quarters, remembers the time as a young undergraduate at Allahabad University in the late 1930s and early 40s, when JOSH was the darling of the young and the dread of the old Raj. His inspiring and aesthetically beautiful poetry sent the young blood coursing through our veins:

Suno ai saakinan khittai-e-khaak
Nida kva as rahi hai gasman se
Ke aazaadi ka ek lamha hai behtar
Ghulami ki hayaat-e-jaavedaan se

(Listen, you people of the Earth below
To the voice coming from up above
That a life span of one moment in freedom Is better than eternal life
without it)

And we took out "Freedom Processions" reciting in chorus his clarion call:

Kaam hai mera taghayyur, naam hai mera shabaab
Mera naara: Inquilaab-o-Inquilaab-o-Inquilaab
(My name is YOUTH, my work is CHANGE My slogan: REVOLUTION,
again and again)

Of course it was not all sloganeering, JOSH has written some of the most subtle, some of the most tastefully erotic poetry to be found, perhaps, in any language. His khumriyat (wine poetry) contain a heady wine as potent as any that Khayyam could brew. He is arguably the greatest romantic poet of Urdu, and as a poet of Nature JOSH has, unquestionably, no equal. He has left a vast corpus comprising over twenty fair sized anthologies, over a dozen long marsiyas (approximately ten thousand lines), hundreds, if not thousands, of rubaiyaat (quatrains), an epic poem: HarfAakhir (The Last Word), with Josh's own take on Genesis, bringing the story of MAN to the present day and pointing the way to an exciting future of quest of the vast universe. Josh's poetic output in Urdu, quantitatively and qualitatively, is surpassed only by the great Anees.

He was also a prolific correspondent and two volumes, to my knowledge, of his letters in his unique style have so far been published. He was editor of several literary journals and an active contributor himself. There are several books of his memorable prose, including his outrageously outspoken Yaadon Ki Baraat (A Cavalcade of Memories), an uninhibited recollection of the main events in his life and of the people inhabiting it. It caused a sensation at the time and continues to raise hackles nearly forty years after its publication.

With all this mind boggling output why has JOSH, one may ask, been so, criminally side-lined? Simple! Like his beloved Urdu, JOSH has become the victim of the politics of Partition. JOSH was at the height of his fame and recognition in India, having been honoured with one of the highest civilian awards (Padma Bhushan) by a grateful country whose Prime Minister (Nehru) was one of the greatest fans of the poet, when in 1955 he was lured by close friends in the Pakistani Establishment (who wanted him as a prize catch) to move to Pakistan where, he was promised , he would be given carte blanche to "to preserve, protect and promote" his beloved Urdu which, at the time, was being systematically eroded in India in the aftermath of Partition.

The move proved disastrous for JOSH and Urdu both and the collateral damage spread to the Muslims of India. If an ardent Nationalist and a great patriot like JOSH could "betray" his country and join hands with "the enemy" then what of the rest of the Muslims in India. Josh's departure dealt a severe blow to the prospects of Urdu in its own motherland, and, by association, to the interests of the Muslims in India who have never forgiven him. As for Pakistan, he finished up there becoming, eventually, a figure of hate, his contempt for narrow religiosity and his eloquently defiant expression of it in parts of his poetry was perceived as blasphemy by an increasingly fanatical and intolerant society. JOSH found the atmosphere in dictator ridden Pakistan choking for his poetry but was too proud to return to India although the option was left open to him by Nehru.

The great bon vivant became a tragic figure, burdened with the responsibility of supporting a vast number of dependents, and no regular income. He lived out the rest of his ageing days in despair and despondency, writing nostalgically of his youth and his beloved Lucknow and calling himself marhoom Josh (the late Josh). He took to writing Marsiyahs and found inspiration in Husain, the Martyr of Karbala. His Marsiyahs are a compelling call for upholding the banner of freedom and justice and a powerful invitation to fight against tyranny and totalitarianism. Yet when he died, a broken man, a mere handful formed a cortege to his grave in Islamabad. Had he stayed in India a whole nation would have mourned his death.
JOSH has been given many sobriquets: Shair-e-Inquilab (Poet of Revolution), Shaire-Shabab (Poet of Youth), Shair-e-Sharab (Poet of Wine), Shair-e-Rabab (Poet of Music) etc.etc. But for many, JOSH will remain the quintessential Shair-e-Fitrat (Poet of Nature). His descriptions and observations of Nature around him and the interaction between Nature and Man, both visual and metaphysical, are sheer genius: aspects and nuances that defy description are unbelievably and exquisitely rendered in a poetic vocabulary sent down from Heaven.
JOSH will live as long as Urdu lives, as the great protagonist of freedom and human dignity and as an eloquent celebrant of Nature in all its glory. Amen!!!

Syed Ali Raza Naqvi

Birth Place: Amroha, UP, India.
Date of Birth: May 14, 1933.

M.A. (Persian), Karachi University, 1955;
Ph.D. (Persian), Tehran University, 1963;

(A special Doctorate given to Iranians as against the one given to foreigners)
Associate Professor & Head, Persian & Islamic Jurisprudence, (1964 – 1993),
Islamic Research Instt, Int'l Islamic University, Islamabad.
Taught Persian Language & "Masnavi" of Maulana Rumi, Iranian Cultural Center, Islamabad, (1978 – 2006)

Awards: 1) Published doctorate thesis awarded,
        "Best Book of the Year 1966" by Shah of Iran.
2) Highest award of "Khidmat-Guzarane Farsi"
by Govt.of Iran, 2007, in recognition of outstanding services for Persian Language in Pakistan spread over 3 decades.

Language &   Himalaya: Persian Translation of Poetical selections
Literature   of 15 modern Urdu poets with biographical
sketches,
        Tehran,1962.
Critical study of 100 Anthologies of Persian Poets written in India
and Pakistan, (Doctorate Thesis in Persian), Tehran,l964.
Beauty of Concealment & Concealment of Beauty: English
Translation of 'Hijabe Islami' by
Z. Rahnavard, (wife of Mr. Mousavi, ex PM of Iran), Islamabad,
1978.
Gulshan-e-Farsi: Persian textBook for beginners, Three Volumes;
Islamabad, 1985.
Farhange Istiqlal: by Jawad Mansuri (ex-Ambassador of Iran in
Pakistan); Urdu Translation,
Islamabad, 1993.
Adabiyyate Pakistan, Persian Translation of Selections from Pakistani
poets and writers, Academy Adabiyat, Islamabad, 1995.
Aasarul Baaqia: Urdu Translation of Alberuni's great book: National
Language Authority,Islamabad, 2003.
        Farhang-e-Jame': Persian-English-Urdu Dictionary, 80,000
words, Islamabad, 1994.
Iqtisaduna (Our Enonomics), English Translation of Baqir Sadr's
monumental work, Vol. II, for PIDE, Quaid-i-Azam University,
Islamabad, (in Press)
Law & Judicial System of Pakistan: Persian Translation,
Jurisprudence (Fiqh')
        Islamabad,1970.
Family Laws of Iran: English Translation with original Persian
text, Islamabad,1971.
Constitution of Islamic Republic of Iran:
English Translation, Islamabad, 1980.
  Shia Penal Laws: Urdu Translation, Islamabad, 1985.
  Islamic Penal Code of Iran: English Translation, Islamabad, l986.
  Tahreerul Waseelah: 4 volumes;
  English Translation of Imam Khomeini's lifelong Research work in
Figh',   .
        Tehran, 2001- 2009
        Shia Personal Laws, English Translation, from original Arabic
sources
        Islamabad, (in Press)

JOSH MALIHABADI

Dr. Syed Ali Raza Naqvi

. Despite the fact that his thought evolved over the years, he remained a progressive till the very end of life. He composed a number of Marsias [of Imam Husain], but his intrepidity and contradiction of generally accepted notions are found in his Marsias too. He has never felt ashamed before his liberal friends and progressive critics for writing Marsias. Unlike Faiz, he nowhere adopted an apologetic attitude. He composed the first Marsia in 1920 and the last in about 1970. During this span of fifty years, his pen had never been slow.

Like Nazeer Akbarabadi and Meer Anees, he ranks among the few poets of Urdu known for their command over the Urdu language. A follower of Lucknow School of poetry, he favored an attitude that lays stress on physical pleasure, gaiety and delicacy of taste, bordering on sensuality and Epicureanism. He was termed "poet of the youth" for his youthful poetry and freshness of thought and diction. A connoisseur of words, he says: "Words stand with folded hands before me and I call any of them wanted by me according to my taste and situation". He coined thousands of new words and gave fresh resonance and color to thousands others, and thus enriched the treasure of Urdu language. According to Dr. Hilal, Josh's smallest poem is "Azaan" (Call for Prayers)in three couplets, while his longest poem: "Harf-e Akhir" (The Last Word) consists of more than twenty thousand couplets. His Marsias also contain various topics in long poetic forms.

Josh sings of nature and liberty and mocks hollow formalism, be it religious or otherwise. The hallmark of his poetry is a complaining and somewhat irreverent attitude towards certain religious and social practices, especially those that denote ostentatious religiosity and show of wealth. His unorthodox views and anti-clerical stance throughout his critical works irked many who in retaliation accused him of agnosticism and atheism. Always averse to any unreasonable authority, and naturally inclined towards sensible rationality, he never backed down in the teeth of insensible opposition from his detractors. His constant devotion to, and veneration for Prophet Mohammad (Peace be upon him and his Progeny), Hazrat Ali (A.S.), Hazrat Imam Husain (A.S.) and some other religious dignitaries always remained unwavering.

Like Byron, he did not care about the rigid discipline framed by the so-called "thekedars" (self-proclaimed dictators) of society, and openly challenged their set of social rules and bravely faced their strong remonstrance in every walk of life. Throughout his life he had extreme hatred for hypocrisy. His works are full of poems in condemnation of persons merely pretending to be pious, honest and fair in dealing. One of his famous poems: "Zakir sey Khitab" deals with the professional preachers who lecture on piety and honesty, but the basic approach to life of some of them is full of dishonesty.

In another poem, Josh has beautifully drawn an interesting picture of a hypocrite Mulla. He says:

> "Yesterday I happened to meet a Molvi,
>
> A symbol of the dome and pulpit (of a mosque),
>
> Who would pretend to deserve the company of Houries in Paradise,
>
> As a reward for his deeds by the Almighty!
>
> A turban on his head, and tooth- brush in pocket,
>
> Wearing a high pant and a coarse coat,
>
> Long beard dyed with henna and eyes blackened by collyrium,
>
> Perfumed locks and scented hair.
>
> Square-neckerchief covering his bent shoulders,

A red rosary hanging from the pocket of his overcoat,

Having a broad chest, and a small neck,

A dreadful stomach, and stature like a spruce,

With disheveled locks, eyes covered with specks,

Mustaches duly cut, beard reaching his belly.

With deep red long overcoat and yellowish green turban.

His mouth full of chewing betel,

His lips red like the blood of a pigeon!

The scar on his forehead, [a sign of worship], black like dark night,

The circumference of his belly round like an ocean!

We are lean and thin like Majnun in the distress of separation from our beloved,

But he was like an ogre in the Love of God.

Reciting with zest the stories of his expected pleasures in heaven,

Holding in his fist his beard dyed in henna.

But in his smile, there was lurking in his eyes

Twinkling lights of hypocrisy! Allaho Akbar!"

Josh never claimed to be a religious or pious person, which, in fact, he never was. "Yadon ki Barat", with a large biographical content, is a clear proof of his tainted life, where, like Rousseau, Byron and Ghalib, he recounts the anecdotes of his love affairs openly and unabashedly, with a tinge of masculine pride, which a lot of other people would rather prefer to leave unsaid and undisclosed. He used to attend the gatherings of religious personalities in his constant search of Truth. On the other hand, Sajjad Zaheer, the famous leftist of the sub-continent in his book: "Rowshana'i" has called Josh the "Peer-e Mughaan" (the top leader) of the Progressives

Despite the fact that his thought evolved over the years, he remained a progressive till the very end of life. He composed a number of Marsias [of Imam Husain], but his intrepidity and contradiction of generally accepted notions are found in his Marsias too. He has never felt ashamed before his liberal friends and progressive critics for writing Marsias. Unlike Faiz, he nowhere adopted an apologetic attitude. He composed the first Marsia in 1920 and the last in about 1970. During this span of fifty years, his pen had never been slow.

Why I like Josh and his poetry

Ikram Brelvi

I feel like a small fry when I think of an intellectual stalwart like Josh Malhiabadi. This is because he was a staunch enemy of imperialism, designed and practiced by the British Rulers of India. I like him because he was a towering beacon of light; honest to himself and resolutely straight forward, and out spoken.

He was uncompromising against his beliefs and tenets as he was not a hypocrite. He had an imaginative mind open to reason and logic.

نہیں مجھ کو پردا، حَرَم ہو کہ دَیر
رسولوں کے مانند نِیَّت بغیر

بجو یندگی اللہ عِباد
مِرا ہَر نفس، اِک مسلسل جہاد
مِرا ہَر تشکک، عبادت گزار
مِرا ہَر تمرّد، اطاعت شِعار
مری سرکشی، انکسارِ ثقاہت
مِرا لمحۂ فِکر، صَوم و صَلوۃ

مِرا ہَر تحیّر، قیام و قُعود
مِرا ہَر تجسّس، رُکوع و سُجود
مِرا قامتِ ذِہن، سَروِ دَلیل
بایماں قصیر و بعرفاں طَویل

With all these qualities of head and heart he was imbued with imagination: Imagination which is no less than God's as he operates in human soul. To Josh it was an act of creativity at once divine and spiritual in nature and intent.

To him primary imagination was prime agent of human perception and living force somehow concerned, with super natural order. At this juncture he festively revels in saying that.

کب سر پہ کسی نبی کا احسان لیا

رازِ کونین، خود بخود، خود جان لیا

انسان کا عرفان ہوا جب حاصل

اللہ کو، ایک آن میں، پہچان لیا

And here I see Josh standing hand in hand and rubbing shoulders with William Blake and Wordsworth. Since it was for them, the very source of spiritual energy, they cannot but believe that it is divine, and that when they exercise it, they in some way, share in the activity of God

میں اور کائنات، اے محرمِ راز

مدت سے اب ایک ہیں، بہ فیضانِ گداز

لے کر جو مرا نام، پکارا کوئی

آفاق سے لبیک کی آئی آواز

Hence this world of imagination assumes the world of eternal reality; the divine bosom into which we all go after death of the vegetated body; and hence the world of imagination becomes infinite and eternal; and exist thereafter in that eternal world as the " permanent reality" of every thing which we see reflected in the vegetable class of nature.

پیدا ہوا، اعصاب میں، اک طرفہ کھنچاؤ

معلوم ہوا متاعِ اسرار کا بھاؤ

ذرّے کو ہتھیلی پہ، جو پل بھر رکھا

محسوس ہوا، نظامِ شمسی کا دباؤ

And to conclude, I admire him for the romantic agony he feels and for the immense love and nobility of "Man" in the core of his heart.

میری نظروں میں ہے وہ فردا کا نظام

جس سے گزر جائیں گے مذاہب کے خیام

جو دیں کہ ہر رہا ہے پیدا اے دوست

ہوگا وہ ماورا اے کفر و اسلام

Translations:

Rubai'at de Josh Malihabadi

Une goutte et l'océan

Dr. Rahat Naqvi

1.

Mes désirs ouvrent des visions illimitées

   et ma voix chante la mélodie des horizons

Longtemps j'ai semé mes pensées

   et j'attends que naisse un savoir nouveau.

اس دُعا میں کہ دل عقل سے شیدا ہو جائیں

آفاق کے اسرار نُویدا ہو جائیں

مدّت سے گزارہا ہوں تخمِ اذکار

شاید کہ نئے درخت پَیدا ہو جائیں

2.

J'ai fouillé les mosquées et les temples,

  je n'ai pas vu la vie obscurcie par le temps qui explore.

J'ai fouillé chaque coin et recoin mais je n'ai pas trouvé Dieu.

  Maintenant c'est à son tour de me chercher

تا چند کوئی دیر و حرم میں کو ڈھونڈے

کب تک مَیں ہستی کے پیچ و خم کو ڈھونڈے

ہم ڈھونڈ چکے بلا کہ نہیں کہیں کو اللہ

اب فرض یہ اس کا ہے کہ ہم کو ڈھونڈے

3.

Nous ne sommes qu'un point dans le monde,

   une goutte de rosée sur laquelle nous régnons.

Quand j'ai cherché dans le grenier des étoiles,

   j'ai vu que notre monde est plus petit que le plus petit grain.

اک ذرّہ مبہم ہے ہماری دنیا

اک قطرہ شبنم ہے ہماری دنیا

تاروں کے جو کنج کھلیاں کھٹکالے تو کھلا

اک جو سے بھی کچھ کم ہے ہماری دنیا

4.

Que le sommeil de l'existence soit bref,

   n'attends pas que le livre de la vie tourne une page

La cité de la joie, tu l'as trouvée en ton coeur,

   ne la laisse pas mourir par la réalité de ton chagrin.

ہستی کو تسلسل سے نہ سونے دیجے

منہ آنسوؤں سے کہیں تو دھونے دیجے

جو شہرِ طرب، دل میں ہوا ہے آباد

اس شہر میں لختۂ غم نہ ہونے دیجے

5.

Chapelets égrenés, prières ferventes et turbans des dévôts,

trône, couronne, tambours, drapeaux, fortifications,

vos pouvoirs sont ligués d'un côté

et la puissance de la Plume est de l'autre.

تسبیح و عمامہ و عبا و حنا تم
تاج و اورنگ و قلعہ و طبل و علم
سب کا اثر متفقہ ایک طرف
اور ایک طرف طاقت سرکار قلم

6.

Mes nerfs furent secoués par une énorme vague,

mon énergie s'est perdue en une immense mesure

A l'instant où j'ai placé un atome au creux de ma main,

j'ai senti me peser tout l'univers.

پیدا ہوا اعصاب میں ایک طرف کھنچاؤ
معلوم ہوا امتناع انکار کا بھاؤ
ذرے کو تہہ میں پہ جو، پل بھر رکھا
محسوس ہوا انظام شمسی کا دباؤ

7.

La recherche dépasse toute espérance,

  elle envisage la poursuite de nouveaux horizons

Le savoir est cette manne miraculeuse

  qui aiguise la faim de l'esprit à l'infini.

تحقیق کے شعلوں کو ہوا دیتا ہے

ہر موڑ نئی راہ دکھا دیتا ہے

اُف علم ہے یہ وہ غذا لئے حیرت انگیز

جو ذہن کی بھوک اور بڑھا دیتا ہے

8.

Les perles de l'intelligence sont rares et dispersées.

La sagesse est légère comme des gouttes de rosée

Les soupçons les plus vils dispensés par le savant

  sont préférables au cadeau de la foi donnée par l'ignorant.

جودت کا گہر، مہر مبیں سے بہتر

حکمت کی حلاوت، انگبیں سے بہتر

عالم کا دیا ہوا گمان بد بھی

جاہل کے عطا کردہ یقیں سے بہتر

9.

J'ai ouvert toutes les portes et libéré tous les mystères,

toutes les inutiles évidences .

J'ai trouvé dans ma coupe le vin de l'ignorance

quand j'ai pressé les raisins de la connaissance.

اسرار سے ہر قفل کو توڑا میں نے

آیات کی ہر شاخ کو چھوڑا میں نے

دیکھا کہ شبنموں میں ہے جہالت کی شراب

جب خوشۂ علم کو نچوڑا میں نے

10.

O mes amis, mes mentors, parlez!

les flammes appellent, vacillent, parlez!

Vous qui êtes cachés derrière la couleur et l'odeur.

Parlez! Parlez! O étoiles du matin! Parlez!

اسے کھلے پیرکے غمگسارو ! بولو

شعلو ! آواز دو شرارو ! بولو

اس پردۂ رنگ و بو میں پوشیدہ کون

بولو اے ڈوبتے ستارو ! بولو

11.

Je suis obsédé par l'idée de posséder la lune et la galaxie,

   Depuis le pôle Nord jusqu'au pôle Sud,

   que tout soit sous mon commandement.

*Les souliers de la connaissance de ce qui est et était sont trop petits
pour chausser mon pied.*

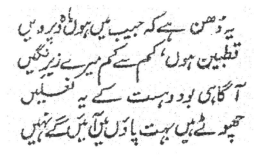

12.

Je sème la tristesse dans mon propre cœur. Pourquoi?

   Personne ne tentera de me piller.

Je ris de mes possessions inutiles

   parce que si le malheur me frappe, je ne pleurerai pas.

تا مزرع دل میں تخم غم بورہ سکوں
جس وقت مجے لوٹ تو کچھ کھونہ سکوں
خالی چیزوں پہ ہنس رہا ہوں کہ ندیم
حب اُس پہ نواں آے توئی روۂ سکوں

13.

Découpe les étoiles et attrape les particules qui s'éparpillent, s'il vous plaît

Bois jusqu'à la lie la coupe des jours et des nuits.

Le temps de vivre est très court, mon ami.

Saisis chaque moment, chaque opportunité.

تاروں میں شگاف ڈال ذرات کو گر وڈ

پیمانہ روز و شب میں اِک بوند نہ چھوڑ

ہاں مہلت زندگی نہایت کم ہے

ہر آن کو دے دوہ ، ہر تشیقے کم پیچوڑ

14.

Vivre ou mourir n'est pas difficile,

ainsi fleurissent les pensées

Le savoir est un riche aliment facile à avaler, difficile à assimiler

اِتنا جینا ہے اور نہ مرنا مشکل

جتنا کب ہے نکر کا کچھ نا مشکل

فن، علم وہ خوں خوڑ غذا ہے جس کا

کھانا آسان، ہضم کر نا مشکل

15.

Il sait vivre, souffrir et mourir,

  il voit l'oiseau du temps prendre son envol et filer.

Les superstitions ont fait de l'idole un dieu

  que seul l'athée renie.

علّت کا' نہ معلول و قضا کا منکر

حاشا' نہ خبر' نہ مبتدا کا منکر

اور ہم نے جس محبت کو بنا یا ہے خدا

الحاد ہے صرف اُس خدا کا منکر

16.

Le cœur plein de malice brûle de sa propre flamme,
malheureusement

Tout être déteste ses ennemis

  mais je suis celui qui prend ses ennemis en pitié.

وہ دَل نہیں کو عناد گر حب تا ہے

بے چارہ خود اپنی لو پہ جلی جاتا ہے

ہر فرد کو ہوتی ہے عدو سے نفرت

اور ہم کو تو دشمن پہ ترس آتا ہے

17.

0 sage! sois heureux même si les malheurs te touchent

  ne cherche pas un confort insaisissable.

La flamme du désir de ce qui n'existe pas te brûle.

  Réjouis-toi, jouis de ce que tu possèdes!

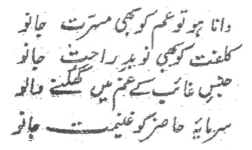

داناہوتوغم کوبھی مسرت جانو
کلفت کوبھی نو بید راحت جانو
جنس غائب کے غم میں گھلنے والے
سرمایۂ حاضر کو غنیمت جانو

18.

J'attends que l'entente entre les hommes émerge

  et moi qui suis là où la flamme de l'existence se consume

Moi, qui ne suis ni confiné à l'Est, ni prisonnier de l'Ouest.

انسان کی توحید کا مشتاق ہوں میں
شمع بزم وحدت کا طباق ہوں میں
مشرق کا پابند نہ مغرب کا اسیر
صد شام کہ باشندۂ آفاق ہوں میں

19.

Connais-moi. J'habite les cieux infinis.

Dans mes pensées, je brise les barrières du jour et de la nuit,

   je suis l'épée qui me découpe comme un gâteau

Soyez témoins de cet événement unique,

   o étoiles! Le monde est endormi et je veille.

هر آن تفکر میں گرفتار ہوں میں

اپنے پہ جو چلتی ہے وہ تلوار ہوں میں

تارو! اس حادثے سے شاہد رہتا

سمنار ہے مجوخواب، بیدار ہوں میں

Rubai'yat of Josh Malihabadi

Selected from

STARS & GEMS

(Najum-o-Jawahir)

Mohammad Yamin

Josh

Khola hay to har aik girah ko kholo

Mantaq kay tarazoo pe har ek shai tolo

Mana kay yeh aalam hay kisi ki eejad

   Aur illat-e-eejad hay kya, ab bolo

☐

   Open each knot, if you must open

   Weigh objects on scale of logic now and then

   I admit, Some One has invented this world

   And now tell me the idea behind the invention

☐

Eeman ki lazzat ki khwahish hay shadeed

Har khairr hay asbaab-tarab ki tamheed

Hooran-e-bahisht-o-dukhtaran-e-kuffar

Baaqi na agar rahein to Ghazi na Shaheed

☐

Behind the virtuous deeds are the spoils of war

   Linked with them are bounties and pleasure

Houris of Heaven and daughters of the vanquished

   If not, neither the crusade nor the crusader

☐

Hay koi jo is dhowain ko gulshan kar day

Tukday is teergi ka daman kar day

Dil per hay wo ghata top andharay ka dabao
Lillah koi chiragh roshan kar day

◻

This ice into a flame of furnace turn
To make hearts abode of vision and foresight, is there none

Darkness of ignorance is so dense all around
For God's sake, light lamp of wisdom and knowledge, someone!

◻

Etna jeena hay aur na merna mushkil
Jetna kay zehn ka nikharna mushkil

Yeh ilm woh kambakht ghaza hay jis ka
Khana aasan, hazm karma mushkil

◻

Living is so nor dyeing difficult
As is thought's flowering difficult

Knowledge is the rich food which
Eating is easy: digesting difficult

◻

Ujlat na kar aiy musafir-e-dasht-e-shsoor
Nafi –o-asbaat ka abhi shahr hay door

Haan saath chala chal kay kaheen thhray ga
Yeh qafla-e-Illat-o- ma'lool zarur

☐

Don't light the candle of faith yet, take care
Time to negate and affirm is still not there

Yes, walk along because surely
This caravan of cause and effect will stop somewhere

☐

Wabasta-e-asmaan na paband-e-zameen
Inkar no eqrar, na dunya hay na deen

Aiy aql-e-ghareeb, yeh siahat kab tak
Tera bhi koi watan banega kay naheen

☐

Bound to the earth nor to the sky's dome
Neither deny nor accept; between faith and disbelief roam

O poor wisdom! How long will you traverse thus
Will any where ever be your home?

☐

Jis des mein aabad hon bhookay insaan

Ehsas-e-lateef ka wahan kya imkan

Ek fikr-e-ma'ash pey nichawar sao ishq

Ek naan-e-jaween pe laakh mukhday qurban

☐

The country with hungry people inhabited

Among men delicate feelings aren't created

Single worry for livelihood hundreds of loves surrenders

For one barley bread millions of charming faces are resisted

☐

Eeeman ko khirad kay rubaro laya hay

Aur bahas ki dil mein aarzu laya hay

Kya is say meray alao per aaegi aanch

Yeh oas ki ek bond jo tu laya hay

☐

Of faith and wisdom confrontation you sought

And many shallow arguments brought

How can the flame of knowledge be quenched

With a drop of dew that you have got

☐

Jab ghurfa-e-ilm ko khola mein nay

Apnay ko naye bant say taola mein nay

Mein hun kay naheen yeh jaanchnay kay liye

Apnay ko kayee baar tatola mein nay

☐

My vision blew up eternal designs

I was released from thought's confines

To examine whether I really exist or not

I touched myself a number of times

☐

Aiy noay basher waqt ki qimat pehchan

Sarmaya-e-Aafaq hay her pal her aan

Her larzish mizgan pey nichawar konain

Her saans pe sao nizam-e-shamsi qurban

☐

O mankind! Recognize the value of time

Every moment is a wealth of heavens sublime

On the movement of eyelashes be sacrificed both worlds

Against a breath hundreds of solar systems not worth a dime

☐

Her satar mein ghaltan hein meray jumla sifat

  Her lafz kay aiwan mein khud hay meri zaat

Jo ghor say padh raha hay meray ash'ar

  Meray dil ki woh gin raha hay zarbat

☐

Every line is with aura of my attributes replete

The chamber of each word is my disposition's retreat

One who reads my verses with intense absorption

Counts my pulse and my heart beat

☐

Farda ki zameen per makan hay mera

  Imroze ek asr-e-bay-zaban hay mera

Boya hi naheen gaya hay abtak jo shajar

  Uski choti per aashian hay mera

☐

My dwellings on the land of tomorrow rest

  My today is a voiceless age at best

  That tree is not even planted in the ground

☐☐

Admirable Research

A Comparative Study of Treatment of Nature by William Wordsworth and Josh Maleeh Abadi

A thesis submitted in partial fulfillment of the degree of Masters in English Literature

Safeer Hussain (2010-KIU-274)

Supervisor: Mr. Muhammad Yasin

Co-Supervisor: Miss

Session 2010-2012

DEPARTMENT OF MODERN LANGUAGES

Karakoram International University

Gilgit, Baltistan

TABLE OF CONTENTS

Only pages marked as (***) included in this book.

*** *Note from the editors of Josh Literary Society of Canada (JLSC):*

Our Current Book was almost print-ready when we found out about Mr. Tafseer Hussain's research paper. We are pleased to include this paper in the book, but not without a regret of adding only the final chapter due to a shortage of space.

We are committed to include selected new research work on Josh andencourage young scholars to submit their Papers directly to us.

Josh Literary Society of Canada (JLSC)

Discussion and Analysis

3.1 Nature to William Wordsworth and Josh Maleeh Abadi

Nature was the foster mother of William Wordsworth. He saw in Nature all the meanings and aspects of life; for him Nature was a teacher, an educator, a mother, a religion, a divinity, a companion and a leader. Nature was the ultimate philosophy for William Wordsworth.

As De Quincy puts it, "Wordsworth had his passion for Nature fixed in his blood. It was a necessity of his being, like that of a mulberry leaf to the silk-worms, and through his commerce with Nature did he live and breathe." [Arthur-Rickett, 308]

In Tintern Abbey, while describing his love for Nature, Wordsworth says,

I cannot paint

What then I was. The sounding cataract

Haunted me like a passion: the tall rock,

The mountain, and the deep and gloomy wood,

Their colours and their forms, were then to me

An appetite; a feeling and a love,

That had no need of a remoter charm,

By thought supplied, nor any interest

Unborrowed from the eye.

In the above lines, Wordsworth's words make his love and passion for Nature explicit. The sounds of the "cataract" excited him; the mighty "rocks" and mountains, the deep and dense "forests"; all the aspects, colors and manifestations of Nature attracted his whole being and existence towards them. He calls all these manifestations of Nature as "appetite"; his deep and uncompromising interest in Nature is shown by these lines, and only Nature could satisfy this appetite. For him, Nature was both an appetite and the food to satisfy this appetite. Nature was a "feeling" for him; a feeling and a "love". Thus he explicitly reveals his love of and love for Nature. He doesn't say that he had love for Nature or love of Nature; rather he calls Nature itself as love. This is the beauty of his expression and this is his intense love for Nature. He was indeed a passionate lover of Nature, more than any other English poet.

Similar to William Wordsworth, Josh was also an ardent lover of Nature. He also found in Nature an appeal that captivated his soul and he could not help but sing the poems in delight and praise of Nature.

Asar Lakhnawi, in his article on Josh, Shaair-e-Fitrat-Josh, is of the opinion that, "Josh is the poet of Nature. His verses have the rush of torrents and waterfalls, the flow of a river, the turbulence of waves and the softness and light-pace of morning air." (Lakhnavi, 122-123)

In برسات کی چاندنی, Josh says,

چرخ پر برسے ہوئے بادل کے ٹکڑے جا بجا

چاندنی ، تالاب ، سناٹا ، پیپہے کی صدا

دشت پر چھائے ہوئے ذوقِ جنوں کے ولولے

چاند میں معصوم بچے کے تبسم کی ادا

فصلِ سرما میں سحر کو غسل کر چکنے کے بعد

رنگ ہو جیسے کسی معشوق کا نکھرا ہوا

[(There are) clouds floating upon the horizon, that have emptied their showers of rain/ (there is) moon-light, pond of water, silence and sounds of a cuckoo/ (there are) the passions of madness brooding over the desert/ (I see) the smile of an innocent child in the moon/...]

The scene presented by him, shows his keen eye and undeniable love for Nature. The skill with which he portrays Nature is enviable. He presents each and every thing in a vivid description; the clouds floating upon the horizon, the moonlight, water, silence. The poet seems to be in love with Nature and this love is as intense as one has love towards children; thus he sees the innocent and angelic smile and bashfulness of a child on the face of the moon. He even compares a dew-wet summer morning to a beloved who has just taken a bath; with her beauty grown more clearly visible and magnified.

In another poem, بدلی کا چاند, Josh says,

خورشید وہ دیکھو ڈوب گیا ، ظلمت کا نشاں لہرانے لگا

مہتاب ، وہ ہلکے بادل سے ، چاندی کے ورق برسانے لگا

وہ سانولے پن پر میداں کے ، ہلکی سی صباحت دوڑ چلی

تھوڑا سا ابھر کر بادل سے ، وہ چاند جبیں جھلکانے لگا

'See the sun has set and darkness has shown its signs/ the moon is spraying silver pages of light from behind a thin layer of clouds/ the dark complexion of the plain has started to get fair/ the moon has raised its forehead a bit by lifting itself from the clouds '

The artistic qualities of Josh make the whole scene alive before our eyes and we feel as if we are beholding that scene in place of Josh. The skill with which Josh portrays Nature is unique, marvelous and unparalleled.

"Josh had a hearty inclination towards the beauty of Nature, from his very child-hood.", says Nisar Azami.

For Wordsworth, Nature was also a healer and a soothing agent. Whenever the poet felt gloomy, sad or blank-minded, the memories of Nature blessed him with a joy, bliss and a new spirit.

For example, in Daffodils, when he sees the flowers of daffodils along the bank of a lake, he feels that,

A poet could not but be gay,

In such a jocund company:

I gazed—and gazed—but little thought

What wealth the show to me had brought:

For oft, when on my couch I lie

In vacant or in pensive mood,

They flash upon that inward eye

Which is the bliss of solitude;

And when my heart with pleasure fills,

And dances with the daffodils.

    With a similar theme, Josh writes in his poem, چڑیوں کا گیت,

مرے قلب کو زندگی دو ، جلاؤ

حقیقت کی محفل سے پردہ اٹھاؤ

میں قطرہ ہوں مجھ کو سمندر بناؤ

کچھ اس طرح تا دیر نغمے سناؤ

یونہی پیاری چڑیو! ابھی اور گاؤ

Burn my heart and bless it with life/Unveil the secrets of Reality/I am a drop, make me an ocean/In this fashion, keep singing songs/Ye Sparrows! Sing more.

    Josh here, addressing sparrows, asks them to keep singing as he finds joy and peace and pleasure in their songs. And the poet considers that their songs, being songs of Nature, will help a person uncover the hidden secrets of Reality and will get transformed from a drop into an ocean; the person will come out of individual sheaths and will merge into the caravan of reality. Thus he pleads and asks the sparrows not to stop and continue to awaken the mind and soul of the poet.

    But a close analysis of The Daffodils by Wordsworth and Chiryun ka Geet by Josh brings out the fact that Nature excites Wordsworth with joy but Josh with a shake and pinch. When we observe and ponder over the following lines by Wordsworth and Josh,

A poet could not but be gay,

In such a jocund company:

I gazed—and gazed—but little thought

What wealth the show to me had brought:

For oft, when on my couch I lie

In vacant or in pensive mood,

They flash upon that inward eye

Which is the bliss of solitude;

And when my heart with pleasure fills,

And dances with the daffodils.

We can vividly observe that Wordsworth feels joy in Nature, whereas Josh pleads the sparrows;

مرے قلب کو زندگی دو ، جلاؤ

Burn my heart and bless it with life…

And further in the same poem he says,

نہیں جاگتی روح میری جگاؤ

میں غفلت میں ہوں دل پہ چرکے لگاؤ

کوئی سرمدی ساز کی گت بجاؤ

مجھے اپنے نغموں کے معنی بتاؤ

It does not wake up; (Ye Sparrows!) wake my soul up;

I am in ignorance; scratch at my heart…

Play tunes of some ever-lasting lyric

Tell me the meaning of your songs…

In another famous poem of Josh, ذی حیات مناظر, we find him saying that,

مجھ سے کرتے ہیں گھنے باغ کے سائے باتیں

ایسی باتیں کہ میری جان پہ بن آتی ہے

گنگناتے ہوئے میدان کے سناٹے میں

آپ ہی آپ طبیعت میری بھر آتی ہے

یوں نباتات کو چھوتی ہوی آتی ہے ہوا

دل میں ہر سانس سے اک پھانس سی چبھ جاتی ہے

'The shadows of the thick garden talk to me/ such things that I feel weary of my life…

In the murmuring silence of plains/ my heart grieves spontaneously'

'The air comes from plants in such a way that something pricks my heart every time I breathe the air in'

Hence we observe that Nature reveals its treasures to Wordsworth through joy but to Josh she blesses a pinching joy of reality.

Thus we find, both in the poetry of William Wordsworth and Josh Maleeh Abadi, a skillful portrayal of Nature and its multifarious phenomena; and also a deep love, affection and an inclination towards Nature and its various manifestations. Nature unveiled its hidden treasure to both the poets; through joy to one and through pinches to the other.

3.2 Nature as a living entity

William Wordsworth regards Nature as a living entity; every object of Nature having a spirit and a soul. "What distinguishes Wordsworth from other poets of Nature is that for him Nature is a living entity. The indwelling spirit in Nature imparts its own consciousness to all objects of Nature." (Mukherjee, 20-34)

As he says in The Prelude,

Low breathings coming after me, and sounds

Of distinguishable motion, steps

Almost as silent as the turf they trod.

Similarly, when he had taken a boat stealthily to explore the silent lake in the evening, he felt as if a huge peak rose and up reared its head,

And growing still in stature the grim shape

Towered up between me and the stars, and still,

For so it seemed, with purpose of its own

And measured motion like a living thing,

Strode after me.

"He conceived, as a poet, that Nature was alive. It had, he imagined, one living soul which, entering into flower, stream, or mountain, gave each a soul of their own." (Mukherjee, 20-34)

Further, Wordsworth writes in Tintern Abbey,

And I have felt

A presence that disturbs me with the joy

Of elevated thoughts; a sense sublime

Of something far more deeply interfused,

Whose dwelling is the light of setting suns,

And the round ocean and the living air,

And the blue sky and in the mind of man;

A motion and a spirit, that impels

All thinking things, all objects of all thought,

And rolls through all things, therefore am I still

A lover of meadows and the woods,

And mountains; and of all that we behold

From this green earth; of all the mighty world

Of eye, and ear, — both what they half create,

And what perceive; well pleased to recognize

In Nature and the language of the sense,

The anchor of my purest thoughts, the nurse,

The guide, the guardian of my heart, and soul

    Of all my mortal being.

    In the above lines, Wordsworth says that Nature is a living entity. It possesses a soul and a spirit that dwells in every object of Nature, in the 'light of setting suns, and the round ocean and the living air, and the blue sky, and in the mind of man'. According to him, this 'motion and spirit' 'rolls through all things'; a spirit or a mighty force that controls each and every thing and dwells within them. Thus Nature is alive and "pervades in all the objects of Nature" [Mukherjee, 20-34]

For this faith in a spirit that dwells in Nature, Wordsworth was also called a Pantheist; one who believes that God is in everything.

Josh Maleeh Abadi has also frequently pointed towards the presence of life and a spirit in different objects of Nature.

For example, in Zee-Hayat Manazir, Josh delineates a detailed and artistic picture of various Natural phenomena. The term Zee-Hayat means the things that are endowed with life; which shows that Josh declares the scenes of Nature, presented in the poem, to be endowed with life. From this poem of Josh we can definitely conjecture that he considers every object of Nature to be alive.

ذی حیات مناظر

خامشی دشت پہ جس وقت کہ چھا جاتی ہے

عمر بھر جو نہ سنی ہو وہ صدا آتی ہے

بھینی بھینی سی مچلتی ہے فضا میں خوشبو

ٹھنڈی ٹھنڈی لبِ ساحل سے ہوا آتی ہے

دشتِ خاموش کی اجڑی ہوئی راہوں سے مجھے

جادہ پیماوں کے قدموں کی صدا آتی ہے

پاس آ کر میرے گاتی ہے کوئی زبرہ جمال

اور گاتی ہوئی پھر دور نکل جاتی ہے

آنکھ اٹھاتا ہوں تو خوش چشم نظر آتے ہیں

سانس لیتا ہوں تو احباب کی بو آتی ہے

دشنہ رکھ دیتا ہے گھبرا کے رگِ جاں پہ کوئی

جب کلی خاک پہ دم توڑ کے گر جاتی ہے

مسکراتی ہے جو رہ رہ کے گھٹا میں بجلی

آنکھ سی کوہ و بیاباں کی جھپک جاتی ہے

کرنے لگتے ہیں نظارے سے جو بادل مایوس

برق آہستہ سے کچھ کان میں کہہ جاتی ہے

جھاڑیوں کو جو ہلاتے ہیں ہوا کے جھونکے

دلِ شبنم کے دھڑکنے کی صدا آتی ہے

مجھ سے کرتے ہیں گھنے باغ کے سائے باتیں

ایسی باتیں کہ میری جان پہ بن آتی ہے

گنگناتے ہوئے میدان کے سناٹے میں

آپ ہی آپ طبیعت میری بھر آتی ہے

یوں نباتات کو چھوتی ہوئی آتی ہے ہوا

دل میں ہر سانس سے اک پھانس سی چبھ جاتی ہے

جب ہری دوب کے مڑ جاتے ہیں نازک ریشے

شیشہِ قلب میں اک ٹھیس سی لگ جاتی ہے

بانسری جیسے بجاتا ہو کہیں دور کوئی

یوں دبے پاؤں بیاباں سے ہوا آتی ہے

حسرتیں خاک کی غنچوں سے ابل پڑتی ہیں

روح میدان کی پھولوں سے نکل آتی ہے

طبعِ شاعر کو روانی کا اشارہ کر کے

نہر شاخوں کے گھنے سایے میں سو جاتی ہے

- [When silence befalls the desert/ Sounds rise that were never heard before/ A faint odour sulks in the air/ And a cool breeze blows from the shore. / When puffs of air poke the bushes/ We hear the throbbing heart of dew... / As if someone afar plays upon a flute/ So gently treads the air from wilderness. /...

  And in the last two lines of this poem, Josh says,

ان مناظر کو میں ہے جان سمجھ لوں کیونکر؟

جوش ! کچھ عقل میں یہ بات نہیں آتی ہے

Why and how shall I consider these scenes as dead?

Josh! It doesn't appeal to my mind. (to call these scenes non-living.)

Thus Josh clearly marks that the manifestations of Nature are not non-living rather they have a powerful and benign spirit. It seems that every leaf, every puff of air, every drop of dew, every ray of moon light is alive and calls us towards the workmanship of a Spirit that has blessed them with life.

Josh himself has said a famous verse,

For the visionary people like us,/ if there was no prophet, morning was enough.

A prophet is one who brings the message of God to His creations; a prophet is one who tells and instructs about God. A prophet is a sign of God. He is one who leads humanity towards God. Here Josh calls morning a poet, which means that he is attributing all the qualities of a prophet to morning; morning is a silent yet a telling message of God; morning is a sign of God; morning is the agent that leads us towards the Divinity. It means that morning recognizes God; thus it is alive and bears a soul that refers us towards the ultimate creator.

"Among all the poems that Josh has written upon Nature, every poem has its own structural/constructive elements in it; but what is common among all is the living-portrayal of the scenes." [Naqvi, 58-60]

But unfortunately nothing has been written on this aspect of Josh except by Dr. Hilal Naqvi, who says, "Josh started his poetry with religious fervor… He ascended the steps of the recognition of God through the study of dawn and the scenes of Nature". [Naqvi, 58-60]

The reason may be that it has been a common practice of Muslim poets that they indicate and point towards the art of Allah Almighty in the beauty and creation of the whole universe and its objects. However no other poet has presented this craftsmanship and art of God in Nature in such a marvelous manner.

"Whether Josh enters into the realm of Nature via spiritual values or realizing the material needs of life, he nowhere neglects the glorious views of Nature and the underlying craftsmanship of God." [Naqvi, 58-60]

3.3 Imagery of Nature

Imagery means the use of figurative language, specially metaphors and similes in poetry, plays and other literary works. Imagery mostly includes detailed illustrations, use of similes and metaphors and sensuousness.

A huge majority of the poems of Josh bear the attribute of imagery and creating beautiful pictorial images. For example, in his poem, جڑیوں کا گیت , Josh describes minutely each and every movement of sparrows so that a vivid picture forms before the eyes of the reader. Descriptions and detailed illustration of every movement of the sparrows marks this poem as highly imagistic and beautiful.

لچکتی ہوی شاخ پر بیٹھ جاؤ   مہکتے ہوے پھول کے پاس أو

کبھی صاف چشمے میں غوطہ لگاؤ   ہوا میں کبھی اڑ کے بازو ہلاؤ

یونہی پیاری چڑیو! ابھی اور گاؤ

چہک کر ادھر سے ادھر پر ہلاؤ   پھدک کر ادھر سے ادھر دوڑ جاؤ

اچھل کر کبھی نہر پر گنگناؤ   چمک کر کبھی شاخ پر چہچہاؤ

'Come to the fragrant flower/ sit over the flexing bough/ flutter your wings by flying in air/ dive into the clean water of the river/ in this fashion, Ye Sparrows! Play on. '

'Jump from here to there/ chirp and flutter your wings from here to there/' shine and sit on the bough and chirp/ jump and sing over the stream. In this fashion, Ye Sparrows! Play on.'

"In the poetry of Josh, there is a multi-colored mood that wraps up the dimensions and variety of beauty and love, irony, facts and knowledge, peace and turmoil. But in this multi-colored rainbow of subjects, the thing that prevails perpetually is his skill of imagery. This is the very skill which being his art, continues to flow through his verses. And this very virtue, which is called imagery, gives him an eminent place among his contemporaries." (Raza, 64-89)

"This art and skill is so fluent in the poetry of Josh that it will not be an exaggeration to call him the poet of imagery." (Raza, 64-89)

"The saying that poetry is a speaking picture wholly applies to the poetry of Josh. (Raza, 64-89)

In another poem, برسات کی چاندنی, Josh uses a multitude of images and an illustrious description of the scene of a dark night, where moon is hiding and showing itself, time and again, behind a thin layer of clouds; that we see the whole scene through his words.

چرخ پر برسے ہوۓ بادل کے ٹکڑے جا بجا

چاندنی، تالاب، سناٹا، پیپہے کی صدا

دشت پر چھاۓ ہوۓ ذوق. جنوں کے ولولے

چاند میں معصوم بچے کے تبسم کی ادا...

سینہِ امواج میں سیالِ چاندی کی تڑپ

طاقِ گل میں قطرہِ شبنم کا چھوٹا سا دیا۔۔۔

کانپتی لہروں سے اٹھتے ہیں نمو کے زمزمے

جھومتے پودوں سے آتی ہے ہے جوانی کی صدا

لرزشِ صبہا میں جھلکے جس طرح نشے کی روح

چاند ہے اس طرح قلبِ آب میں ڈوبا ہوا۔۔۔

[(There are) clouds floating upon the horizon, that have emptied their showers of rain/ (there is) moon-light, pond of water, silence and sounds of a cuckoo/ (there are) the passions of madness brooding over the desert/ (I see) the smile of an innocent child in the moon/…]

The pictorial images used by Josh in the above mentioned lines of the poem are: Josh calls the hide and seek of the moon in the clouds to be like the bashfulness and innocent smile of a child; flower a pot and dew a candle kept in it; sounds of chanting and singing of growth arise from trembling waves; the fluttering plants exclaim of youth; the (image of) moon is immersed in water like the way the soul of intoxication spills over from liquor.

The spectacular images of Josh describe the scene extremely minutely and vividly.

Another poem بدلی کا چاند presents a stunning example of imagery.

خورشید وہ دیکھو ڈوب گیا، ظلمت کا نشاں لہرانے لگا

مہتاب، وہ ہلکے بادل سے، چاندی کے ورق برسانے لگا

وہ سانولے پن پر میداں کے، ہلکی سی صباحت دوڑ چلی

تھوڑا سا ابھر کر بادل سے، وہ چاند جبیں چھلکانے لگا۔۔۔

بادل میں چھپا، تو کھول دیے، بادل میں دریچے ہیرے کے

گردوں پہ جو آیا تو گردوں، دریا کی طرح لہرانے لگا۔۔۔

پردہ جو اٹھایا بادل کا، دریا پہ تبسم دوڑ گیا

چلمن جو گرائ بدلی کی، میدان کا دل گھبرانے لگا۔۔۔

'See the sun has set and darkness has shown its signs/ the moon is spraying silver pages of light from behind a thin layer of clouds/ the dark complexion of the plain has started to get fair/ the moon has raised its forehead a bit by lifting itself from the clouds / when the moon hid itself in clouds; it opened doors of diamond in the clouds/ when came to the sky, the sky wavered like a river/ when raised the curtain of clouds, a smile ran over the river/ when dropped the veil of the clouds, the heart of the plain got worried (dark)…'

Josh has employed certain similes, metaphors, personification and minute description to present the scene. He calls moonlight as pages of silver and the pouring moonlight as rain of pages of silver. When the moon shows itself from behind the clouds, he says that the moon is showing its forehead and its light runs upon the plain. When the moon inhabits the clear sky, the sky wavers like a river. When the moon raises the curtain of clouds, a smile ran over the river and when it dropped the veil, the heart of the plain rended.

Masoom Raza, in an article named, "Josh- Imagery ka shair (Josh-the poet of imagery)", written for the fifth edition of "Josh Shinasi", says that Josh Maleeh Abadi is a multi-faceted poet. In his poetry one finds a rainbow of themes and subject matters. Especially Josh presents nature very minutely in a way that the pictures he draws come alive before the eyes of the readers.

He compares "Marg-e-Moseeqi" of Josh with the "Solitary Reaper" of William Wordsworth.

"In his poem Josh speaks about a beggar who is lying in sun on a road. He is unaware of his own condition. He is neither happy nor morose and is singing something from quite some time. His song is wandering with the dust of the street.

کچھ سر و پا کا جس کو ہوش نہیں	دھوپ میں اک گدائے راہ نشیں
دیر سے ہے سرود میں مشغول	نہ تو بشاش ہی ہے، اور نہ ملول
دف کی آواز ہے ستار کے ساتھ	نغمہ آوارہ ہے غبار کے ساتھ

A similar situation is presented by William Wordsworth in his poem, "Solitary Reaper".

Behold her, single in the field

You solitary Highland lass!

Reaping and singing by herself,

Stop here or, gently pass!" [(Raza, 64-89)]

Comparing some other fragments of Josh and Wordsworth's poetry, Masoom Raza writes;

"In a poem of Josh, where he has said about a sister, who was parted from his brother, sees a little brother and his little sister quarrelling on something, her own childhood flashes back in his mind when she and her brother were used to be mischievous and quarreled on petty matters.

On the other side, when Wordsworth observes a butterfly, he remembers his own childhood when he and his sister used to run after butterflies.

Josh has ended the poem in the following way:

اس جنگ کے آئنے کے اندر

بچپن ہے ہمارا جلوہ گستر

کرتے تھے شرارتیں، اودھم بھی

لڑتے تھے، اسی طرح ہم بھی

In this mirror of quarrels, our childhood resides when we were mischievous and made a lot of mess; quarreled in the same way as these children are.

While Wordsworth ends his poem in a similar fashion:

Oh! Pleasant, pleasant were the days, the time

When in our childish plays

My sister Emmeline and I, together chased the butterfly." [(Raza, 64-89)]

William Wordsworth also is well-known for his imagery of Nature. "We may notice the power and truth of Wordsworth's imagery. Seldom does he employ mere conventional classical comparisons. In one place, indeed, we find him reproducing Milton's archaic astronomy, where blinded Samson complains that for him the sun is dark—

And silent as the moon,

When she deserts the night,

Hid in her vacant interlunar cave:

Sometimes Wordsworth's imagination prompts him to felicitous descriptive metaphors, as in the snake-like convulsions of the yew tree's trunk (yew trees, 16-18), the green moss-grown stones that lie scattered under the shady trees 'like a flock of sheep' (Nutting, 35-37)…" [Mukherjee, 79-80]

Further, "Clouds often furnish Wordsworth with his happiest comparisons. The poet himself wanders 'lonely as a cloud' (The Daffodils, 1); the Knight rides 'with the slow motion of a summer cloud' (Hart-Leap Well, 2); kingdoms are to 'shift about like clouds' (Rob Roy's Grave, 91)…" [Mukherjee, 79-80]

In The Solitary Reaper Wordsworth has used two beautiful images of Nature;

Behold her, single in the field,

Yon solitary Highland Lass!

Reaping and singing by herself;

Stop here, or gently pass!

Alone she cuts and binds the grain,

And sings a melancholy strain;

O listen! for the Vale profound

Is overflowing with the sound.

Two contrasted images suggest Nature's vastness and solitude—one, vivid, dynamic, vibrating with life; the other, desolate, lonesome, wrapped up in mystery.

The imagistic qualities of Wordsworth can further be exemplified from A Night Piece, in which the description of night, darkness, moon, moon-light, clouds and stars is indeed illustrious and bears a striking resemblance with the poem چاند کا دلی of Josh;

With a continuous cloud of texture close,

Heavy and wan, all whitened by the Moon,

Which through that veil is indistinctly seen,

A dull, contracted circle, yielding light

So feebly spread, that not a shadow falls,

Chequering the ground—from rock, plant, tree, or tower.

    While Josh says,

خورشید وہ دیکھو ڈوب گیا، ظلمت کا نشاں لہرانے لگا

مہتاب، وہ ہلکے بادل سے، چاندی کے ورق برسانے لگا

وہ سانولے پن پر میداں کے، ہلکی سی صباحت دوڑ چلی

تھوڑا سا ابھر کر بادل سے، وہ چاند جبیں جھلکانے لگا۔

'See the sun has set and darkness has shown its signs/ the moon is spraying silver pages of light from behind a thin layer of clouds/ the dark complexion of the plain has started to get fair/ the moon has raised its forehead a bit by lifting itself from the clouds /'

At length a pleasant instantaneous gleam

Startles the pensive traveler while he treads

His lonesome path, with unobserving eye

Bent earthwards; he looks up—the clouds are split

Asunder, —and above his head he sees

The clear Moon, and the glory of the heavens.

There, in a black-blue vault she sails along,

Followed by multitudes of stars, that small

And sharp, and bright, along the dark abyss

Drive as she drives: how fast they wheel away,

Yet vanish not!—the wind is in the tree,

But they are silent;—still they roll along

Immeasurably distant; and the vault,

Built round by those white clouds, enormous clouds,

Still deepens its unfathomable depth.

لو، ڈوب گیا پھر بادل میں، بادل میں وہ خط سے دوڑ گئے

لو، پھر وہ گھٹائیں چاک ہوئیں، ظلمت کا قدم تھرانے لگا

بادل میں چھپا تو کھول دیے، بادل میں دریچے ہیرے کے

گردوں پہ جو آیا تو گردوں، دریا کی طرح لہرانے لگا۔۔

'Behold! The moon got immersed in the clouds again and rays emerged in the clouds/ Behold! The clouds cleaved and the feet of darkness started shaking/ when the moon hid itself in clouds; it opened doors of diamond in the clouds/ when came to the sky, the sky wavered like a river/ when raised the curtain of clouds, a smile ran over the river/ when dropped the veil of the clouds, the heart of the plain got worried (dark)…'

Thus we see a similar imagery of Nature in Wordsworth and Josh, but Josh exceeds Wordsworth because of his striking and stunning similes and metaphors and detailed and minute illustration of the Natural phenomena.

Chapter IV

Conclusion

4.1 Nature to William Wordsworth And Josh Maleeh Abadi

As we have seen in the chapter of Data Collection and Analysis, Nature is a teacher, a soothing and healing agent, a living entity, "an appetite, a feeling and a love" for both the poets. Nature forbade Wordsworth when he stealed a boat, Nature followed him in the form of "low breathings" and "silent steps" when he did something wrong; Nature blessed him with joy in times of gloom and sadness. For him, Nature was a code of conduct, a law, a discipline and a guide to follow footsteps. He was the most ardent and passionate lover of Nature.

Similar to Wordsworth, Josh was also a passionate lover of Nature and its manifold manifestations. Nature aslo blessed him with joy; but through pinches. Josh also saw in Nature, a spirit, a life, a universal message; and he regarded it as a messenger of Divinity. His heart danced with the dancing waves of river; his soul grew worried with the spreading darkness after the hiding of moon behind clouds. He considered Nature to be alive and pointing towards a Power that created it and blessed it with the beauty and soul that captivated and appealed him. And we can surmise that Nature,being a messenger of God, was a code of conduct, a guide and a law to follow, as was the case with William Wordsworth.

4.2 Nature As a Living Entity

Both Wordsworth and Josh considered Nature and its objects as alive; having a spirit and life. Where Wordsworth feels 'a presence' in Nature, an indwelling spirit and life; Josh also calls the scenes and objects of Nature as alive. Where Wordsworth speaks of Nature's teaching as if a human taught him, Josh also pleads the objects of Nature (Chiryun ka Geet) to reveal to him the meaning of their songs, the reality; he pleads them to wake his soul up. In his poem, 'Zee-Hayat Manazir' (Alive Scenes) Josh clearly marks that the manifestations of Nature are not non-living rather they have a powerful and benign spirit. It seems that every leaf, every puff of air, every drop of dew, every ray of moon light is alive and calls us towards the workmanship of a Spirit that has blessed them with life. The title of the poem itself vividly and clearly tells us that Nature, the scenes of which he presents, is alive.

4.3 Imagery of Nature

As far the imagery of Nature is concerned, Josh excels Wordsworth in his unparallel imagery of Nature. Though both present same type of scenes of Nature, yet the similes, metaphors and description that Josh employs are far more vivid, marvelous and captivating than that of William Wordsworth.

Josh has employed certain similes, metaphors, personification and minute description to present the scenes of Nature. In a few lines of one of his poems, he gathers a lot of similes, metaphors and detailed description. He calls moonlight as pages of silver and the pouring moonlight as rain of pages of silver. When the moon shows itself from behind the clouds, he says that the moon is showing its forehead and its light runs upon the plain. When the moon inhabits the clear sky, the sky wavers like a river. When the moon raises the curtain of clouds, a smile ran over the river.

Wordsworth has also used various tools of imagery in his poems. Often he employs descriptive metaphors and similes, as in the snake-like convulsions of the yew tree's trunk (yew trees, 16-18), the green moss-grown stones that lie scattered under the shady trees 'like a flock of sheep' (Nutting, 35-37)…"

Further, "Clouds often furnish Wordsworth with his happiest comparisons. The poet himself wanders 'lonely as a cloud' (The Daffodils, 1); the Knight rides 'with the slow motion of a summer cloud' (Hart-Leap Well, 2); kingdoms are to 'shift about like clouds' (Rob Roy's Grave, 91). Also in The Solitary Reaper, Wordsworth has employed the tool of detailed description to present the scene of a village girl, reaping crops alone in a field and singing to herself.

Thus we see, in the poems of William Wordsworth and Josh Maleeh Abadi, a very similar treatment, passion and inclination towards Nature. However, they differ in the effects that Nature impressed upon them; one with joy and the other with a pinching joy. They both have employed beautiful imagery of Nature in their poems but we see a difference in their images. All these similarities may be because human nature and its response to Nature is very similar throughout the world; whereas the differences may be attributed to their personal caliber and thinking, the difference in the civilization and culture they belonged to and the society in which they were born and bred. However, poets, especially good poets are always universal and thus similar; and we find the same universality and similarity in these two outstanding poets of Urdu and English Literature.

BIBLIOGRAPHY

Aazamee, N. (1986). Josh: Husn-e-Fitrat ka Muganni. In Khan A., A. (Ed.), Josh Shinasi (p. 170). Nizami Press Lakhnaw

Arthur Compton-Rickett, A History of English Literature (Thomas Nelson & Sons Ltd./London, 1963), p. 308

Basil Willey, The Eighteenth Century Background, p.283

Clements, Robert J. "Romanticism." Microsoft® Encarta® 2009 [DVD]. Redmond, WA: Microsoft Corporation, 2008.

Dr. Naqvi, H. (2007). Pakistani Adab k Me'mar: Josh Maleeh Abadi: Shakhsiyat aur Fann. (pp. 58-60). Islamabad: Academy Adabiyat Pakistan.

Lakhnavi, A. (1961, October). Josh: Shair-e-Fitrat. Afkaar Monthly, Josh No. 122-123.

Mukherjee S.K. (Ed.). (2007). William Wordsworth: The Prelude I & II & Tintern Abbey (pp. 20-34,79,80). Lahore: Famous Products

Raza M. (2009, August). Josh: Imagery ka Shaair. Josh Shinasi. (5), 64-89.

www.123HelpMe.com. 18 Jan 2012

www.cliffsnotes.com/WileyCDA/study_guide/literature/The-Prelude-Poem-Summary.id-235,pageNum-3.html

www.gradesaver.com/wordsworths-poetical-works/study-guide/major-themes/

www.SparkNotes.com. SparkNotes LLC. 2002. Web. 16 Jan.

Inspiring Youngsters

MY TRUE LOVE*

Nadia Kazmi

All the hearts of man are in my heart

All the sands of time they flow through mine

All the blood of life flows through my veins

Of my enemies, my friends alike

All the people are my kin - my true love

With all the virtue all their sin - my true love

From the grass below to the sky above

Everyone my love

Even in the madness I rejoice

Even in the terrors there are many joys

Even in the madness there is a voice

In life there is always a choice

Chorus

At my depth of sorrow, I still feel alive

Though you may see nothing but the bleakest night

In feeling this too, you must feel alive

In feeling this...

Chorus

Spoken word:

The winds of storm and the passing breeze

They do flow through the same trees

All the soil beneath is within me

Everyone old and young

Every song that's sung is my mother tongue

Sister daughter father mother

Everyone is someone's other

Myself and humankind are of one mind

In loving you, I'm loving me

And that's the way it's got to be

Chorus

* A song written, composed and rendered by promising young Artist Nadia Kazmi - Inspired by **Josh's Nazm Ektaara**

Josh – The hidden treasure

By Nida Haider

All my life, I have grown up hearing about Josh, and how great of a poet he was. I was never able to participate in my dad's gratification of this man because of the language barrier. Recently, I had the opportunity to read Josh's poetry because there was a book that was translated in English. After 30 years, I was finally able to appreciate what my dad had idolized my entire life. By being able to read these poems, I feel like I have been able to connect with my dad on a level I would not have been able to without this book.

In many of his poems, it is quite evident that he longed to find answers, and was driven by his hunger for knowledge. His way of thinking was also very unique. I read one poem where he described a baby's birth, a joyful occasion to most, as a very sinister occasion.

Stating that, all the firsts of a child, that we celebrate so blissfully could also be seen as the baby's first steps towards death. He seemed to have a very satirical way of thinking, which I think furthered his brilliance and added to the controversy that surrounded him.

Another detail I noticed is the amount of sorrow that lies behind his poetry. I could feel his pain as I read through his lines. With every poem I read I felt like I knew what he was going through in his life at the time that he wrote it. In one of his poems, he speaks of the death of his parents; the last line of this poem vividly illustrates the pain he was feeling at the time. He said "On your sadness we be sacrificed", this to me illustrates that he felt his parents were taken from him in spite of his sadness. There is such sorrow in his words that it is impossible to not feel what he is saying. One of my favorite lines by him was when he said "The words that once were glittering pearls on lips; On tips of eyelashes, are sparkling tears." This not only shows the intensity of his writings but also the pain behind the man.

Despite his anguish, his poetry also demonstrated his utmost appreciation of life and its beauty. In one of his poems, he says, "The honey of beauty and the wine of looks; Like tongue, I taste with my eyes." His use of taste as vision and vice versa shows an excellent use of the imagery that he was so known for.

When reading this man's poetry, it is hard not to become engaged in his every word. Not only did it make me realize how brilliant this man really was; but also it opened my mind to think of things in a different way, that may have not crossed my mind had I not read this book. It also made me appreciate what my dad had been harping about for so many years. I was able to see many similarities in the kind of man my dad has become, and how Josh influenced him throughout his life. My dad's thirst of knowledge and his urgency for his kids to live life to their fullest became very apparent to me after sharing in his passion. I always knew my dad was influenced by Josh, but after reading and learning more about Josh myself, I was actually able to see the influence this man had on my dad. Not only was I able to learn about the man my dad had idolized all my life, but I was also able to learn about myself, and most importantly, my dad. And that is something that I will cherish forever.

Now I would like to share with you some of my more favorite short poems of Josh. I am greatly indebted to Mr. Yamin Qureshi who translated some of this remarkable work. It is definitely a great service to not only Josh but also to the second generation of Urdu Diaspora around the globe.

Ujlat na kar aiy musafir-e-dasht-e-shsoor

Nafi –o-asbaat ka abhi shahr hay door

Haan saath chala chal kay kaheen thhray ga

Yeh qafla-e-Illat-o- ma'lool zarur

☐

Don't light the candle of faith yet, take care

Time to negate and affirm is still not there

Yes, walk along because surely

This caravan of cause and effect will stop somewhere

☐

Aiy noay basher waqt ki qimat pehchan

Sarmaya-e-Aafaq hay her pal her aan

Her larzish mizgan pey nichawar konain

Her saans pe sao nizam-e-shamsi qurban

O mankind! Recognize the value of time

Every moment is a wealth of heavens sublime

On the movement of eyelashes be sacrificed both worlds

Against a breath hundreds of solar systems not worth a dime

Eeman ki lazzat ki khwahish hay shadeed

Har khairr hay asbaab-tarab ki tamheed

Hooran-e-bahisht-o-dukhtaran-e-kuffar

Baaqi na agar rahein to Ghazi na Shaheed

☐

Behind the virtuous deeds are the spoils of war

Linked with them are bounties and pleasure

Houris of Heaven and daughters of the vanquished

If not, neither the crusade nor the crusader

Ocean: Plunging into the al,

A Review of the Rubai'yat of Josh Malihabadi

By Hamna Jamal

University of Toronto

My verses are attired in the robes of gold
Mysteries of rhythm my thoughts unfold

Words take the shape of my charming beloved
It's the grace of my voice, lo and behold!

Josh Malihabadi
(1896/1899 – Feb. 22, 1982)

Recently, I had the pleasure of reading the Rubai'yat of Josh
Malihabadi, subtitled A Drop and the Ocean and translated by
Mohammad Yamin. If you have no clear idea as to who I am referring
to when I speak of Josh Malihabadi, allow me to lessen the intensity
of the ignorance you are feeling that is likely strikingly similar to the
type I felt when my father first handed me the chronicle of Josh's
work compiled by Mr. Yamin.

Josh Malihabadi, full name Shabbir Hasan Khan, became a renowned
writer and poet during the colonial era. His fans rose from amongst
those in the sub-continent who shared a love of Urdu Poetry, having
fallen in love with his skillful mastery of the language as well as with
his variety. And why wouldn't have Josh gained at least some literary
skill, coming from a family of renowned writers and poets? Both his
father and grandfather were published poets in their own right, and his
grandmother was related to the family of renowned poet Mirza
Asadullah Khan Ghalib.
Josh came to be versed in Arabic, Urdu, Persian, as well as English.
In terms of education he dabbled in everything from Literature,
History and Philosophy to Science and Religion, and did not simply
restrict himself to Urdu writings and figures but also investigated the
works of persons such as Shakespeare, Socrates and Marx.

Josh Malihabadi's defining forms of writing were poems and
Rubai'yat, for which he garnered immense fame. If you don't know
what Ruba'iyee is (I didn't prior to reading the book), it is a form of
Urdu and Persian poetry consisting of four lines, written in one meter
("an arranged pattern of rhythm in a line of verse" (Encarta
Dictionary), identified by syllables) and one scale. They are almost
like miniscule stories, where the first line acts as the introduction, the
second line as the relaying of the central theme, third line as the rising
towards climax, and the fourth line as the dramatic conclusion. It
would seem simple enough thus far, right? Four lines? Telling a
story? Pfft, easy. Well, here's the icing on the literary cake: the first,
second, and fourth lines are required to rhyme (look back at the
example given above, my friends). If the lines don't rhyme, well,

you've essentially written a short blank verse have you not? Anyhow, now that you've been given a brief introduction, let's delve into the work of the man himself.

In A Drop and the Ocean, Josh takes us into his perceptions of Power and Existence, Anguish, and Beauty and Glamour (coincidentally, also the section titles in the book). Josh kept to the rule of storytelling rather strictly – rather, his writings exude him as a born storyteller. Each Ruba'iyee flows with much confidence and surety. As you may have observed with the example given at the beginning of this article, Josh was not short in confidence. Here is another example from the section entitled, "Anguish":

How afflictions strike and happiness flee?
What turns lips in desert and eyes in sea?

    Why ask the experts in divine law?
    About the benevolence of God, ask me.

Josh's ample use of personification adds a hint of drama and romanticism to his writings. In the first line, you may observe that grammar has been sacrificed for the sake of form; this is done a few times and with reason. However, I also found that even the form was sacrificed in a way, as Josh seemed to stray from the perceived meter in his poems. You will find this in the above example as well as the coming ones. Where one would expect perhaps pentameter (10 syllables/line) or tetrameter (8 syllables/line), which I have read are most common in Rubai'yat, there is inconsistency. Whether this is seen as laziness or freedom or even passionate rebellion, is up to the pros.
The ruba'iyee above makes reference to nature, emotion, as well as god and religion. These are some of the prevailing themes throughout the book. Josh also seems to have stressed the importance of knowledge and wisdom. Here is an example from the section, "In the Name of Power and Existence":

My cravings untapped visions bring
And lips melody of horizons sing

For long, I'm sowing the seed of thoughts
Wait until the new trees of knowledge spring

It is apparent that grammar is being sacrificed once more, and again there is significant emphasis on nature. Not only that, but when it comes to nature, the environment, and our world, Josh seems to have been quite fond of making reference to astronomy and biological concepts such as atoms and other particles:

My nerves were seized by a strong current
In an immense measure my energy spent

    The moment I placed an atom on my palm
    The weight of the entire solar system descent

Through descriptions such as these, we are treated to his numerous experiences and varying knowledge. The use of exaggeration, or in poetical terms, the use of hyperboles, seems to be a technique used by Josh to add that drama and romanticism I mentioned previously. All in all, his work gives you an impression of him being a rather romantic individual. He was actually born into an Afridi family and, being a Jagirdar, indulged in drinking, rich living, and was known to be quite the flirt. This part of his personality is quite evident in the section, "Beauty and Glamour," where a number of his poems dedicated to romance, amore, and women are showcased. One such example:

Bellowing, echoing bright and fair
A youthful face glowing with qualities rare

    This book of infidelity to hold in his thoughts
    Even Gabriel, the trusted, wouldn't dare

You become lost in Josh's lush, romantic world, enraptured by his vivid imagery and impressive diction. His use of enjambment, that is, the lack of use of any punctuation at the end of lines, actually enhances the poetic flow. His style has a type of Shakespearean feel, but it is still unique to him as he applied all of his knowledge and experience into his work. In the last line of the Ruba'iyee above, Josh refers to Gabriel from the Bible. As previously mentioned, there is emphasis on god and religion in this collection, and that may be uncomfortable for some. Josh not only wrote about Christianity, but also Islam, Hinduism, and other religions, with referral to Holy Scriptures and figures. It is entirely up to the individual reader to decide whether or not the content is suitable for him/her. However, I would certainly encourage giving Josh's work a try. If you are indeed a writer yourself, you may benefit from delving into Josh's world and his frame of thought. The ruba'iyee strikes me as a short, sweet, yet elegant form of poetry, and it may prove a good form of exercise for the budding writer.

Once again, in accordance to form, Josh made use of repetition to add emphasis and even a sense of humor, sarcasm and irony to darker subjects (it also makes rhyming easier! Even Josh seems to have had a little trouble in that department). You may also observe some religious undertones to this piece:

You pious! Assert soul's purity. Well done!
Self-righteousness is your identity. Well done!

> *The path that's stained with the blood of mankind*
> *You tread that path and claim chastity. Well done!*

Despite the flowing lines of his poems which incite dreamy visions, it is apparent from the above example that Josh knew how to approach realism and truths of life. He was especially adept at wording human emotion as he went about exploring so many of his own feelings through his work. There is also a sense of loneliness depicted in some of the rubai'yat. We all have that part of our lives where we rue some aspect of our age – be it perhaps seeming too young, or, largely, too old. Aging, one of the inevitable thresholds of life, is something Josh seems to have viewed with a sense of foreboding, perhaps due to his busy and adventurous life as a youth:

Times passed and moments flew
Events grabbed my desires and slew

> *With hope's colour, I kept painting my cheeks*
> *Yet wrinkles of despair grew and grew.*

A wide spectrum of emotions is relayed through Josh's skillful wording and passion. Despite some of the more somber poems in the collection, there are certainly hopeful messages that the poet often attempted to give to his readers; each piece never seems to be written simply for the sake of being written. There are life lessons to be taken away from them. It appears that Josh was attempting to do what any true artist is trying to accomplish through their craft – and that is to find some clarity in life and all of its obstacles.

In closing, I attempt a ruba'iyee in honor of Josh Malihabadi. May he not be thoroughly disappointed in me. Amen.

In observing Josh's work I found
Beauty, knowledge and adventure unbound

> *Precious jewels and pearls unearthed shone*
> *On the ignorance in which I was wound*

Komal Zaidi

A Reflection on "A Drop and the Ocean by Josh Malihabadi"

Since my childhood and throughout my educational experience I have been exposed to

the great work of poets such as Theodore Giesel, Jack Kerouac and Homer. All of them being unique and having different views from each other contributed to my understanding of the world in different ways.

However, up until now I had not read the works of a poet from my own culture. The rubai'yee of Josh Malihabadi were my first experience of reading this distinguishable genre of oriental poetry and it is completely unique from the work I have read in the past.

Josh Malihabadi's work to me is distinct because of the fact that I can relate to the work differently than any other poets' that I have encountered.

Unlike the majority of western poets whose books and poems I have read, Josh captures the cultural aspect of the life that I have been brought up in. Due to this, Josh's work has educated me a little further than most poets I was familiar with, as well as introduced me to different aspects of my culture that I had otherwise never encountered. Through this connection to my culture, I found that I was able to relate to many of Josh's views on religion.

Being brought up in a western society, in a family with deep ties to Pakistani culture and Islam, it is hard to find a balance between the two cultures. In Josh's rubai-yee, a lot of his statements are how I have sometimes thought or felt to help me deal with the imbalance and confusion that the two cultures can cause.

Josh's Rubai'yee expresses:

"You have faith, but lack in benevolence;
I lack in faith and excel in good deeds."

This quote was found in A Drop and the Ocean by Josh Malihabadi, and I found that it is a thought that comes across quite often in my mind. Perhaps this is a way that I try to make sense of, or even make up for some of the quarrels that I have with certain aspects of religion.

Most of the time it is how I truly feel about life. This quote also relates to how one can feel when they are a part of a culture in which they are so deeply rooted, but are raised somewhere where that culture is not predominant.

When a culture or religion is so strongly followed within a family, it is hard for people to accept anything other than what they already know and understand.

The experience of reading A Drop and the Ocean is one that has helped me to grow and

Understand my life in a cultural aspect. Josh, being a Pakistani writer, brought many things to my attention that had never occurred to me in the past. It also helped me to understand my parent's and family's point of view on life and why they encourage certain behaviours or ways of thought.

Overall, A Drop and the Ocean was an insightful and very unique literary experience for someone raised in a western society.

Henna Haider

Henna Haider hand-painted a picture of Josh at the conference. Unfortunately it did not pass the test of time and could not be transformed into a computer photo. So we selected one of her early works, against her wishes.

Do not revere tattered traditions

Do not look down upon inquisitions

You even embrace their religion as such

Do not love your parents ever so much

Josh

A Drop and the Ocean
By Ijmal Haider

In this particular collection of Quatrains Josh Malihabadi focuses on comparisons between the world around us, and the power of religion versus the power of language and knowledge within this world.

He proposes that the infinite ego, collective life, living among others and human mind should be seen as a whole. He focuses a lot on our struggles with our collective-self versus our individual-self.

He challenges minds to realize that we only know a fraction of the universe and there are many things we can put aside to fully take in what the cosmos and the life has to offer.

The interpretation I gather from his work is that throughout life we do come across many struggles and battles, internally or among rivals but at the end of the day the problems are just a mere grain in this life and the world we live in.

Josh Malihabadi spends a lot of time painting picturesque backdrops as he sets the tone for his art, he searches for God around him, but can find no real evidence of his existence. I find that he highlights the beauty of the world and struggles of day to day just to refute all of its importance, reassuring us that our egos have made us feel like the centers of the universe, in turn coming back to discussing our individual power. Our time in this world is so preciously little that we must not waste it fighting over gods who we may or may not find.

O mankind! Recognize the value of time
Every moment is a wealth of heavens sublime
On the movement of eyelashes be sacrificed both worlds
Against a breath hundreds of solar systems not worth a dime

As humans we do good deeds to ensure our place in after life but he counters that with the creation of war and unrest that we promote in the name of our people. Having knowledge is far more powerful in this world than power we hold through violence and war.

The knowledge we hold from reading, whether it be a holy book or just a novel is only partial knowledge and to act out based on what is read would be doing ourselves an injustice, especially considering all literature is open for interpretation as well. It is important we explore life through our own physical research, and we use not only our minds but all of our senses that we have been blessed with.

 The empirical knowledge we can gain from this beautiful, yet small grain in the universe, is far superior to the power we gain through ruling over people through intimidation and individual belief systems. If we, as people, were able to come together collectively and enjoy the world that we are given, and appreciate the wonders it has presented us our affirmation of 'oneness' be far exceeding anything we could gain through fighting (collective power). If there is a God why would he have produced something so beautiful to be ignored, and the egos wanting to rule one another?

We owe it to the world not to take it for granted and live a life where we actually take the time to explore and appreciate the differences in one another, and differences in the world. Those differences were not made to empower us over each other, but in turn to teach us and broaden our minds, teach us the importance of humility, acceptance, camaraderie, and in his words 'oneness.' It is important we take the time to learn about as much as we can in the short time we are given in this world. Although this is my interpretation of this particular piece, I feel as though I tapped into an underlying message or theme, however it is open for interpretation but I believe every interpretation has validity to it and should be explored by those who do appreciate his work and respect real art. Josh Malihabadi was definitely a very forward thinker and it shows in this piece particularly well.